Malign Neglect—Race, Crime, and Punishment in America

MALIGN NEGLECT— RACE, CRIME, AND PUNISHMENT IN AMERICA

MICHAEL TONRY

New York   Oxford
Oxford University Press
1995

Oxford University Press

Oxford   New York
Athens   Auckland   Bangkok   Bombay
Calcutta   Cape Town   Dar es Salaam   Delhi
Florence   Hong Kong   Istanbul   Karachi
Kuala Lumpur   Madras   Madrid   Melbourne
Mexico City   Nairobi   Paris   Singapore
Taipei   Tokyo   Toronto

and associated companies in
Berlin   Ibadan

Copyright © 1995 by Oxford University Press, Inc.

Published by Oxford University Press, Inc.,
198 Madison Avenue, New York, New York 10016-4314

Library of Congress Cataloging-in-Publication Data
Tonry, Michael H.
Malign neglect—race, crime, and punishment in America / Michael Tonry.
p.   cm.   Includes bibliographical references and index.
ISBN 0-19-507720-2
1. Criminal justice, Administration of—United States.
2. Discrimination in criminal justice administration—United States.
I. Title.   HV9950.T66   1995   364.973—dc20   94-16342

Table 2–3: Reprinted by permission of Alfred Blumstein.
Tables 2–4 and 2–5: Reprinted by special permission of
Northwestern University School of Law, Volume 76, Issue 3,
Journal of Criminal Law and Criminology, pp. 675, 677, (1985).
Figures 3–10 and 3–11: Reprinted by permission of the American Society of
Criminology. Figure 3–14: Reprinted by permission of the
National Council on Crime and Delinquency, 1989.

3 5 7 9 8 6 4 2

Printed in the United States of America
on acid-free paper

Preface

Few subjects are more important or more sensitive than the interactions between race and crime. Crime, guns, gangs, and drugs ravage deteriorated inner-city areas where too many black and Hispanic Americans live; concern for the well-being of minority victims and communities requires that they be taken seriously. At the same time, crime and drug control policies since 1980 have greatly increased the numbers of young minority citizens, especially males, who are entangled in the justice system's tentacles, thereby fundamentally undermining social policies aimed at fuller integration of disadvantaged people into the fabric of American life. The prison population nearly tripled during the 1980s, and by 1990 a quarter of young black males were in jail or prison, on probation or parole. The chance that a black male was in jail or prison was seven times that of a white male. Poor minority communities cannot prosper when so many of their young men are prevented from settling into long-term personal relationships, getting or keeping jobs, and living conventional lives.

Conservative crime control policies emphasizing harsher penalties were ostensibly designed to enhance public safety. They failed to do that, but they did ruin countless lives and weaken numerous communities. It was foreseeable that wars on crime and drugs would worsen racial disparities in jails, courts, and prisons. Any experienced police officer, for example, would have known that the War on Drugs' emphasis on arrests of low-level drug dealers would have little lasting effect on the drug trade but would result in many more arrests of young males from deteriorated inner-city neighborhoods. And that is what happened. Any experienced prosecutor or judge would have known that enactment of harsh mandatory penalties for street-level drug offenses would result in greatly increased incarceration of young males from inner-city neighborhoods, and that too is what happened.

There are better ways to attack crime and vindicate victims' rights, while doing less harm to disadvantaged members of minority groups. This book attempts to demonstrate why American crime control polices from 1980 onward did so little good at such great cost and how policies in coming years can do more good at less cost and with much less racial disparity.

Whether the time is right for a book on this subject remains to be seen. Social welfare scholars avoided questions of race for nearly two decades after the publication of Daniel Patrick Moynihan's *The Negro Family* (1965) because of fierce attacks on Moynihan for "blaming the victim" and perpetuating negative stereotypes of blacks. Criminologists likewise long avoided the subject of "race and crime" for the same reasons and also to avoid being labeled a racist. Several times from the late 1970s onward, I tried to commission essays on race and crime for *Crime and Justice,* a book series I edit for the University of Chicago Press that specializes in state-of-the-art reviews of knowledge on important research and policy subjects. Most qualified scholars turned me down cold. Two took on the subject and later withdrew because it was just too controversial. Serious writing on race and crime resumed only in the mid-1980s and continues at a trickle.

I suspect that this book will offend readers on the left and right fringes of American political life. Those on the far left are likely to be offended by my conclusion that racial differences in patterns of offending, not racial bias by police and other officials, are the principal reason that such greater proportions of blacks than whites are arrested, prosecuted, convicted, and imprisoned. Those on the far right are likely to be offended by my conclusion that cynical policies of the Bush and Reagan administrations, and not racial differences in patterns of offending, are the principal reason that racial disparities in the justice system steadily worsened after 1980.

Two final prefatory explanations are in order concerning the book's focus on blacks and on males. Problems of bias and stereotyping affect many minority groups. Some, including some Hispanic and Native American groups, are disproportionately involved in the justice system. Nonetheless, black Americans are our most numerous minority group, the group that longest and most cruelly suffered the pains of slavery and legal discrimination and that today experiences the sharpest disparities in the justice system. The stories of other groups are important and warrant attention, but for this book, in order to maintain focus and restrain length, I discuss only the experience of black Americans. Fortunately for readers interested in knowledge about crimes and justice system experiences of other minority groups, Coramae Richey Mann's *Unequal Justice* (1993) exhaustively discusses research concerning many different groups.

The rationale for focusing on men is slightly different. Racial disproportions are about as bad in women's prisons as in men's. Like men, about half of female prisoners are black. However, women make up only 6 to 7 percent of the total number of prisoners. Because one of my central arguments is that by removing so many young black men from their families and communities, crime control policies are undermining efforts to ameliorate the conditions of life of the black urban underclass, the focus on black men is necessary. The story of black women as offenders and as prisoners is important, but it is a different story.

Finally, I have the good fortune to be able to thank many friends and colleagues for their advice, which I sometimes took, and for their patience, which I often tested. Norval Morris and Lloyd Ohlin, as always, read what I wrote and helped me try to say it better. Kate Hamilton spent countless hours analyzing data and developing figures and tables. Among my colleagues at the University of Minnesota, I benefited from the advice of David Bryden, Daniel Farber, Barry Feld, Richard Frase, Daniel Gifford, Victor Kramer, Michael Paulsen, and Susan Wolf. Among colleagues elsewhere, I owe thanks to Roy Brooks, Kathleen Daly, Mark A. R. Kleiman, Patrick A. Langan, Roxanne Lieb, Coramae Richey Mann, Marc Mauer, Sheldon L. Messinger, Mark H. Moore, Peter Reuter, Andrew von Hirsch, William Wilbanks, and Franklin E. Zimring.

This book attempts to demonstrate why we must begin to think about crime and social welfare as different facets of the same problem and to illustrate why and how we must begin to develop policies that understand crime as a consequence of social disorganization and adversity and criminal justice policies as a cause of disorganization and adversity. To do these things I bring together literatures from criminology, social welfare policy, drug control policy, criminal law, jurisprudence, and the philosophy of law. The book consists of seven chapters. The first, for those in a hurry, offers a summary of the whole. The second provides basic data on crimes and punishments of blacks and whites, shows that black/white punishment differences are enormous and growing, and considers whether so relatively many more blacks are in prison and jail because of racial discrimination in the criminal justice system, racial differences in patterns of criminality, or both. The third examines the disastrous consequences for American blacks of the War on Drugs launched and carried out by the Reagan and Bush administrations. Criminality is born in conditions of disadvantage and deprivation, conditions that unhappily characterize the lives of too many black children. Chapters 4, 5, and 6 consider the significance of offenders' disadvantaged backgrounds for criminal-law analysis, punishment philosophy, and sentencing. The seventh proposes how criminal justice policies should be recast so as to do less harm to black Americans and to be less obstructive to the achievement of social welfare policy goals.

Castine, Maine   M.T.
June 1994

Contents

Malign Neglect—Race, Crime, and Punishment in America

1

Malign Neglect

Throughout this century, black Americans, especially men but increasingly also women, have been more likely than whites to commit violent and property crimes. They have also been more likely to be in jail or prison, on probation or parole. People of goodwill, from W. E. B. Du Bois at the turn of the century through Gunnar Myrdal in the 1940s, to most contemporary scholars of crime, agree that disproportionate black criminality is the product of social and economic disadvantage, much of it traceable to racial bias and discrimination, more overt in earlier times than today.

For at least seventy years, scholars have differed on how much more involved in crime blacks are than whites. Bias in police arrest and crime-recording practices, insufficient sympathy for black victims, exaggerated sympathy for white victims, and official practices adverse to blacks are often said to distort official statistics. The disagreements, however, have principally concerned the extent, not the existence, of higher levels of black crime.

Racial disparities in prisons, jails, and other corrections programs trigger larger and harsher disagreement. Some argue that the disparities result from racial bias operating at every criminal justice stage from arrest to parole release. However, although no one denies that there is bias in the system, many scholars and most officials believe that racial disproportions result largely from different racial patterns of criminality and that bias is a relatively small, though immensely important, part of the problem.

So summarized, it might appear that these are chronic problems about which broadly shared understandings have emerged. That appearance would be deceptive. Crimes and punishments of blacks

3

are acute social problems; their ramifications dig deeply into the fabric of American life; and there is no agreement on their solution. Crime by blacks is not getting worse. The proportions of serious violent crimes committed by blacks have been level for more than a decade. Since the mid-1970s, approximately 45 percent of those arrested for murder, rape, robbery, and aggravated assault have been black (the trend is slightly downward). Disproportionate punishments of blacks, however, have been getting worse, especially since Ronald Reagan became president. Since 1980, the number of blacks in prison has tripled. Between 1979 and 1992 the percentage of blacks among those admitted to state and federal prisons grew from 39 to 54 percent. Incarceration rates for blacks in 1991 (1,895 per 100,000) were nearly seven times higher than those for whites (293 per 100,000). Widely publicized studies in 1990 showed that 23 percent of black males aged 20 to 29 in the United States were under criminal justice system control (as were 23 percent in New York and 33 percent in California). Studies by the National Center on Institutions and Alternatives showed that in 1991 in Washington D.C., and Baltimore, 42 and 56 percent, respectively, of black males aged 18 to 35 were under justice system control.

Those numbers are, or ought to be, shocking to every American. It is not hard to understand why many interpret them as *prima facie* evidence of a racist criminal justice system. Disturbing though the numbers are on the surface, what lies below is even more disturbing, for three reasons. First, the rising levels of black incarceration did not just happen; they were the foreseeable effects of deliberate policies spearheaded by the Reagan and Bush administrations and implemented by many states. Anyone with knowledge of drug-trafficking patterns and of police arrest policies and incentives could have foreseen that the enemy troops in the War on Drugs would consist largely of young, inner-city minority males. Blacks in particular are arrested and imprisoned for drug crimes in numbers far out of line with their proportions of the general population, of drug users, and of drug traffickers.

Although damaging the lives of countless young blacks was probably not their primary aim, the architects of the War on Drugs no doubt foresaw the result. Any conventional ethical analysis would hold them accountable for the consequences of their policies. For most purposes, an action taken to achieve a result is ethically indistinguishable from an action taken with knowledge that a result will almost certainly occur. In the criminal law, for example, if death results, setting fire to a house for the purpose of killing the sleeping occupants is first-degree murder, as is setting fire to a house for the purpose of defrauding an insurance company, but with knowledge that the occupants will most likely die. In equal employment opportunity law, use of screening criteria for job applicants with knowledge that they will exclude proportionately more minority than white applicants is as objectionable as use of a device intended to achieve that result, and is allowable only if exacting tests can be met to show that the screening criteria validly measure qualities related to successful job performance.

Sometimes, of course, undesirable side effects are an inevitable consequence of socially desirable policies. Using automobiles predictably results in traffic fatalities, and building skyscrapers predictably results in the deaths of construction workers, so knowledge of undesired side effects is not always a basis for ethical indictments. Undesired side effects like these can be distinguished from the racial disparities caused by recent crime control policies. Although automotive engineers and architects try to minimize the collateral harms their activities cause, crime controllers made no effort to minimize foreseeable racial disparities. Although automakers and builders are involved in self-evidently useful activities, the effectiveness of recent crime control policies is far from self-evident. Finally, foreseeable racial disparities in human suffering are, in the late twentieth century, a uniquely undesirable side effect.

Race Matters (1993), the title of Cornel West's recent book reminds us. Howell Raines, a *New York Times* editor, writes of the shame that he and his family felt on meeting a former, much loved family maid thirty-four years after she left them. Her life had been hard, and her opportunities for developing talents and improving material conditions had been few. The family, however, could easily have paid to send her to college, and if they had, her life would have been very different.

Raines writes:

> Mother said at dinner last night, "If we had just known, we could have done something." Mary Jo said: "Well, how could we not have known?"
>
> Yes, precisely, how could we not have known—and how can we not know of the carnage of lives and minds and souls that is going on among young black people in this country today?

In the 1950s, Raines's family may well have been blind to the interests of blacks around them. Government officials in the 1980s cannot credibly claim to have been similarly blind.

Second, and worse, support for repressive crime control policies, with their foreseeable disproportionate impact on blacks, has been national Republican policy at least since the presidential campaigns of Richard Nixon, part of what Thomas Edsall calls "a conservative politics that had the effect of polarizing the electorate along racial lines." The text may be crime. The subtext is race. The infamous Willie Horton ads run to support George Bush's presidential election campaign in 1988, ostensibly a critique of Michael Dukakis's criminal justice policies, again quoting Edsall, "tapped these concerns through a particularly threatening and dangerous archetype: of the black man as the rapist of a white woman."

Third, and perhaps worst of all, the crime control policies of recent years have undermined achievement of the overriding national goal of full unbiased incorporation of black Americans into the nation's social, political, and economic life. No modern social policy subject has received more attention than the black urban underclass, living in pockets of concentrated poverty, unemployment, and disadvantage, in which illegitimacy, teenage pregnancy, single-parent households, and welfare dependency are at record and growing levels. As one indicator of the problems of the black underclass, William Julius Wilson developed an index that shows changes over time in the number of employed males per 100 females for whites and nonwhites. Among whites, the number of employed men per 100 women has been stable or increasing for every age group. Among nonwhites, the number of employed men per 100 women has been declining since 1960 for every age group, with the sharpest declines among those under twenty-five. There is disagreement, especially from radical feminists, about the normative relevance of Wilson's index (after all, it implies that marriage is a good thing), but it captures a commonsense reality. Men who have no jobs, no prospects, and few skills are not attractive candidates for marriage or a long-term relationship.

Particularly since 1980, the effects of crime control policies have been a major contributor to declining levels of lawful employment by young black males. The extraordinary levels of black male involvement with the justice system—far, far higher than twenty years ago—are a serious impediment to the achievement of welfare policy goals. Many disadvantaged black males start out with bleak life chances, and disadvantaged young men ensnared in the criminal justice system have even bleaker prospects. No solution to problems of the urban underclass or, more broadly, of black poverty can succeed if young men are not part of it. The crime problem is no longer simply a criminal justice system concern. Unless America can devise ways to make its crime control policies less destructive of poor black males and poor black communities, there can be no solution to the problems of the black underclass.

The traditional left/right disagreement over whether crime control efforts should concentrate on root causes or on the preventative effects of punishment, exemplified by then Attorney General Richard Thornburgh's acerbic remark at a 1991 "Crime Summit," "We are not here to search for the roots of crime or to discuss sociological theory," is obsolete. The issue is no longer whether social disorganization and economic disadvantage predispose the people affected by them to crime; it is whether crime control policies and justice system practices can be made less socially destructive.

This introduction has three aims: first, to demonstrate that crime control and social welfare policies are inextricably connected; second, to show that blacks disproportionately bear the burdens of the crime control policies of the Reagan and Bush administrations; and third, to sketch the elements of a crime policy that would reduce conflicts with social welfare policies and begin to undo the damage caused by twelve years of indifference.

Social welfare is an elastic term that could encompass virtually any domestic social policy from economic development to prenatal health care. Here I use it more narrowly to refer generally to social programs aimed at improving the living conditions and incomes of disadvantaged people and specifically to programs like Aid to Families with Dependent Children that provide cash payments to enable recipients to cover their basic living costs.

Crime and Social Welfare

Intellectual dishonesty and political cynicism have long characterized both crime control and social welfare policies in the United States. We are unlikely to improve either until we become less cynical and more honest. Both crime and social welfare are conundra, because they provoke conflicting emotions. We are at once afraid and resentful of criminals and yet troubled by our understanding of the miseries that shaped them. We are at once disdainful and resentful of welfare recipients and yet troubled by our understanding of the miseries of their lives, especially the lives of the children.

Welfare dependence elicits different reactions from the stony puritannical side of our national pysche and from the sunny optimistic side. We sympathize with people whose work cannot support them and their children, and yet wonder whether they ought not to have gotten more education or delayed having children until they could afford them. We want to help those in need, without patronizing those who are struggling barely to get by. We want to boost the incomes of those whose work cannot support them, without giving them incentives to work less. We empathize with mothers and children in disadvantaged, single-parent households, but do not want to encourage the births of more such children or the formation of more such households.

Crime likewise elicits contradictory reactions. Crime and fear of crime corrode our collective sense of well-being. We want our streets safe, our homes secure, our children protected. We want government to devise ways to prevent crime, the police to come when we call, the courts to convict wrongdoers, and punishments to work. However, we also know that experiences of physical and sexual abuse, poverty, and single-parent homes as a child are strongly associated with offending as an adult. We wish that children could be spared those experiences, and we wish that erring adults could be helped to become self-supporting, law-abiding citizens.

These all are hard problems without easy answers. That is why, as anyone who has spent time around criminal courts knows, many trial judges' ideological preconceptions disappear soon after they begin hearing cases. Whether newly selected judges are liberal Democrats or conservative Republicans, they are soon disabused of simplistic stereotypes by the suffering of victims, the sadness of the lives of most victims and offenders, and the limited ability of the legal system to rebuild broken lives or make a safer society. (Appellate judges are a different matter; they see lawyers and paper, not defendants; it is far easier to believe in stereotypes when you never see the people they purportedly describe.)

And so it is with the American public. Notwithstanding the sensationalism of media coverage of crime and the simplicities of pandering politicians, the public has the same conflicted reactions to crime and criminals that practitioners do: Crime is inexcusable and should be punished; if we can rehabilitate offenders and make them less likely to offend again, we should, for our sake and theirs.

Most people believe that a deprived background is the primary cause of criminality. According to Julian Roberts of the University of Ottawa, the leading North American authority on research on public opinion about crime, "Gross economic factors predominate in public explanations of crime." A 1989 Gallup survey found that when asked to choose between improving law enforcement and "attacking social and economic problems that lead to crime," 61 percent of a representative national sample of adults would rather attack social problems. Thirty-two percent preferred law enforcement measures. Similarly, the Public Agenda Foundation, a nonprofit research organization that uses focus groups in order to get richer, fuller views of public opinion, found the same thing in Delaware. When asked to identify the most important or major causes of crime, 94 percent cited drug use, followed by a breakdown in family structure (71 percent) and lack of education (67 percent). By contrast, half or fewer cited "the belief that crime pays," "bad or greedy people," or "not enough emphasis on basic law and order."

Similarly, although National Opinion Research Center surveys for many years have shown that large majorities of respondents say they believe that sentences are insufficiently harsh, large majorities of Americans also want prisons to rehabilitate offenders. When the Gallup survey just mentioned asked respondents to choose between punishment and rehabilitation as the primary goal of imprisonment, by 48 percent to 38 percent they chose rehabilitation. When the Public Agenda Foundation asked Delawareans whether the state should "build more prisons and pay for them by raising taxes," only 32 percent answered yes. Yet when the same Delawareans were asked whether taxes should be increased to pay for drug treatment for every drug addict, 67 percent answered yes.

Crime and poverty are part of the human condition and likely always will be. In most Western countries, public safety is not a partisan political issue on which electoral campaigns are based, but is one of the unglamorous continuing responsibilities of government, like public health or public transportation. Public officials, with such expert assistance as is available, work to prevent crime and to manage decent, efficient justice system institutions. In the United States, by contrast, especially in the last twenty years, both criminal justice and social welfare have been converted by conservative politicians from subjects of policy to objects of politics.

Americans have negative feelings and resentments about both subjects, and conservative politicians have exploited them. In doing so, they have relied on racial stereotypes that have fanned the embers of racial enmity. In the politics of racial division, Willie Horton is to crime control as the Welfare Queen is to welfare policy. Willie Horton is known to anyone who lived through the 1988 presidential campaign. The person caricatured by Ronald Reagan in his 1976 campaign for the Republican nomination and in the 1980 general election was Linda Taylor, a Chicago woman who reportedly collected welfare benefits under several aliases and, as mythology has it, traveled to the welfare office in a rented limousine to pick up her checks. Both Willie Horton and Linda Taylor were black.

These two black people were used as metonyms to caricature in their blackness and in their behavior entire areas of government policy. Their blackness reminded voters that in 1991 there were slightly more non-Hispanic black (38.8 percent) than non-Hispanic white (38.1) families among AFDC recipients and that slightly more than half of those admitted to prison that year were black.

Willie Horton and the Welfare Queen communicate to voters that the foreseeable failures of criminal justice and welfare policies are the most important things about them, rather than unhappy but inevitable aspects of human institutions. No program that distributes things of value—export subsidies, public works contracts, subsidized loans to disaster victims, or welfare benefits—can avoid fraud. If men were angels, none would be tempted to take more than is their due, but men are not angels. When the subject is defense contracts or compliance with environmental laws or securities regulations, conservative politicians tend to regard fraud as a predictable but regrettable side effect of otherwise worthy programs. Of course, we should work to prevent, discover, and punish fraud, the argument goes, but we should not let it obscure the value of important programs or policies. Equally foreseeable and regrettable welfare cheating, however, is used to symbolize both the nature and the problems of income maintenance programs for the nonelderly.

Similarly, no program that relies on predictions of human behavior can avoid making bad predictions. To the rue of bankers and merchants, predictions of creditworthiness are often wrong. So are predictions from the Educational Testing Service and college admissions offices about prospective students' academic performance. So are doctors' prognoses about their patients' future health and psychiatrists' predictions about their patients' likely dangerousness to themselves or others. Inevitably, decisions by criminal justice officials are sometimes wrong.

Willie Horton's is a terrible story, but it shows the cynicism of racial politics. Horton, who in 1975 had been convicted of the 1974 murder of a seventeen-year-old boy, failed to return from a June 12, 1986 furlough. In April of the following year, he broke into an Oxon Hill, Maryland, home where he raped a woman and stabbed her companion.

Lee Atwater, George Bush's campaign strategist, decided in 1988 to make Willie Horton a "wedge" issue for the Republicans. Atwater reportedly told a group of party activists that Bush would win the election "if I can make Willie Horton a household name." He reportedly told a Republican gathering in Atlanta, "There's a story about a fellow named Willie Horton who, for all I know, may end up being Dukakis's running mate." For a time, Atwater denied making both widely reported remarks. In 1991, however, when he was dying of cancer, he apologized for the "naked cruelty" of the attacks on Dukakis: "In 1988, fighting Dukakis, I said that I would 'strip the bark off the little bastard' and 'make Willie Horton his running mate.' I am sorry for both statements."

The sad reality is that tragedies like the crimes of Willie Horton are inevitable. So are airplane crashes, 40,000 to 50,000 traffic deaths a year, and Defense Department cost overruns. Every person convicted of a violent crime cannot be held forever. Furloughs are used in most corrections systems as a way to ease offenders back into the community and to test their suitability for eventual release on parole or by commutation. (Another politically awkward truth: The sentences of most prisoners serving life sentences are eventually commuted or otherwise shortened.) While Horton had been granted nine previous furloughs, from each of which he had returned without incident, under a Massachusetts program established in 1972 under a Republican governor, Francis Sargent. The tenth was a disaster, but it should not have been used to exacerbate racial tensions and caricature corrections policies.

Public discourse about crime and social welfare has been debased by the cynicism that made Willie Horton and the Welfare Queen major participants in presidential campaigns. That cynicism has made it difficult to develop sensible public policies.

Policy and Mendacity

Crime control and welfare policies of recent years have been based on false premises. Welfare policies have been based on the premise that benefit levels will allow a modest living standard of safety and decency. They won't, as even a cursory look at benefit levels and policy research shows and as every honest politician knows. Crime control policies have been based on the premise that harsh penalties and escalating prison populations will make Americans safe. They won't, as the accumulated research in this and other countries shows and as every honest politician knows.

Social Welfare

Conservative critiques of social welfare programs focus mainly on Aid to Families with Dependent Children, commonly known as AFDC, and on the claim that experience with AFDC shows that social welfare programs foster dependence, sap character, and provide perverse incentives to recipients to have illegitimate children and to form single-parent households.

Focusing on AFDC is itself a distortion, since AFDC is a tiny part of federal social welfare spending. In 1992, the federal share of AFDC benefits was a little over $12 billion. In 1990, AFDC spending for children totaled $7 billion, and Social Security spending for the elderly exceeded $193 billion. Social Security spending for children totaled $9 billion.

American social welfare policies, notably Medicare and Social Security, have greatly improved the lives of older Americans, who vote. The story concerning children, who do not vote, is not so encouraging. If there is one point on which conservatives and liberals agree, it is that expansion of Social Security coverage and annual cost-of-living–indexed increases in benefits have greatly diminished poverty among the elderly. The percentage among those over sixty-five living in poverty fell from 29.5 percent in 1967 to 12.4 percent in 1991, according to the Census Bureau. Among children, the shift was in the opposite direction: 16.6 percent lived in poverty in 1967, a level that rose to 21.8 percent in 1991.

Most of the details of conservative critiques even of AFDC, such as those in Charles Murray's *Losing Ground* (1984) and Lawrence Mead's *The New Politics of Poverty* (1992), are wrong or misleading, as important recent books by Andrew Hacker and Christopher Jencks show. High rates of illegitimacy among recipients, for example, are often blamed on AFDC. Illegitimacy rates, however, have been rising for twenty-five years, for a variety of reasons, in every racial group and income class. During much of that period, fertility rates (live births per 1,000 women) were declining, but an increasing proportion of births were out of wedlock. The same pattern held for poor women, including AFDC recipients: By 1991, the average AFDC household contained 2.9 people; 42 percent consisted of a woman and one child, and another 30 percent consisted of a woman and two children. For comparison, among all households with children in 1992, 41 percent had one child and 38 percent had two, numbers not much different from those for AFDC families.

The largest percentage increase in illegitimate births between 1980 and 1990 was not among teenage women but among women aged 35 to 39, with the next largest increases among those 40 and over and those aged 30 to 34. In all age groups, the percentage increases in illegitimacy were higher among white women than among blacks. So in the end, the honest conclusion is yes, increasing percentages of children born to AFDC recipients were illegitimate, but they were having fewer children overall, and the patterns mirrored those occurring throughout American society.

Many of the detailed conservative critiques are similarly misleading. But this is a book about crime control policy, not social welfare, and so I do not discuss other examples. Interested readers should consult Andrew Hacker's *Two Nations* (1992) and Christopher Jencks's *Rethinking Social Policy* (1992).

Those arguments, however, obscure the more important point that AFDC is a fundamentally dishonest program premised on the notion that benefits provide an adequate subsistence income. Failure to report additional income is a crime and is the basis of many allegations of cheating by AFDC recipients. The reality, however, is that women cannot raise children in minimum standards of comfort and security on AFDC benefits. This can be seen by contrasting benefit levels with the federal poverty level and by considering a recent study by Kathryn Edin and Christopher Jencks of the household economies of AFDC recipients in Chicago.

In January 1993, not one state provided AFDC benefits for a single-parent household of three people that reached the Bureau of the Census's 1992 poverty threshold of $11,187 ($932 per month) for a household of that size. The median monthly benefit level nationally was $367, ranging from $120 and $164 in Mississippi and Alabama to $703 in Suffolk County, New York, and $923 in Alaska (where living costs are the nation's highest). In Mississippi, AFDC benefits equal 13 percent of the federal poverty level. In only fourteen states did benefits reach even half the federal poverty level.

The inadequacy of AFDC to provide even a poverty-level income should be no surprise. Unlike Social Security, AFDC payments are not adjusted to take account of changes in the Consumer Price Index. As a result, adjusting for inflation, the average monthly benefit per family fell from $644 in 1970 to $388 in 1992, a 40 percent decline.

A critic might argue that focusing on AFDC benefit levels understates recipients' incomes because other federal programs provide support. Some, like Medicaid and Head Start, do provide valuable services but do not put food in children's stomachs, roofs over their heads, or shoes on their feet. The exception is the federal food stamp program, which provides certificates that can be exchanged for food. When food stamps and AFDC benefits are combined, recipients' incomes in Alaska and Hawaii reach the federal poverty level, and those in a few other states exceed 90 percent. But even taking food stamps into account, only in nineteen states do recipients' incomes reach 75 percent of the poverty line. The national median is 70 percent. Thus, the picture changes slightly, but the final conclusion is unchanged: AFDC, augmented by food stamps, does not provide enough money for people to live on.

In 1988 and 1990, Kathryn Edin interviewed fifty women living in Chicago and Cook County about their incomes and expenses. It was not a representative sample. Many women would understandably be reluctant to discuss possibly felonious behavior with a stranger and would be unlikely to cooperate, thereby ruining the representativeness of a scientifically selected sample. Instead, Edin asked people she knew to refer her to AFDC recipients and then moved through networks of acquaintances. Fifty of fifty-nine women contacted were willing to talk to her. As the findings indicate, they were apparently willing to trust her.

Four crucial findings stand out. First, each of the fifty women had outside sources of support, ranging from unreported jobs to support from families to illegal income from prostitution and drug dealing. Second, not one reported all her additional income and support to the welfare authorities, and only four reported any of it. Third, adding together AFDC benefits, food stamps, housing subsidies that a few received, and unreported income, most nonetheless had below-poverty-line incomes, and living standards that few Americans would willingly endure. Fourth, they felt morally entitled to ignore the income-reporting rules because otherwise there was no way they could support their children or improve their and their children's lives through working.

Edin and Jencks concluded that without cheating, an AFDC-dependent big-city mother "will almost inevitably end up in a public shelter." Legal income and outgo just do not match. To reach this conclusion, they looked in detail at the women's finances. Some of the women were slightly better off because they lived in subsidized housing. Of twenty-eight who did not, Edin found that their AFDC checks averaged $327 monthly and their combined rent, heat, and electricity averaged $364. For all fifty mothers, food costs exceeded food stamp allowances by $50 per month. Thus before paying for clothing, laundry, cleaning supplies, school supplies, telephone, transportation, and all the other things besides housing and food that families need, a typical AFDC mother was $90 in the hole each month. These other expenses averaged $351 per month, meaning that the household ran a monthly deficit of $440. Almost all this money came from unreported income.

The fruits of the women's welfare crimes did not include lavish living. Six families escaped absolute deprivation because of earnings from drug dealing and theft, undisclosed support from family or boyfriends, an unreported $8.00-an-hour job, or a $7,000 award in an auto accident. The other forty-four families

> did without things that almost everyone regards as essential. Half lived in very bad neighborhoods. Half lived in badly run-down apartments, where the heat and hot water were frequently out of order, the roof leaked, plaster was falling off the walls, or windows fitted so badly that the wind blew through the apartment in the winter. One in four did without a telephone. . . . Most said their food budgets were too tight for fresh fruit or vegetables.

Edin and Jencks's most powerful finding, however, is that the welfare mothers operated on the same moral principles as do other Americans. They believed they were obligated to feed, dress, house, and love their children. When following welfare rules would make that impossible, they felt entitled to ignore the rules. Many wanted to improve their circumstances by working. When welfare rules denied them any benefit from working, by reducing their benefits dollar-for-dollar, they felt entitled to ignore the income-reporting rule.

The genius of the Edin and Jencks study is its systematic demonstration that AFDC benefits and food stamps do not provide enough money for recipients to live on, a conclusion that should be numerically evident from comparing benefit levels with the poverty level. Edin and Jencks, however, converted numbers into people. Anyone who has struggled to provide for a child or who has been unable to pay for a child's eyeglasses or school trip or videogames or whatever clothes "everyone else" is wearing can empathize with a mother who, month after month, can do few or none of those things.

The scandal of American welfare policy is that policymakers know this. Whether they be cabinet secretaries, Department of

Health and Human Services bureaucrats, legislators, or staffers to congressional subcommittees, and whether they be liberals or conservatives, anyone who has worked with welfare policy knows that benefit levels do not support people in decency and that as a result many or most recipients must cheat to survive. When, therefore, conservative politicians try to define welfare cheating as the central welfare problem and the Welfare Queen as the typical welfare recipient, they are indulging in a particularly cruel form of intellectual dishonesty, and one that disproportionately injures black Americans.

Crime Control Policy

Crime control policy has similarly been debased. For at least twenty-five years, researchers have shown and honest politicians have known that manipulations of penalties have relatively little or no effect on crime rates. In 1993, for example, a National Academy of Sciences report commissioned and paid for by the Reagan administration's Department of Justice, noting that the average prison time per violent crime had *tripled* between 1975 and 1989, asked, "What effect has increasing the prison population had on levels of violent crime?" The answer, "Apparently, very little."

No one doubts that society is safer having some penalties for crime rather than none at all, but that choice is not in issue. On the real-world question of whether increases in penalties significantly reduce the incidence of serious crimes to which they attach, the answer is maybe, a little, at best, but usually not. Minor misconduct is a different matter. Parking patterns do change, for example, when ticketing becomes more common, towing is more often used, or "boots" immobilize illegally parked vehicles. Financial crimes involving extensive planning and calculation likewise are susceptible to influence through penalties. This is why the Internal Revenue Service initiates tax evasion prosecutions each spring, shortly before income tax returns are due, and it is why great prominence is given to securities law and antitrust prosecutions.

The evidence concerning the limited influence of penalties on ordinary crimes against people and property comes from research in many countries on the deterrent and incapacitative effects of penalties, from evaluations of mandatory penalty laws in the

United States, and from governmental surveys in the United States, Canada, Australia, and England of knowledge concerning the effects of penalties.

That the question is not even close is shown by official statements of conservative national governments in other English-speaking democracies. In Margaret Thatcher's England, for example, a 1990 White Paper (an official policy statement of the government), based on three years' study, called for a major overhaul of sentencing laws to emphasize the reduction of sentencing disparities as a primary objective. The government expressed its skepticism about the preventive effects of penalties:

> Deterrence is a principle with much immediate appeal. . . . But much crime is committed on impulse, given the opportunity presented by an open window or unlocked door, and it is committed by offenders who live from moment to moment; their crimes are as impulsive as the rest of their feckless, sad, or pathetic lives. It is unrealistic to construct sentencing arrangements on the assumption that most offenders will weigh up the possibilities in advance and base their conduct on rational calculation.

Canada is the other English-speaking democracy that recently had a conservative government. In Brian Mulroney's Canada, the Committee on Justice and the Solicitor General of the Canadian House of Commons, chaired by a member of Mulroney's party, proposed in February 1993 that Canada shift from an American-style law enforcement approach to crime to a European-style preventative approach. The report observed that "the United States affords a glaring example of the limited impact that criminal justice responses may have on crime. . . . If locking up those who violate the law contributed to safer societies then the United States should be the safest country in the world." Six years earlier, the Canadian Sentencing Commission had premised its recommendations on similar conclusions: "Evidence does not support the notion that variations in sanctions (within a range that could reasonably be contemplated) affect the deterrent value of sentences. In other words, deterrence cannot be used, with empirical justification, to guide the imposition of sentences."

American governments have not always been outside the mainstream of knowledge about the effects and limits of criminal penalties. In 1967, the President's Commission on Law Enforcement and Administration of Justice concluded that measures directed expressly at crime and criminals could have little effect without much larger simultaneous efforts being directed at crime's underlying social and economic causes. "The Commission . . . has no doubt whatever that the most significant action that can be taken against crime is action designed to eliminate slums and ghettos, to improve education, to provide jobs. . . . We will not have dealt effectively with crime until we have alleviated the conditions that stimulate it." In 1978, the National Academy of Sciences Panel on Research on Deterrent and Incapacitative Effects concluded more narrowly, "In summary . . . we cannot assert that the evidence warrants an affirmative conclusion regarding deterrence." The panel's principal consultant on the subject, Daniel Nagin of Carnegie–Mellon University, was more categorical: "The evidence is woefully inadequate for providing a good estimate of the magnitude of whatever effect may exist. . . . Policymakers in the criminal justice system are done a disservice if they are left with the impression that the empirical evidence . . . strongly supports the deterrence hypothesis."

Nonetheless, from 1981 onward, the Reagan and Bush administrations repeatedly called for tougher penalties, mandatory penalties, death penalties, more prisons, and reduced habeas corpus rights—as if those policies would make a safer America. And in arguing for those proposals, they repeatedly made claims that defied well-established knowledge. Three warrant discussion: that the greater use of imprisonment reduces crime rates, that 95 percent of those in prison are violent or other dangerous offenders, and that building prisons saves, not costs, money.

REDUCING CRIME RATES

The clear weight of the evidence in every Western country indicates that tough penalties have little effect on crime rates. In addition, in 1993, after the most exhaustive and ambitious analysis of the subject ever undertaken, the National Academy of Sciences Panel on the Understanding and Control of Violent Behavior concluded that greatly increased use of imprisonment has had little effect on violent crime rates. Recent national administrations, however, on the basis of deceptive and distorted presentations of data, have claimed the contrary. The baldest claims came from Steven D. Dillingham, director during the Bush administration of the Department of Justice's Bureau of Justice Statistics, an agency that should be a nonpartisan source of statistical knowledge concerning criminal justice in America, and from William Barr, attorney general during the Bush administration's final months. At the Attorney General's 1991 Crime Summit, Dillingham claimed that "statisticians and criminal justice researchers have consistently found that falling crime rates are associated with rising imprisonment rates, and rising crime rates are associated with falling imprisonment rates." For authority, he cited the 1978 report of the National Academy of Sciences Panel on Research on Deterrent and Incapacitive Effects which, as I demonstrated a few paragraphs ago, found no such thing. Barr, in a tract entitled "The Case for More Incarceration" that was released late in his administration, made the same claim in much the same language. Because Barr's claims purport to be well documented, I discuss them in some detail.

Before presenting Barr's evidence, a look at data on crime trends provides a necessary backdrop, because Barr's claims refer to it. Figure 1-1 shows police data from the FBI's *Uniform Crime Reports* on aggravated assaults, robberies, burglaries, thefts, and total index crimes from 1970 to 1992. Rates for burglary, theft, and total index crimes have been divided by 10 in order to show trends for all these offenses in a single figure. The broad pattern is of an increase in rates for most crimes until the early 1980s, followed by declines until the mid-1980s and increases thereafter. Among important offenses not shown in Figure 1-1, the homicide rate in 1980 was 10.2 per 100,000 population, falling to 7.9 in 1984 and 1985 and returning to 9.3 in 1992. The rape rate in 1980 was 36.8 per 100,000 and in 1992 was 42.8. Because public attitudes have rightly become less tolerant of assaults and sex offenses, in recent decades most analysts believe that significant parts of the apparent increases for rape and aggravated assault result from the greater likelihood that incidents will be reported to the police and that the police will record them as crimes. That this is so for assaults can be seen by comparing the steadily growing rates for assault with the mild decline for homicide. A homicide is a lethally successful assault. Given the greater availability of ever-more-lethal firearms, the proportion of assaults proving fatal (that is, the ratio of homi-

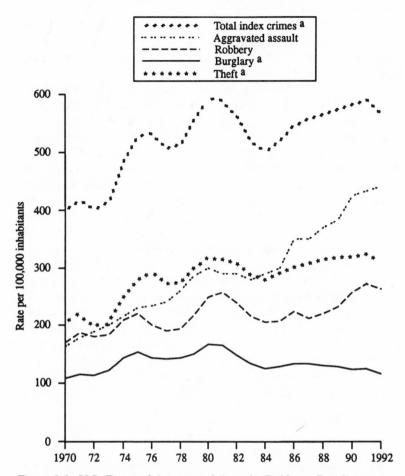

Figure 1-1. U.S. Rates of Aggravated Assault, Robbery, Burglary, Theft, and Total Index Crimes and Offenses Known to Police, 1970–92

[a]Rates for these offenses have been divided by 10 to fit to scale. "Total index crimes" include homicide, rape, robbery, aggravated assault, burglary, theft, and auto theft.

Sources: Maguire, Kathleen, Ann L. Pastore, and Timothy J. Flanagan, *Sourcebook of Criminal Justice Statistics—1992* (Washington, D.C.: U.S. Government Printing Office, 1993); Federal Bureau of Investigation, *Uniform Crime Reports for the United States—1992* (Washington, D.C.: U.S. Government Printing Office, 1993), Table 1, p. 58.

cides to assaults) should be increasing. To the contrary, it has steadily fallen. This suggests that much of the apparent rise in assault rates reflects higher reporting and recording rather than a higher incidence of assault.

Barr's "Case for More Incarceration" came from deceptive presentation of some of the data shown in Table 1-1. Barr explained that Table 1-1 shows a declining incarceration rate in state and federal prisons in the 1960s, when crime rates increased, and sharply increased incarceration rates in the 1970s and 1980s, when violent crime rates also rose but at lower percentage rates; the rates for "all crimes" fell slightly during the 1980s. From this comparison, Barr claimed that reduced use of incarceration led to the substantial increase in rates for "all crimes" between 1960 and 1970 and that the 112 percent increase in incarceration between 1980 and 1990 led to a 2 percent decline in crime rates.

The problems with Barr's analysis can be seen in Table 1-2, which repeats Table 1-1 but in highlighted form fills in missing data so that differences are shown at five- rather than ten-year intervals. It becomes apparent that the years Barr compared were chosen deceptively. For example, had he compared the crime rates in 1985 with those in 1990, a five-year period when the percentage and absolute increases in prison populations were the largest in the nation's history, he would have found it difficult to claim a cause-and-effect relation between incarceration and crime rates. Crime

Table 1-1. Crime and Incarceration Rates, State and Federal Prisons, 1960–90 (per 100,000 population)

	1960	1970	% Change 1960–70	1980	% Change 1970–80	1990	% Change 1980–90
"All crimes"	1,887	3,985	+111	5,950	+49	5,820	−2
Violent crimes	161	364	+126	597	+64	732	+23
Incarceration	117	96	−18	138	+44	292	+112

Sources: William P. Barr, "The Case for More Incarceration" (Washington D.C.: U.S. Department of Justice, Office of Policy Development, 1992), table 2.; Bureau of Justice Statistics, *Prisoners in America*, various years.

Table 1-2. Crime and Incarceration Rates, State and Federal Prisons, 1960–90 (per 100,000 population)

	1960	1965	% Change 1960–65	1970	% Change 1965–70	1975	% Change 1970–75	1980	% Change 1975–80	1985	% Change 1980–85	1990	% Change 1985–90
"All crimes"	1,887	**2,449**	**+30**	3,985	**+63**	**5,282**	**+33**	5,950	**+13**	**5,206**	**−13**	5,820	**+12**
Violent crimes	161	**200**	**+24**	364	**+82**	482	**+32**	597	**+24**	**556**	**−7**	732	**+32**
Incarceration	117	**108**	**−8**	96	**−11**	111	**+16**	138	**+24**	**200**	**+45**	292	**+46**

Note: **Bold** data not provided in "The Case for More Incarceration."

Sources: William P. Barr, "The Case for More Incarceration." (Washington, D.C.: U.S. Department of Justice, Office of Policy Development, 1992), table 2; FBI, Uniform Crime Reports, various years; Bureau of Justice Statistics, Prisoners in America, various years.

rates overall rose 12 percent, and violent crime rates climbed more than 32 percent. There is little to celebrate in a one-third increase in violent crime.

Barr also deceptively selected the crime rates to be compared: "From 1960 to 1970, the crime index rate [for all crimes] more than doubled, increasing by 111 percent; from 1970 to 1980, it rose by 49 percent; but from 1980 to 1990, it actually *declined* by 2 percent" (emphasis in original). By focusing on 1980 and 1990 rates for "all crimes," Barr could claim that a decade's more-than-doubling of incarceration rates had produced a slight decrease in crime rates (from 5,950 per 100,000 population to 5,820). Had he focused on changes in violent crime rates during the same years, he would have had to acknowledge (and explain away) a 23 percent increase.

A critic might suggest that it is unfair to subject a politician's numbers to close scrutiny. In this case, however, "The Case for More Incarceration" was more than an unstudied speech by a politician. It was, after all, a formal public statement by the attorney general of the United States. Moreover, it was an official, widely disseminated publication of the U.S. Department of Justice, and as an accompanying press release made clear, it was prepared under the direction of Stephen R. Schlesinger, for many years director of the department's Bureau of Justice Statistics. Between them, Schlesinger and Steven Dillingham, whose Barr-like claims were quoted earlier, were directors of the bureau through most of the Reagan and Bush presidencies. They are the most sophisticated conservative students of criminal justice statistics in America, and Barr's claims are theirs. Thus, the "Case" is probably the best statement of their position that can be made. It does not provide a very strong basis for explaining why, alone among the governments of the major English-speaking countries, the United States government long claimed that harsh law-and-order policies would decrease crime rates.

WHO IS IN PRISON?

A second defense of law-and-order imprisonment policies is the claim that any sympathy with prisoners is misplaced because the vast majority of those sent to prison are dangerous people who have committed very serious crimes. In speeches, the claim is usually made that only 5 percent of offenders are nonviolent first offenders. In writing, the statements are slightly more careful. Thus Steven Dillingham at the Attorney General's 1991 Crime Summit: "National statistics reveal that 95 percent of state prisoners have been convicted of violent crimes, or are recidivists." This suggests that prisons are used parsimoniously and are reserved for violent and other serious offenders. That impression is false, for two reasons.

First, the combination of violent offenders and "recidivists" in one category suggests that both are equally threatening. They are not. Numerous minor nonviolent offenders have been convicted before of theft, shoplifting, passing bad checks, selling small amounts of marijuana or other drugs, or other trifling crimes. This makes them recidivists, but neither very important nor very scary ones, and certainly not ones who need to be held in expensive prisons.

So what proportion of the 95 percent are violent offenders, most of whom presumably deserve to be in prison, and what proportion are recidivists who may or may not deserve to be in prison? We know the answer for 1991, the latest year for which sufficiently detailed national data have been published. In that year, 46.6 percent of those in state prisons on a census date had been convicted of violent crimes (another 25 percent had been convicted of property crimes, 21 percent of drug crimes, and 7 percent of "public-order" crimes). And of those in prison in 1991, 38 percent had not been incarcerated before. In other words, well over half of state prisoners had been convicted of crimes not involving violence, and two-fifths had never before been sentenced to jail or prison. The claim that only 5 percent of prisoners are nonviolent first offenders begins to take on a different, less threatening, hue.

Second and more important, the 95 percent claim confuses prison populations with prison admissions. Because people convicted of violent crimes deservedly receive longer sentences than do people convicted of most property crimes, they remain in prison longer. On any day, the proportion of violent prisoners among those in prison is larger than the proportion of violent offenders among those admitted to prison. The proportion of those admitted to prison for violent crimes has been declining steadily (down from 42 percent in 1977 to 35 percent in 1985 to 27 percent in 1990).

Perhaps the most extreme claims about the threatening nature of modern prisoners were made by John DiIulio of Princeton University, who ought to know better. In a January 26, 1994, column in the *Wall Street Journal,* DiIulio wrote, "More than 95 percent of state prisoners are violent criminals, repeat criminals (with two or more felony convictions), or violent repeat criminals." Pretty scary, if true, but it is not true. Here is what the U.S. Department of Justice had to say in its report on the 1991 survey of state prisoners: "About 38% of all inmates had not been incarcerated before: 19% were sentenced for the first time [hence this was a first conviction]; 19% had [previously been sentenced] to probation." DiIulio's numbers do not add up.

In thinking rationally about imprisonment policies, what we should want to know is who goes to prison, not what percentage of those in prison are "nonviolent first offenders." We know the answer for 1990. Twenty-seven percent were violent offenders; 32 percent each were property and drug offenders; 8 percent were "public-order" offenders, and 1 percent were "other." There is lots of room for debate about the wisdom of contemporary patterns of prison use.

THE COST-EFFECTIVENESS OF IMPRISONMENT

The final disingenuous explanation for why more imprisonment is appropriate is that incarcerating offenders saves money and that building more prisons will save more money. As former Attorney General Barr put it in the 1992 "Case for More Incarceration", "inadequate prison space *costs* money" (emphasis in original). This implausible proposition is based on a series of discredited cost–benefit analyses of prison use. The first, by Edwin Zedlewski of the Justice Department's National Institute of Justice, claimed that locking up one additional prisoner, net of criminal justice system and prison costs, would save $430,000. His estimate was based on the assumption that each confined offender would otherwise have committed 187 offenses and thus that each offense avoided would save $2,300. His use of the number 187, taken from a RAND Corporation survey in the late 1970s in which prisoners were asked about their past criminality, involved, however, a number of confusions. It was an average, for example, and half the inmates surveyed admitted to offending at less than one-tenth the average rate. More important, because only a small percentage of offenders are highly active, as more people are sent to prison, their average criminal activity declines. The RAND survey was done in the 1970s when the average state prisoner was a much more serious offender than today.

Franklin Zimring and Gordon Hawkins of the University of California at Berkeley soon published a rejoinder to Zedlewski's analysis, pointing out his mistakes. They also reran his analysis by applying it to 1977 FBI data on reported crime and showed that, given Zedlewski's assumptions, the 237,000 increase in the American prison population between 1977 and 1986 should have "reduce[d] crime to zero on incapacitation effects alone . . . On this account, crime disappeared some years ago." Zedlewski's analysis lost all credibility, except in the eyes of the U.S. Department of Justice.

A series of later, similar analyses were made by John DiIulio of Princeton University and Mark A. R. Kleiman and David Cavanagh of Harvard's Kennedy School of Government. These studies used methods and assumptions similar to Zedlewski's and reached similarly implausible conclusions. The Kleiman and Cavanagh anaysis, though never published, was cited by Barr as demonstrating "benefits of incarcerating that *one inmate* for a year at between $172,000 and $2,364,000" (emphasis in original).

The Kleiman–Cavanagh findings in turn were premised on a farfetched cost–benefit analysis of imprisonment by economist Mark Cohen of Vanderbilt University. Cohen attempted to calculate the "true" cost of crimes by taking account of the economic value of victims' "pain and suffering." To do this, he obtained data from jury awards in accident cases and applied the resulting dollar estimates to crime. There were, however, two fundamental problems in doing this, and they paralleled Zedlewski's mistakes. First, contested tort actions that are resolved by jury trials are that small percentage of cases in which the liability is so clear, the plaintiff so sympathetic, or the damages sought so large as to make worthwhile the time and expense of years-long civil litigation. In other words, such cases are far from representative of run-of-the-mill accident claims or, by implication, of ordinary crimes. Second, civil damage awards are inflated to take account of enormous transactions costs, including attorneys' fees and expenses that frequently equal one-third to one-half of any award.

On the basis of Cohen's estimates, raised to take account of inflation since the time of Cohen's analysis, Barr claimed that the total cost in 1990 to victims of ordinary crimes (that is, excluding white-collar crimes, environmental crimes, and so forth) was $140 billion. That this is somewhat exaggerated may be seen by comparing it with an estimate prepared by Barr's own Bureau of Justice Statistics—direct economic losses to victims in 1992 of $17.6 billion.

None of these financial or empirical claims about the need for or benefits of harsh crime control policies withstands scrutiny. Even Princeton's DiIulio eventually backed away from the most exaggerated claims:

> A debate has raged over the cost-effectiveness of imprisonment. This debate has been waged as a numbers game, with conservatives citing figures to show that "prison pays," and liberals citing figures to insist that it doesn't. The truth, we find, lies in between, though arguably closer to the liberal than to the conservative view.

Reasonable people disagree over what penalties should attach to what crimes and over the general directions that crime control efforts should follow. There are, however, important costs to alternative choices, and one of the most important is the effects of policies of historically unprecedented harshness on members of minority groups. The claims of the Reagan and Bush administrations notwithstanding, these are and should be hard choices, not easy ones.

The Burden on Black Americans

American crime policies since 1980 have had disastrous consequences for black Americans. On any given day, blacks are six to seven times more likely than whites to be in jail or prison. Astonishingly high percentages of young black males are under the control of the criminal justice system. These patterns, all of which have worsened steadily since 1980, do not result from increases in the proportions of serious crimes committed by blacks.

Black Americans are far more likely than whites to be in prison or jail. Although blacks make up less than 13 percent of the U.S. population, they comprise nearly half of the populations of U.S. prisons and jails and, in recent years, more than half of those sent to jails and prisons. Most people's first reaction is to compare 13 percent of the general population with 50 percent of the prison population and to be surprised that black imprisonment rates are four times higher than they ought to be. Although the surprise is warranted, the calculation is misleading because it understates racial disparities.

What should be compared is the likelihood, relative to their numbers, that black and white Americans will be locked up. In 1991, the black rate was 6.47 times higher than the white rate. Among black Americans, 1,895 per 100,000 were in prison or jail on the counting dates. Among white Americans, 293 per 100,000 were in prison or jail. Between December 1991 and December 1993, the number of jail and prison inmates grew by more than 150,000. Both the incarceration rates by race and the black–white differentials have also grown.

Another, even more remarkable pattern of black–white disparities has been revealed by a series of studies attempting to determine the proportions of blacks under the control of the criminal justice system on a given day. Of all the people in prison or jail, on probation or parole, or released on bail or recognizance pending trial, what percentage are black? The first such analysis, in 1990 by Marc Mauer of The Sentencing Project, showed that nationally 23 percent of black males aged 20 to 29 were under justice system control. Table 1-3 shows the findings of five such recent studies.

Two studies done at the state level have been widely reported. The Correctional Association of New York found that 23 percent of black males aged 20 to 29 were under justice system control in 1990. California's Center on Juvenile and Criminal Justice found in 1990 that 33 percent of black males aged 20 to 29 were under justice system control.

Two studies at the city level were carried out by Jerome Miller of the National Center on Institutions and Alternatives. In Washington, D.C., Miller found that 42 percent of black males aged 18 to 35 were under justice system control in 1991. In Baltimore in

Table 1-3. Percentages of Young Black Males Under Justice System Control

Source	Area	Coverage	Year	Ages	Percent
Correctional Association of New York (1990)	New York State	JPPP	1990	20–29	23
Mauer (1990, The Sentencing Project)	United States	JPPP	1990	20–29	23
Center on Juvenile and Criminal Justice (1990)	California	JPPP	1988/89	20–29	33
Miller (1992a, National Center on Institutions and Alternatives)	Washington, D.C.	JPPP, PTAW	1991	18–35	42
Miller (1992b, National Center on Institutions and Alternatives)	Baltimore	JPPP, PTAW	1991	18–35	56

JPPP = Jail, prison, probation, parole.
PTAW = Pretrial release or sought on arrest warrant.

1991, the corresponding figure for 18- to 35-year old black males was 56 percent.

All of these estimates are based on readily available statistical data. Some of them may be slightly exaggerated because of the double counting of people who are simultaneously in two corrections populations. Louis W. Jankowski, a senior career statistician at the Bureau of Justice Statistics, however, estimates the effects of double counting at between 3 and 10 percent and probably nearer the lower estimate: "The number of inmates double counted may be small relative to the total population under correctional control." This is because there is little chance of double counting between people in prison and jail or between people in jail and released before trial. There is some chance of overlap between offenders in confinement and those in parole and probation caseloads. People committing new offenses may be in jail and, until news of the arrest reaches a probation or parole officer, may continue to be counted in a supervision population. However, because new arrests typically result in revocation proceedings and because justice system records in most jurisdictions have been computerized, the likely overlap is small.

In addition, there is a special problem with the city analyses. If the justice system control percentage—56 percent in Baltimore—is thought of as a fraction—56/100 of young blacks—the numerator and denominator will not match up. First, the Census Bureau is known to undercount mobile, inner-city young people, which means that the denominator is too small. There are more young blacks in Baltimore than the Census Bureau knows about. Second and more important, the numerator is too large because it includes all young blacks under justice system control, whether they are residents of Baltimore City, Baltimore County, the District of Columbia, or anywhere else.

The problems of double counting and, in the city studies, with identifying the relevant populations to be compared do not in any significant way deprive these studies of their force. Even if the correct national level of justice system control of black 20 to 29 year olds is *only* 21 percent or the Baltimore 18 to 35-year-old figure is *only* 46 percent, they still are astonishing figures that should disturb anyone who thinks about them.

The punishment patterns underlying those different rates are explained in Chapters 2 and 3. Since 1980, the black incarceration rate has been rising much faster than the white rate; the proportions of blacks among those admitted to prisons and jails have been climbing to historic highs; and the proportions of blacks among those held in prisons and jails have been growing also to historic highs.

Justifying the Unjustifiable

It seems a bit odd in the 1990s to have to explain why the adoption of policies with foreseeable racially disparate impacts is a bad thing. Avoiding undesirable side effects and rejecting iatrogenic policy options seem obviously right. Consider, for example, the questions of registering of persons who are HIV positive and of notifying family members and other inmates of the infection. Homosexuals have consistently opposed registration laws and notification policies because of fears that they would be stigmatizing and would adversely affect them as a group. Public health officials' views have changed over time. In the mid-1980s, many supported registration policies and contact tracing. More recently, because registration might deter people from being tested for HIV, most public health officials have been opposed, and few such policies have been adopted, in part from respect for homosexuals' concerns about their disparate impact.

Other examples are available of policy realms in which the desirability of avoiding disparate impacts is generally seen as self-evident. In employment discrimination law, proof of a disparate impact on women or members of minority groups is enough to create inferences of discriminatory intent and to shift burdens of proof. Likewise, on constitutional grounds, statistical evidence that jury-selection criteria or processes create racial disparities is enough to create an inference of bias and, often, to win a jury-composition lawsuit.

As a matter of policy, de facto discrimination on racial or ethnic grounds is as damaging to the people affected as is de jure discrimination; the law's failure to treat them identically results not from a judgment that one form of discrimination is less harmful than another but from practical concerns. Whether or not remediable by the courts, many claims of innocent de facto discrimination meet with skeptical reactions from bystanders.

There are a number of other ways to think about the ethical justification of law-and-order crime policies' disparate impact on blacks. The criminal law's mens rea analyses, for example, offer the law's most highly developed schema for analyzing culpability and moral responsibility. In the criminal law, purpose and knowledge are equally culpable states of mind. An action taken with a purpose to kill is no more culpable than an action taken with some other purpose in mind but with knowledge that a death will probably result. Blowing up an airplane to kill a passenger is equivalent to blowing up an airplane to destroy a fake painting and thereby to defraud an insurance company, knowing that the passenger will be killed. Both are murder. Most people would find the latter killing more despicable. By analogy with the criminal law, the responsibility of the architects of contemporary crime control policies is the same as if their primary goal had been to lock up disproportionate numbers of young blacks.

The architects do no better under criminal law actus reus analysis. Although the common law imposed no criminal responsibility for harms caused by omissions, unless the actor put the victim at risk or had some duty regarding that person's care, this is almost universally seen as a retrograde doctrine. If with no significant risk to himself a person can save a child from drowning in a shallow pool, why should he not be expected to do so? In any case, whatever the criminal law provides, most people would hold the bystander morally responsible. If the crime control architects could have adopted policies that would not have damaged the lives of so many young black Americans, as of course they could have done, why should they not have done so? Are they not morally responsible for having omitted to do so?

One last argument using a criminal-law analogy involves the defense of necessity. In most American legal systems, an action that produces harm can be justified if a greater harm is thereby avoided. A classic example is of people who open a swollen dam and divert its flow into a valley, thereby destroying a farm and perhaps killing its inhabitants, in order to prevent the dam's breaking and jeopardizing an entire town and its inhabitants. Whether the defense of necessity applies depends on balancing the harms caused and avoided. Given the absence of credible evidence for believing that harsh crime and drug policies would significantly reduce crime rates, the harms that those policies have caused to black Americans cannot be justified.

There are thus a number of modes of analysis that condemn the conscious adoption of policies foreseeably detrimental to blacks. One final step, however, is to examine three defenses that have been or could be put forward by conservative crime controllers.

The "Don't blame us" defense is that in a democracy, public officials respond to the fears and preferences of the electorate and, in the 1980s, the "public" was concerned about crime and drug abuse. The public wanted harsh penalties and a drug war, and the federal government (and those state governments that followed the federal lead) were simply, and rightly, giving the public what it wanted. In his *No Escape* (1991), Princeton's DiIulio argued that "the sensitivity of politicians to the will of a persistent majority of their constituents should be a cause for celebration, not lamentation."

The defect of "Don't blame us" is that it gets the causal chain backward. Throughout the 1980s and earlier, conservative politicans used "law and order" (remember Willie Horton?) as an emotional issue to curry favor with voters, in effect heightening their fears and then promising to assauge them. Common-law and street criminals do not vote very much and do not attract much sympathy from those who do vote. It is easy to provoke voters' fears, and, as both Michael Dukakis's fumbling of the crime issue in the 1988 presidential campaign and the immobilizing fears of many elected officials to be portrayed as "soft on crime" attest, it is difficult for others to dampen them.

Almost all the premises underlying the "Don't blame us" defense were wrong. First, as explained above, there is no basis for claiming a good-faith belief that harsh crime control policies can achieve their ostensible objectives.

Second, although politicians' harping on rising crime rates made the public believe that crime was increasing, all of the evidence points the other way. FBI data on reported crimes showed that reported rates of most serious crimes fell from 1980 through 1986 and slowly rose thereafter (during the height of toughened crime control initiatives) to levels that in 1993 for most offenses remained below those in 1980. The other source of national data on crime trends—data on victimization published by the Bureau of Justice Statistics of the U.S. Department of Justice—showed that victimization rates for all serious crimes, except murder, fell throughout the 1980s. (Murder rates did decline during the 1980s, but murder victims do not participate in victimization surveys.) Most crime statistics experts consider the victimization data a more dependable indicator of crime trends because they are not affected by changes in victims' willingness to report crimes to the police or in police willingness to record reported incidents as crimes. Although the data sources have different strengths, weaknesses, and uses, the critical finding for present purposes is that neither shows a significant overall increase in crime since 1980.

Third, politicians' claims that the public "wanted" tougher crime policies were disingenuously based on misleading poll results. It is true that, when asked simplistic questions like "Are the sentences that judges impose too harsh, too lenient, or about right?" most people answer "too lenient," and they have done so for as long as such questions have been asked. Relying on such results as the basis for policy is no more warranted than relying on similar, uninformed, off-the-cuff answers to pollsters' questions about foreign policy or support for DNA research. The problem is not that people answering pollsters do not know what they think. It is that people's uninformed first reactions often change once they give informed consideration to a problem.

A huge body of public opinion data is available that shows that Americans have complicated opinions about crime and punishment, just as most practitioners do. Most people want to see offenders punished, for example, but they also want to see them rehabilitated. Americans believe that many offenders should be sentenced to meaningful community-based penalties rather than to prison. Americans believe that a disadvantaged upbringing is the primary cause of crime and want to see efforts made to rehabilitate offenders. Surveys show that people who do not want their taxes increased to pay for more prisons do support tax increases to pay for drug treatment and other rehabilitative programs. Americans are not alone in harboring ambivalent feelings about offenders. Similar results were found in Australia, England and Wales, Canada, Germany, Scotland, and the Scandinavian countries. Complicated problems elicit complicated reactions.

The point is not that Americans lack punitive instincts. They have them. But they also have other more generous instincts that policymakers can encourage or ignore. The architects of recent crime control policies chose to ignore them.

A second defense, "It's not unconstitutional," is that despite their foreseeable disparate impact on blacks, punitive crime control strategies were not wrong, in the sense that they were not unconstitutional. This is a non sequitur. It is true that since *Washington v. Davis,* 426 U.S. 229 (1976), an intent to discriminate must be shown to establish a civil rights claim under the Constitution. Since courts will not look behind the ostensible crime- and drug-use reduction goals claimed for the anticrime and antidrug policies, the unconstitutionality claim can be set aside. However, that a policy is not unconstitutional does not make it right, or even not wrong. One need only look at the U.S. Supreme Court's death penalty jurisprudence to see that law and morality sometimes march in different directions.

Last, there is the "We are concerned about black victims and black communities" defense. As Attorney General Barr put it in his *Case for More Incarceration,* perhaps in ill-chosen words, "The benefits of increased incarceration would be enjoyed disproportionately by black Americans." Fleshed out, the argument is that most crime is intraracial, that drug trafficking is associated with guns, gangs, and violence, that drug markets ruin neighborhoods and make it nearly impossible for law-abiding people to enjoy the peace and stability that should be every person's right, and that wars on crime and drugs were launched to vindicate that right. All the empirical statements that precede the last comma are true. What is false is the final clause. The cure does not follow from the diagnosis, as previous parts of this chapter demonstrate.

A variation on the concern-for-black-victims defense is the assertion that black inner-city residents want the police to close down street drug markets and to arrest drug dealers and that failing to do these things would be a form of bias against blacks. This also is a half-true argument. No one wants to live in a neighborhood in which drug dealing is common, in which gangs are active, in which children cannot be allowed to go outdoors, in which ordinary citizens feel at risk. Minority citizens want help from the police in dealing with acute problems, even if the young men and women who will be arrested are their neighbors' sons and daughters, nieces and nephews. In a crisis, people need help and ask for it, and the police are often the only source of available help. There is little reason to doubt that minority citizens want order brought to their communities.

Requesting help in a crisis and supporting harsh crime and drug control strategies with racially disparate impacts, however, are not the same thing. The relevant distinction is between acute and chronic problems. Recent crime control policies treat crime and drug trafficking as if they were only acute problems: Apply a deterrence and incapacitation poultice and the problem will be solved. But inner-city crime and drug abuse and related social pathologies are not acute problems amenable to easy solutions. Rather, they are symptoms of chronic social and economic conditions shaping disadvantaged inner-city communities and the life chances of the people in them.

Law-abiding minority citizens would much prefer policy solutions that preponderantly treated crime and drug abuse as chronic rather than as acute conditions. This may explain, for example, why the Congressional Black and Hispanic Caucuses opposed the harsh crime bills under consideration in the winter of 1993/94 and why they have consistently favored more spending on drug treatment, early childhood programs, and crime prevention initiatives. A recent *New York Times* story reports on a January 1994 meeting of black politicians, academics, ministers, and civil rights leaders to consider solutions to crime problems affecting black communities: "While they agreed that the problem was spinning out of control, they condemned the solution most often offered to deal with it: stiffer prison sentences and more jail cells." Representative John Conyers, Jr., observed that "we've got to take the initiative . . . to move government and the country away from this simplistic approach to the crime problem."

That people in frustration and desperation want to see their neighbors' children and their children's friends locked up (virtually no one wants to see his or her own children incarcerated) does not mean that they would not prefer policies that made the locking up less likely. Given the choice, minority citizens would greatly prefer social policies that made it much less likely that so many minority young people would wind up living lives in which crime and drugs are common. Most parents I know want good lives and rich opportunities for their children and for other people's children. People who live in disadvantaged minority communities do not hope for less for their children. "Hello Brother—What a Wonderful World," a staple in Louis Armstrong's repertory, gets it right:

> You can travel all around the world and back.
> You can fly or sail or ride a railroad track.
> But no matter where you go—
> You're gonna find that people have the same things on their
>   mind.
>
> A man wants to work for his pay.
> A man wants a place in the sun.
> A man wants a gal proud to say that she'll become his loving
>   wife.
> He wants the chance to give his kids a better life.

There is some evidence to support the preceding speculations. First, there are chilling reports that large percentages of black Americans see contemporary crime and drug policies as a near-genocidal effort by whites to control blacks. University of Chicago law professor Norval Morris describes a seminar with black maximum security inmates in Stateville Prison in Illinois in which patterns of race, crime, and punishment were discussed. Of twenty-six prisoners present, only three doubted that American drug and crime policies were a genocidal (their word) assault on blacks by whites. In their 1991 book *Chain Reaction: The Impact of Race, Rights, and Taxes on American Politics*, Thomas and Mary Edsall describe focus groups held in the late 1980s under both Democratic and Republican party auspices; in every session with black participants, the view was expressed that crime and drug control policies were a deliberate effort to destabilize black communities. A Democratic pollster, Ed Reilly, reported a belief among northern, urban blacks "that there is an organized approach to keep them [blacks] isolated from mainstream America, that the government system is rigged to keep them in poverty." A *New York Times*/WCBS-TV poll in 1990 found that 29 percent of blacks (only 5 percent of whites) thought it was true or might be true that the HIV virus was "deliberately created in a laboratory to infect black people," that 60 percent (16 percent of whites) believed it was true or might be true that government makes drugs available "in poor black neighborhoods in order to harm black people," and that 77 percent of blacks believed the government "singles out and investigates black officials in order to discredit them." (The poll results were reported in an October 29, 1990 *Times* article by Jason DeParle.)

Second, evidence from public opinion surveys over many years shows that much larger percentages of blacks than whites believe that the government has social welfare responsibilities to its citizens. In 1986 in surveys conducted as part of the University of Michigan's National Election Studies, blacks by 64 to 36 percent said they believed the federal government had a responsibility to guarantee every adult a job and a good standard of living (whites came out the other way, by 66 to 34 percent). During most of the 1980s, whites split evenly on whether the government should increase spending for improved services; blacks were in favor by margins as high as 77 to 23 percent (These data are reported in

Warren E. Miller and Santa A. Traugott's *American National Election Studies* [1989]). According to National Opinion Research Center surveys conducted from 1975 to 1989 and summarized in a book by Floris Wood, among blacks, 53 to 70 percent believed that the government has a "special obligation to help blacks improve their living standards." Only 12 to 20 percent of whites agreed, and 60 percent of whites disagreed. With similar and sometimes sharper racial contrasts, blacks supported and whites opposed more spending on welfare, on income redistribution, and on improving conditions in cities.

Crime and drug abuse do disproportionately affect disadvantaged minority communities. Amelioration of their effects should be a paramount policy priority. So much is clear. Racially sensitive policies would, however, take account of foreseeable racially disparate impacts as well as the policies' likely instrumental effects.

All that is left is politics. The War on Drugs and the set of harsh crime control policies in which it was enmeshed were undertaken to achieve political, not policy, objectives. It is the adoption for political purposes of policies with foreseeable disparate impacts, the use of disadvantaged black Americans as means to achieving politicians' electoral ends, that must in the end be justified. It cannot.

Doing Less Harm

Basic changes in the social and economic conditions that shape the lives of disadvantaged black Americans and cause their disproportionate involvement in crime are beyond the power of the criminal justice system. However, although we do not know much about using the criminal justice system to do good, we do know how to change its policies so that they do less harm. Such a harm-reduction strategy would have six elements.

First, be honest. Admit that no war against crime will ever be won, that criminal sanctions have at most a modest influence on short-term crime rates, and that locking up many more people is not likely to produce a demonstrably safer America. Crime is part of all human societies and is shaped by the ways in which societies organize themselves. If crime rates in America are to decline in the long term, the causes will lie in major changes in social policies toward job creation, income maintenance, medical care, housing, education, drugs, and firearms.

If the insight that crime rates are the product of fundamental social and economic forces were to be ignored, it would be easy to blame the Reagan and Bush administrations for increasing crime rates. Here is how the argument would go. Both administrations openly and successfully fought to reduce federal funding for social, educational, and housing programs and for aid to cities. Authorized federal spending on low-income housing programs, for example, fell by 75 percent between 1981 and 1989. Presidents Reagan and Bush promoted a strategy of federal disinvestment in the inner cities, which accelerated their deterioration and diminished the scope and quality of urban public services. The Reagan and Bush administrations thereby increased criminogenic pressures in the cities.

The only reason that this Republican crime-causing process is not widely recognized is that Republican crime control strategies simultaneously raised the number of people in jail or prison from under 500,000 in 1980 to nearly 1.5 million in 1994. Crime rates in 1993 were at about the same level as in 1980. There are two plausible explanations for the contrast between stable crime rates and soaring incarceration rates. The first is a proposition that Reagan and Bush administration spokesmen would reject, that increased incarceration has had little effect on crime rates. Second, crime rates would have risen to unprecedented levels between 1980 and 1993, but increased incarceration prevented this, in effect soaking it up. But why would crime rates have climbed to unprecedented levels? Something must have happened during the 1980s that would have caused more crimes to take place. Disinvestment in the cities and in social services for poor people are the most probable answers. Increased violence surrounding drug trafficking, a result of the punitive policies of the War on Drugs, no doubt would be part of the explanation, as would the refusal, for political reasons, to adopt serious gun control measures. Thus, if the second explanation is the right one, increased incarceration has prevented the rise in crime that the social and drug policies of the Reagan and Bush administrations would otherwise have caused.

There is probably some truth to this Reagan-and-Bush-policies-cause-crime argument. Crime rates are highest in the most disadvantaged neighborhoods and policies that create more disadvantaged neighborhoods and make the existing ones worse are likely to be criminogenic. The problems of poverty, social disadvantage, and the black underclass existed, however, when Ronald Reagan took office, and they would exist had he never taken office. There are no quick or easy solutions to crime, and we debase policy discussions when we pretend there are.

As long as politicians continue to make cynical and disingenuous appeals to the deepest fears and basest instincts of the American people, and to make crime-preventive promises that police, courts, and prisons cannot keep, the prospects of reducing racial disparities in the criminal justice system will remain small. There is considerable evidence in this country and others that most people are deeply ambivalent about crime, fearful and wanting wrongdoers to be punished and yet sympathetic and wanting wrongdoers to be rehabilitated. Appeals to only one side of that ambivalence with allusions to Willie Horton and similarly visceral and powerful stereotypes make honest policymaking impossible.

Second, think about the foreseeable effects of crime control policies on members of minority groups. When policies are likely to burden members of minority groups disproportionately and, through them, their families and communities, reconsider the policies. One extreme example is the 100-to-1 distinction made between crack and powder cocaine in federal law and the federal sentencing guidelines. Presumptive sentences vary directly with the amount of illicit substance involved, and the guidelines direct judges to multiply quantities of crack by 100 in order to determine the amount on which the sentence will be based. The problem is that crack, though it is pharmacologically indistinguishable from powder, tends to be used and distributed by blacks, and powder by whites. One federal court of appeals reported that 95 percent of federal crack defendants are black and 40 percent of powder defendants are white. As could have been expected, blacks convicted of crack offenses receive much harsher sentences in federal courts than do whites convicted of powder offenses.

Another extreme example is the War on Drugs. All sources of relevant knowledge, ranging from experienced police narcotics squad members to ethnographers studying inner-city street life, supported predictions that the enemy troops would consist mostly of young minority males. Any experienced police official could have predicted that policies of wholesale arrests of dealers would sweep up mostly young minority user-dealers in the cities. This is not necessarily because more members of minorities use or sell drugs, but because arrests are easier to make in disorganized inner-city areas where many minority dealers operate than they are in middle- and working-class neighborhoods where white dealers operate. As could have been expected, the number of blacks in prison for drug crimes has risen sharply. In 1986, among white non-Hispanic state prisoners, 8 percent had been convicted of drug crimes, compared with 7 percent of black non-Hispanic prisoners. By 1991, the white percentage had increased by half to 12 percent, and the black percentage had increased by three and one-half times to 25 percent.

The examples of policies with foreseeable racially disparate effects could go on and on and include the effects of refusing to make drug abuse treatment available on demand, underinvestment in other treatment programs, greater use of capital punishment, and sharp increases in penalties for crimes for which blacks are disproportionately likely to be arrested. Asking whether contemplated policies will adversely affect blacks and other members of minority groups will seldom provide easy answers, because the problems that crime poses are difficult. Much serious crime, for example, is intraracial, and the interests of black victims, especially of violent crimes, need to be considered. Nonetheless, routinely asking the race-effects question should provide some easy answers: The 100-to-1 crack/powder cocaine punishment differential is hard to defend once challenged. So is the death penalty: Death rows are nearly as disproportionately black as are prisons generally. At least in Georgia, research whose validity even the death penalty–promoting U.S. Supreme Court in *McCleskey v. Georgia,* 107 S. Ct. 1756 (1987) accepts, shows that blacks who killed whites were, in that state, twenty-two times more likely to be sentenced to death than were blacks who killed blacks.

Third, establish sentencing guidelines with strong presumptive upper limits on punishment severity. Experience with guidelines in the United States has been mixed. Some guidelines are broad and flexible and place few constraints on judges' discretion. Others are narrow and rigid and greatly constrain judges' options. Most have reduced sentencing disparities and racial differences in sentencing. Some are followed most of the time; others are often ignored. In every system on which data are available, we know that judges much more often impose sentences less severe than the guidelines direct than more severe, and that sentences more severe than the guidelines direct are everywhere uncommon.

The worst injuries that biased sentencing can produce are cases in which racial bias or judicial idiosyncrasy results in the imposition of aberrantly severe penalties. In American systems of indeterminate sentencing that existed in every state before 1976, maximum lawful penalties were often extremely long. Twenty-year, thirty-year, and life maximums were not uncommon. The rationale was that the maximum had to cover the worst imaginable instance of any crime and had to allow for sentence reductions for good behavior (often one-third to one-half the maximum) and for release on parole (eligibility often ripened after serving one-third the sentence). Thus a thirty-year sentence meant ten to twenty years served, and sometimes less if good-behavior time reduced both maximum and minimum terms. In many modern determinate sentencing systems, good-behavior time has been reduced and parole release eliminated. In the federal system, for example, a nominal twenty-year sentence means at least seventeen years in prison. In both indeterminate and determinate sentencing systems, a willfully biased judge can easily impose an exceedingly harsh sentence, but the risk is greater under determinate sentencing.

There are two solutions. First, cut the statutory maximums. The difficulty is that a move to cut a twenty-five year maximum for burglary to a more realistic five years will open legislators to accusations of reducing sentences and being soft on crime. The second solution is to establish sentencing guidelines that, if past experience is repeated, will reduce sentencing disparities in general to some degree and will greatly lower the risk of aberrantly long, racially motivated sentences. Even if the guidelines are exceptionally harsh, like the current federal guidelines, they will lessen the risks of even longer extraordinary sentences.

Fourth, abolish all mandatory penalties. The evidence is overwhelming that mandatory penalties for serious crimes have few if any deterrent effects (which, if they exist, soon waste away), are

frequently circumvented by judges and lawyers, and sometimes result in imposition of penalties that everyone involved believes are
too severe. Moreover, they are often applied to drug and other
crimes with which blacks are disproportionately likely to be charged
and accordingly have a disproportionate impact on blacks.

Mandatory penalties are an especially pernicious part of contemporary punishment policies. Their principal purposes are political
and short term—to allow officials at a time of heightened concern
about crime to show that they are "tough on crime." Such laws,
however, once passed, are seldom repealed and continue to affect
the lives of offenders long after the concern that produced them
has dissipated. For at least two centuries, the failures of mandatory
penalties to achieve their ostensible purposes have been well documented and well known. There are no bases other than cynical
politics to justify their retention.

*Fifth, empower and encourage judges to mitigate sentences to take
account of individual circumstances.* Minority offenders would especially benefit from broadened judicial discretion. The movement
in the last twenty years toward systems of rigid sentencing standards based solely on offenders' crimes and criminal records, and
premised on just-deserts theories, was a mistake. Ethically and
humanly relevant differences among offenders extend well beyond
their crimes, and most judges and many prosecutors want to take
account of some of those differences. Examples include distinctions between user and nonuser drug dealers, between offenders
from distressed and privileged backgrounds, between offenders
with and without dependent spouses and children, between offenders motivated by want and motivated by greed, and between
stranger and nonstranger assailants.

Part of the rationale in many jurisdictions for limiting judges'
powers to mitigate sentences was the just-deserts argument that
crimes, not criminals, should be punished and that basing punishments only on crimes and criminal histories will ensure equality in
sentencing, that "like cases are treated alike." The second half of
the equality maxim, "and treat different cases differently," high-
lights the problem. Criteria must be prescribed by which cases are
deemed alike and unlike, and crimes and criminal histories offer
only an impoverished set of criteria. As Nigel Walker, the English
criminologist, pointed out, a system of punishment truly premised

on notions of moral culpability and morally deserved punishments would take account of all the particulars of an offender's life, just as the Recording Angel would for purposes of grander judgments.

A second rationale for limiting judges' powers to mitigate punishments was that the resulting discretion would be exercised for the benefit of middle-class defendants. This is why many sentencing guidelines systems expressly forbid judges to take into account employment prospects, education, and family status as mitigating considerations. The problems are that there are very few "middle-class" defendants in most felony courts and that the offenders who might benefit from mitigating consideration of personal circumstances are mostly disadvantaged people who to some degree have overcome the odds against their establishing a conventional pattern of life. Thus the people most likely to benefit from increased powers of mitigation are mostly disadvantaged, and many are from minority backgrounds.

Sixth, greatly limit the use of imprisonment, and use part of the money saved to support enhanced community corrections and treatment programs. The rest can be applied to putting state and federal budgets back in balance. If the combined prison and jail population was lowered to 1980 levels, adjusted for population increase and a bit more, $10 billion to $20 billion a year could be saved on institutional corrections budgets, and additional billions could be saved (or reallocated) on police, prosecutorial, and court operations. Crime rates in 1993 were about the same as in 1980 when the prison and jail population was under 500,000, which makes 600,000 a reasonable target to set for 1999. Between 1980 and 1993, the resident population of the United States rose by less than 12 percent. Thus 600,000 inmates would allow for population growth and still permit some increase over 1980 levels. It would also generate a national incarceration rate of 225 per 100,000 population, which is somewhat higher than the 1980 rate and would still be two to five times higher than that of any other country with which the United States ordinarily wants to be compared. Many would still find these levels unacceptably high in light of recent evidence that American crime rates, except for gun crimes, are about the same as those of most Western nations.

Several questions arise. How could inmate populations be cut so sharply? If my first two proposals, be honest and worry about race effects, were taken seriously by policymakers, the answers would be easy. Stop imprisoning most user-dealers and most property offenders. Revise sentencing standards and guidelines to prescribe prison sentences for violent offenses at 1980 levels. Rescind all mandatory penalty laws retroactively. Create special parole boards with the power to consider the release of every prisoner who is over age fifty and has served at least five years and every prisoner who has served ten years or more. The only valid general criterion for denying release would be that, on actuarial grounds, the offender presents an unacceptable risk of future violent criminality. Denying release might also be justified for especially notorious offenders like political assassins and serial murderers.

How much money would be saved? At a modest estimate of $25,000 in annual operating costs per inmate, the gross savings from 900,000 fewer inmates would be $22.5 billion. The net would be less; experience with deinstitutionalization of mental health programs demonstrates that governments have difficulty terminating employees and closing facilities that are no longer needed. However, many new jobs would open up in community corrections and in treatment programs for which current corrections workers would be qualified. There would also be one-time charges as outmoded facilities were closed forever, offset to some extent by gains from converting some prisons and jails to other uses. Whatever the details, in the end the annual net savings would permit a massive rise in funding for community corrections and treatment programs and still lower government spending by many billions.

What would be done with the diverted offenders? For some, nothing. Most former prisoners over age thirty-five present little threat of violence or other serious offending. The best thing to do is to let many of those released early get on with their lives. For current offenders, depending on the gravity of their crimes, confinement or community penalties are the answer. Those confined should receive sentences scaled down at least by half from current levels of time served to 1980 levels and never more than is commensurate with the relative severity of their offenses. Most, however—again depending on the gravity of their crimes—should be sentenced to community penalties like intensive supervision probation, community service, house arrest, daytime or nighttime confinement, and financial penalties coupled when appropriate with compulsory participation in treatment programs. When it is feasible, restitution or community service should routinely be ordered. Conditions of community penalties should be vigorously enforced, with prompt but graduated consequences attaching to violations.

From a public safety perspective, a combination of community penalties and greatly expanded treatment programs for offenders is more effective than the current program of excessive incarceration and insufficiently supported community punishments and treatment programs. Community penalties do no worse than prisons in regard to recidivism, and sometimes better. Well-managed drug treatment programs have repeatedly been shown to be capable of reducing both drug use and offending by drug-dependent offenders. Sex offender programs likewise have been shown to lessen later offending when the programs are well run and appropriately targeted. A number of types of programs for young offenders have been shown to lower reoffending. Educational and vocational training programs must enhance peoples' employment prospects, or millions of people would not pay to participate in them. Even public-sector programs like manpower training and the Jobs Corps, although often badly managed and insufficiently funded, have modest positive effects.

My first two proposals, be honest and think about the foreseeable race effects of policy decisions, are odd in a way, because they should go without saying. If they were widely accepted, the rest of my proposals would be uncontroversial. There are no sound, knowledge-based justifications for current crime control policies, and they create disastrous racial disparities, with all the accompanying negative consequences. Only the proposal to roll back prison and jail populations to slightly above 1980 levels is likely to be startling, but that need not even be a separate goal. It would happen as the other proposals were implemented.

So there are things that could be done to make current criminal justice policies less destructive of the lives and life chances of disadvantaged black Americans and their children. Of course, disadvantaged Americans of all races would benefit, but that is a happy product of nondiscriminatory public policies. All Americans would benefit from saving the tens of billions of unnecessary dollars now spent on crime control policies that are cruel and destructive and that do not make America a safer place. All Americans would also benefit from living in a kinder, gentler country.

2

Racial Disproportion in the Criminal Justice System

Three findings about race, crime, and punishment stand out concerning blacks. First, at every criminal justice system stage from arrest through incarceration, blacks are present in numbers greatly out of proportion to their presence in the general population. In 1991, for example, blacks made up a bit under 13 percent of the general population but 44.8 percent of those arrested for violent felonies and nearly 50 percent of those in prison on an average day. Second, although black disproportions in the front of the system—as offenders and arrestees—are essentially stable, since the early 1980s they have steadily grown worse at the back. Between 1979 and 1990, for example the percentage of blacks among persons admitted to state and federal prisons grew from 39 to 53 percent. By contrast, 44.1 percent of violent crime arrests in 1979 were of blacks, virtually the same as the 1992 figure. Third, perhaps surprisingly, for nearly a decade there has been a near consensus among scholars and policy analysts that most of the black punishment disproportions result not from racial bias or discrimination within the system but from patterns of black offending and of blacks' criminal records. Drug law enforcement is the conspicuous exception. Blacks are arrested and confined in numbers grossly out of line with their use or sale of drugs.

Do not misunderstand. A conclusion that black overrepresentation among prisoners is not primarily the result of racial bias does not mean that there is no racism in the system. Virtually no one believes that racial bias and enmity are absent, that no police, prosecutors, or judges are bigots, or that some local courts or bureaucracies are not systematically discriminatory. The overwhelming weight of the evidence, however, is that invidious bias explains much less of racial disparities than does offending by black offenders. Much offending is intraracial, which means that a failure by the state to take crimes by blacks seriously depreciates the importance of victimization of blacks—discrimination little less objectionable than bias against black offenders. Virtually every sophisticated review of social science evidence on criminal justice decision making has concluded, overall, that the apparent influence of the offender's race on official decisions concerning individual defendants is slight.

That bias does not explain most racial disparities does not mean that the justice system treats blacks and whites indistinguishably. Black Americans suffer from what social welfare scholars call "statistical discrimination," the attribution to individual persons of characteristics of groups of which they are members. A recent statement by the Reverend Jesse Jackson (quoted on December 21, 1993 by *Washington Post* columnist Richard Cohen) is illustrative: "There is nothing more painful to me at this stage in my life than to walk down the street and hear footsteps and start thinking about robbery—then look around and see somebody white and feel relieved." Because young black men are members of a group in which crime is high, many people of all races react to the stereotype and unfairly judge individuals.

Not only young black men suffer from stereotypes about black criminals. Newark Judge Claude Coleman, for example, a policeman-turned-judge, experienced a nightmare of false accusation and public humiliation when he was arrested in December 1993 in Bloomingdales in Short Hills, New Jersey, while Christmas shopping. A black man earlier in the day—who bore no physical resemblance to Judge Coleman—had tried to use a stolen credit card. After making a purchase with his own credit card, Judge Coleman was followed by security guards to an adjacent store where he was detained. According to a *New York Times* article by David Margolick:

> When the officers arrived, Judge Coleman protested his innocence, asked to see his accusers, and showed identification. He was nonetheless handcuffed—tightly and behind his back—and was dragged through crowds of shoppers to a police car. At the

station house, he was chained to a wall and was prevented from calling a lawyer.

Eventually, he was released and exonerated, and apologies came from all quarters. To Judge Coleman, the moral was sobering, "no matter how many achievements you have, you can't shuck the burden of being black in a white society."

Nearly every contemporary black writer tells similar stories. In *Parallel Time: Growing up in Black and White* (1994), Brent Staples, a member of the editorial board of the *New York Times,* recounts numerous incidents of stereotyping that he encountered as a college and graduate student and since. Journalist Ellis Cose, in *The Rage of a Privileged Class* (1993), tells of being tossed out of a restaurant because a waiter mistook him for another black man who had earlier been obstreperous. Harvard philosopher Cornel West writes in *Race Matters* (1993) of being stopped "on false charges of trafficking in cocaine" while driving to Williams College and of "being stopped three times in my first ten days in Princeton for driving too slowly on a residential street with a speed limit of twenty-five miles per hour." Early in 1993, Brian Roberts, a University of Minnesota law student in a three-piece suit, visiting a white St. Louis judge as part of a class project, was pulled over by the police soon after his rental car entered the judge's affluent neighborhood. He was then followed, the squad car leaving only after he was admitted to the judge's home.

Being victimized by racial stereotyping is galling and humiliating. But that police and others too often for no reason other than skin color or style of dress are suspicious of blacks does not, according to the best available evidence, mean that blacks as defendants and convicted offenders are treated fundamentally differently than whites.

How can these seemingly contradictory findings be reconciled? How is it possible that black participation in serious crime has not increased while rising numbers and proportions of blacks are in prison or jail, and yet racial bias not pervade the system? Most lawyers would see the disproportions as *prima facie* evidence of discrimination. There is an answer, and it lies not in the criminal justice system but in the policies of the Reagan and Bush administrations and their tough-on-crime followers in many states. The aggressive promotion of punitive crime control policies and a "War on Drugs," in the face of overwhelming evidence that these policies would not produce a safer America, has caused the ever harsher treatment of blacks by the criminal justice system, and it was foreseeable that they would do so. Just as the tripling of the American prison population between 1980 and 1993 was the result of conscious policy decisions, so also was the greater burden of punishment borne by blacks. Crime control politicians wanted more people in prison and knew that a larger proportion of them would be black. This chapter reviews the evidence regarding patterns of black criminality and the increasing blackness of American jails and prisons and examines the social science literature on racial bias in the system.

Black Offenders, Black Prisoners

For as long as the FBI has collected and reported national arrest data in its *Uniform Crime Reports,* blacks have experienced substantially higher arrest rates than whites relative to their respective shares of the population. This should surprise no one. Criminality and other serious antisocial conduct flow from social disorganization and social and economic disadvantage.

No ethnic or racial group in America except blacks has suffered the disadvantages of legally countenanced racial discrimination over sustained periods, continuing but widespread private discrimination, and objectification in Welfare Queens and Willie Hortons into archetypal enemies of working and middle-class white Americans. No experienced observer of American life, in any major city, would have any difficulty, even if there were no people around, guessing which neighborhoods were crime ridden; much too often, when the people appeared, many would be seen to be black. The legacy of legal racism, modern discrimination, and the failures of government to provide opportunities to the disadvantaged have combined to create criminogenic conditions in which too many black Americans are forced by circumstances to live.

Since the turn of the century, scholars and others have been writing about the causes and consequences of black criminality, and most diagnoses have been consistent. In 1899, W. E. B. DuBois, the pathbreaking black intellectual and political leader, argued that crime rose and fell with economic and social conditions and that, in bad times, blacks suffered extreme fluctuations:

> This is what we would naturally expect: we have here the record of a low social class, and as the condition of a lower class is by definition worse than that of a higher, so the situation of the Negroes is worse as respects crime and poverty than that of the mass of whites. We have in all probability an example of this in the increase of crime since 1890; we have had a period of financial stress and industrial depression. The ones who have felt this most are the poor, the unskilled laborers, the inefficient and unfortunate, and those with small social and economic advantages. The Negroes are in this class, and the result has been an increase in Negro crime and pauperism.

No more in 1899 than today were only economic conditions at fault, as Du Bois hastened to add: "It is certain that Negro prejudice in cities like Philadelphia has been a vast factor in aiding and abetting all other causes which impel a half-developed race to recklessness and excess."

Thirty years later, in 1928 in *The Negro Criminal*, Thorsten Sellin, for nearly half a century America's preeminent criminologist, offered a litany of "social factors" the explained disproportionate black criminality:

> Lack of formal education, the deleterious effects of the contact of the illiterate and unskilled Negro migrant with the city life of the North, the injustice of our agencies of justice, poverty, and a host of other conditions are brought forth as generators. The important fact, however, is the belief in the Negro's higher criminality. . . . In the case of the Negro, stranger in our midst, all beliefs prejudicial to him aid in intensifying the feeling of racial antipathy engendered by his color and social status.

After another decade, in 1941 in "The Negro and Crime," another classic article, Guy B. Johnson of the University of North Carolina summarized the subject:

> If it were possible to compute some sort of objective index of social disorder as a basis for predicting probable crime ratios, there can be little doubt that the index for the Negro would be higher than that for any other large group in the Nation. . . .

The position of the Negro in American society, with all that
means in terms of subordination, frustration, economic insecu-
rity, and incomplete participation, enters significantly into almost every aspect of Negro crime causation. Indeed, it is so
important as to constitute virtually a special and major set of
sociological and pyschological factors which can "explain" Negro
crime in so far as it needs special explanation.

Finally, in 1944, Gunnar Myrdal, in *An American Dilemma—The
Negro Problem and Modern Democracy,* still the most famed and
exhaustive account of race relations in America, offered an account
not greatly different from Du Bois's: "We suspect that the 'true'
crime rate—when extraneous influences are held constant—is
higher among Negroes. This is true at least for such crimes as involve personal violence, petty robbery, and sexual delinquency—
because of the caste system [Myrdal's label for systematic social and
economic subordination] and the slavery tradition [Myrdal's label
for systematic racial subordination]."

If I seem to be belaboring these antique analyses, some of which
use language that grates on modern ears and employ stereotypes
that modern minds reject, it is to stress that rates of crime by
blacks have for at least a century been higher than those for whites
and that the reasons for this difference have long been understood.
That a significant majority of modern black Americans are manag-
ing to win in social and economic games in which history stacked
the cards against them is cause for rejoicing. That a minority still
struggle in criminogenic conditions faced by few other Americans
is cause for regret. That a high rate of participation in crime is a
result is to be expected.

Today it is widely accepted that rates of criminality among blacks
are higher than those of whites, but it was not always so. Although
Du Bois observed in 1899 of crime, "to the minds of many, this is
the real Negro problem . . . that it is a vast problem a glance at
statistics will show," only in recent decades has there been broad
agreement that higher levels of black arrests result substantially
from higher levels of black crime and not preponderantly from
officials' bias. Sellin in 1928 was doubtful whether the higher black
criminality apparent in official records reflected behavior or racial
discrimination, particularly by police and court officials:

[Discrimination must] be taken into account when crime statistics dealing with the Negro are interpreted because it distorts the rate of apparent criminality to such a degree that no comparison with the rates for whites is possible unless it be in some way estimated and the rates corrected in light of the findings.

Although skeptical of the inferences to be drawn from official records, Sellin also believed that black crime rates in his time probably were, if knowable, higher than whites': "It would be extraordinary indeed if this group were to prove more law-abiding than the white, which enjoys more fully the advantages of a civilization that the Negro has helped to create."

Both Guy Johnson and Gunnar Myrdal, who relied heavily on work by Johnson in *The American Dilemma,* were of like mind.

[Myrdal:] In general, our attitude toward crime statistics must be that they do not provide a fair index of Negro crime. . . . We suspect that the "true" crime rate—when extraneous influences are held constant—is higher among Negroes.

[Johnson:] Most discussions of Negro crime have been concerned with the biases and the inadequacies of criminal statistics as a measure of the actual criminality of the Negro. . . . Our survey of the factors which might be expected to affect Negro criminality lends strength to the presumption that the Negro crime rate is actually considerably higher than the white.

There the matter stood for a very long time: higher black arrest rates coupled with widespread belief in justice system bias against blacks, confirmed by both common experience and numerous early statistical studies of sentencing that showed systematically harsher sentencing of blacks, especially concerning the death penalty and especially in the South. The conventional wisdom began to change in the 1970s because of two research developments. The first, beginning with work by University of Toronto sociologist John Hagan, was a series of surveys of the earlier research that concluded that much of the apparent discrimination they seemed to document resulted from overly simple analyses. When less simple analyses were undertaken that, for example, took offenders' prior criminality into account and controlled for other differences among cases, the apparent discrimination often was substantially reduced. The second was a pair of analyses in the late 1970s by the late Michael Hindelang of data from newly available victimization surveys of eight cities and of a representative sample of the national population to learn whether victims' identifications of their assailants' race in serious crimes matched up with arrest data. They did, which suggests that police arrests for serious crimes, whatever their other defects, are not badly distorted by racial considerations; but I get ahead of the story. Before looking at analyses of whether black disproportions in the criminal justice system reflect black criminality or official bias, and in what balance, I present descriptive data on long-term racial patterns in arrest, jail, and prison statistics.

The critical question is why proportionately so many more blacks than whites are in prison. The polar answers are "because blacks commit proportionately more crimes that typically result in prison sentences" and "because criminal justice officials make decisions that are racially biased." Which is true or, more likely, in what balance both are true cannot be answered without first looking back at what is known about different patterns of involvement in crime by black and white Americans.

Patterns of Crime Participation

Official criminal justice records are at least as much an indicator of bureaucratic policies and officials' discretionary decisions as of criminal events. For example, when the police are called to a domestic incident, for which policy tells them to separate and counsel the parties but not to write up an assault, it never happened, as far as official records are concerned. Nor did drunken blows among friends when the responding officer decides that a drive home is a more appropriate response than an arrest. More broadly, the nearly 50 percent of prisoners who are black could result from a series of compounding racially biased decisions and bear no resemblance to comparative racial patterns of crime. Because of these and other failings of official records, scholars have long recognized that the closer records are to events, the less distorted the picture is that they will paint.

Nonetheless, because the starkest disproportions in the criminal justice system—which most powerfully support a *prima facie* inference of discrimination—occur in the prisons and jails, Figures 2-1, 2-2, and 2-3 start there and show demographic trends in selected American correctional populations. Because of variations in statistical and reporting systems, the data for different populations cover different periods. Recent changes and inconsistencies in reporting data on Hispanics complicate some trend reports. Until 1980, Hispanics generally were included in black and white counts, sometimes with separate supplementary counts of Hispanics alone. More recently, some reports count non-Hispanic whites, non-Hispanic blacks, Hispanics, and others (sometimes also reporting data on Asians and Native Americans). When possible, I have included Hispanics in racial groupings.

A few words about sources of information are needed. Data on correctional trends over time must be cobbled together from disparate sources. There are two major problems. First, America's federal system of government and state-by-state differences in division of correctional responsibility among state, county, and municipal agencies create a national pattern of dizzying complexity. Unlike in England, for example, where the English Prison Service, a component of the Home Office, operates all correctional institutions for pretrial detainees and sentenced offenders (except short-term lockups in police stations), in the United States, pretrial detainees and convicted offenders are distributed among federal, state, and local authorities. The U.S. Bureau of Prisons handles all federal confinement, including pretrial. In most states, the state prison system houses offenders sentenced to terms of one year or longer, and county institutions house pretrial detainees and offenders sentenced to less than one year. There are, however, exceptions. Some states, like Connecticut and Delaware, have unified state departments of corrections that house detainees and all convicted offenders. In other states, local jails house offenders serving longer sentences; Pennsylvania's county facilities, in which terms up to five years can be served locally, are the extreme case.

The organization of corrections in the United States presents problems for counting offenders. If, for example, a count of all confined convicted offenders is wanted, data must be obtained from the Federal Bureau of Prisons, fifty state departments of corrections, the District of Columbia, and more than 3,300 county jails. Those data, which are voluntarily provided, may be furnished on time, late, or never, or they may be furnished complete and accurate, incomplete and sloppy, or not at all.

The second problem is that there are no comprehensive counts of persons incarcerated in jails and prisons, except as incidental to the decennial censuses of the U.S. Bureau of the Census. Instead, there are separate efforts to count jail and prison inmates. For many years, a succession of federal agencies has compiled and published annual, and recently semiannual, reports that give data on confined offenders under the jurisdiction of the Federal Bureau of Prisons and the departments of corrections of the fifty states and the District of Columbia. Counts are provided for total populations on a census date (including detainees and short-term prisoners in unified systems) and prisoners serving sentences of one year or longer. In addition, the Bureau of Justice Statistics of the U.S. Department of Justice in recent years has annually published more detailed prison population data in two publication series called the "National Corrections Reporting Program" and "Correctional Populations in the United States," which also present annual data on jail and parole populations. Finally, data were reported from national prison inmate surveys conducted by the Bureau of Justice Statistics in 1974, 1978, 1986, and 1991.

Jail populations are less reliably known. There have been a number of jail inmate surveys (in 1978, 1983, and 1989) and, since the early 1980s, the Bureau of Justice Statistics has published an annual "Jail Inmates" report, based partly on estimates.

The only feasible way to calculate national incarceration rates is to combine the annual-count population data reported for a given year for prisoners and jail inmates. So calculated, both aggregate and racially disaggregated incarceration rates climbed steadily between 1972 and 1992.

Figure 2-1 shows admissions to state and federal prisons by race from 1960 to 1991, the most recent date for which national admissions data on race have been published. White percentages declined and black percentages rose. Between 1986 and 1991, the racial mix in admissions reversed, from 53 percent white and 46 percent black to 53 percent black and 46 percent white. (Of those committed to state prisons in 1990 following a conviction, 54 percent were black and 45 percent were white.) The black population

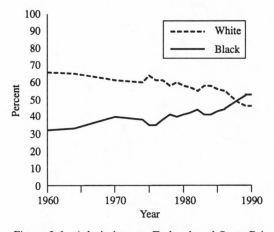

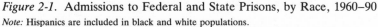

Figure 2-1. Admissions to Federal and State Prisons, by Race, 1960–90

Note: Hispanics are included in black and white populations.

Sources: Darrell K. Gilliard, *National Corrections Reporting Program, 1987* (Washington, D.C.: U.S. Department of Justice, Bureau of Justice Statistics, 1992); Patrick A. Langan, *Race of Persons Admitted to State and Federal Institutions, 1926–86* (Washington, D.C.: U.S. Department of Justice, Bureau of Justice Statistics, 1991); Craig Perkins, *National Corrections Reporting Program, 1989* (Washington, D.C.: U.S. Department of Justice, Bureau of Justice Statistics, 1992); Craig Perkins, *National Corrections Reporting Program, 1990* (Washington, D.C.: U.S. Department of Justice, Bureau of Justice Statistics, 1993); Craig Perkins and Darrell K. Gilliard, *National Corrections Reporting Program, 1988* (Washington, D.C.: U.S. Department of Justice, Bureau of Justice Statistics, 1992).

has continued to grow. Preliminary estimates are that 54 percent of new admissions in 1992 were black.

Figure 2-2 shows the racial composition of state and federal prison populations on counting dates for selected years from 1960 to 1980 and successively from 1985 to 1991. The trend is one of decreasing white and increasing black percentages. By 1991, American prisons housed more blacks than whites. Reported black numbers in recent years are an understatement because many Hispanics, some of whom are black, are reported as "race unknown" by some states, including Florida and Texas, which have sizable Hispanic populations.

Figure 2-3 shows the racial composition of jail populations for selected years from 1960 to 1978 and for successive years from 1983 to 1992. The trend again is one of a steady decrease in whites and an increase in blacks in the population's composition. In 1992, 44

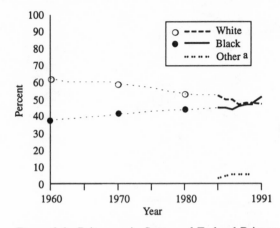

Figure 2-2. Prisoners in State and Federal Prisons on Census Date, by Race, 1960–91

[a] Hispanics in many states, Asians, Native Americans.

Sources: For 1960, 1970, and 1980, Margaret W. Cahalan, *Historical Corrections Statistics in the United States, 1850–1984* (Washington, D.C.: U.S. Department of Justice, Bureau of Justice Statistics, 1986), Table 3.31; for 1985 to 1991, Bureau of Justice Statistics, *Correctional Populations in the United States, 1985; 1986; 1987; 1988; 1989; 1991* (Washington, D.C.: U.S. Department of Justice, 1987, 1989a, 1989b, 1991b, 1991c, 1993).

percent were black non-Hispanic, 40 percent were white non-Hispanic, and 15 percent were Hispanic. When Hispanics are reclassified by race, nearly half of all inmates were black.

The patterns shown in Figures 2-1 to 2-3 for adult offenders also characterize juveniles. The proportion of whites in custody in public juvenile facilities fell from 70 percent in the 1950s to 60 percent in the late 1970s. By 1980, 42 percent of confined juveniles were black, 40 percent were white, and 15 percent were Hispanic (if adult patterns hold, roughly two-thirds are white and one-third are black). Between 1987 and 1989, the number of confined white juveniles fell by 5 percent while the number of confined black juveniles grew by 14 percent.

Most people are instinctively uneasy about black rates of incarceration that appear to be three to four times higher than white rates. The uneasiness is warranted, but the disproportion is far greater than three or four to one. The initial tendency to compare American blacks' proportion of the general population (13 per-

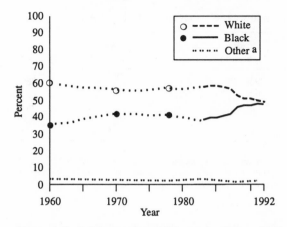

Figure 2-3. Jail Inmates at Midyear, by Race, 1960–92

[a] White and black figures for 1988, 1991, and 1992 are estimated; white non-Hispanic, black non-Hispanic, and Hispanic reported; Hispanic racial breakdown assumed to be the same as 1990, for which racial data were reported.

Sources: For 1960 to 1983, Margaret W. Cahalan, *Historical Corrections Statistics in the United States, 1850–1984* (Washington, D.C.: U.S. Department of Justice, Bureau of Justice Statistics, 1986), Tables 4.15, 4.21; for 1984 to 1992, Bureau of Justice Statistics, *The 1983 Jail Census* (Washington, D.C.: U.S. Department of Justice, 1984); Bureau of Justice Statistics, *Jail Inmates, 1983* (Washington, D.C.: U.S. Department of Justice, 1985); Bureau of Justice Statistics, *Census of Local Jails, 1988* (Washington, D.C.: U.S. Department of Justice, 1991a); Bureau of Justice Statistics, *Jail Inmates, 1991* (Washington, D.C.: U.S. Department of Justice, 1992); Bureau of Justice Statistics, *Correctional Populations in the United States, 1991* (Washington, D.C.: U.S. Department of Justice, 1993).

cent) with their presence in the prison and jail populations (48–50 percent) is understandable but misleading, and it greatly underestimates the dimensions of racial disparities. A better comparison is between racially disaggregated incarceration rates measured as the number of confined persons of a racial group per 100,000 population of that group. By that measure, black incarceration rates in recent years have been six to seven times higher than white incarceration rates.

Table 2-1 shows racially disaggregated jail and prison incarceration rates for the United States for 1990. For every 100,000 white Americans, 289 were in jail or prison on a typical day in 1990. For every 100,000 black Americans, 1,860 were in jail or prison. The racial differences in incarceration rates can be expressed as a ratio.

Table 2-1. U.S. Black, White, and Other Incarceration Rates, 1990

	General Population	Prison Population	Jail Population	Prison + Jail Population	Rate 100,000
White	199,686,000	369,485	206,713	576,198	289
Black	29,986,000	367,122	190,500	557,622	1,860
Other	19,038,000	37,768	8,106	45,874	241
Total	248,710,000	774,375	405,319	1,179,694	474

Sources: Louis W. Jankowski, *Correctional Populations in the United States, 1990* (Washington, D.C.: U.S. Department of Justice, Bureau of Justice Statistics, 1992), Tables 2.1, 2.3, 5.6; Bureau of the Census, *Statistical Abstract of the United States—1992* (Washington, D.C.: U.S. Government Printing Office, 1992), Table 16.

When divided by the white rate of 289 per 100,000, the black rate of 1,860 per 100,000 results in a ratio of 6.44 in population-adjusted incarceration rates (1860/289) = 6.44). The incarceration rates and ratio can be thought of as racial differences in the risk of incarceration. Thus the 6.44 ratio of racial incarceration rates in 1990 means that in that year the likelihood that a black American was in prison or jail on any given day was 6.44 times higher than the equivalent likelihood for a white American.

The 6.44 racial incarceration ratio raises a series of "why?" questions. Why is the ratio so high—discrimination against blacks in the criminal justice system, much more crime by blacks, or something else? If blacks do commit many more serious crimes that are ordinarily punished by imprisonment than whites do—what might be thought of as "imprisonable crimes"—why is this so?

Others would append other "why" questions that I do not explore. Why, for example, do the criminal law and the criminal justice system treat those crimes—homicide, robbery, rape, aggravated assault—which blacks commit relatively more often as imprisonable crimes rather than white-collar and business crimes, which whites commit relatively more often? Issues that this question raises are patently important. No doubt the self-interest of the white majority that dominates American social, economic, and political life is part of the answer. But it does not follow from the proposition that the criminal law should take consumer fraud, financial crimes, income tax evasion, and water and air pollution more seriously that it should take rape, robbery, and homicide less seriously. During the 1970s in both England and the United States, self-styled "radical," "critical," and "Marxist" criminologists and political activists attacked the criminal justice system on precisely the grounds that it unfairly, for class and political reasons, focused too much attention on poor people's crimes. That movement has largely withered away, to be replaced in England by "Left Realism," the realism referring to the inexorable insight that poor people no more than the wealthy want their property taken or destroyed or themselves and their loved ones sexually or violently assaulted.

If, however, it were the case (it is not) that the 6.44 racial imprisonment rate resulted solely from a 6.44 ratio of rates of black and white commission of traditional imprisonable crimes, many people would consider that to be a persuasive explanation for the imprisonment ratio. But this would be oversimplistic, since other things besides the crimes that people commit influence punishment. The offender's prior record is one: Imprisonment patterns cannot meaningfully be compared with patterns of commission of imprisonable crimes unless offenders' criminal records are taken into account. Or to take account of a different kind of consideration, if crime participation is partly the product of social and economic disadvantage or of being a member of a minority that has suffered sustained invidious discrimination, ethical arguments can be developed that those offenders should not be punished as severely as should more privileged offenders who have committed the same crimes. For example, if both had no prior record, a nineteen-year-old Mexican-American from a single-parent, welfare-dependent, inner-city background might warrant more solicitous sentencing on a burglary charge than would a nineteen-year-old white from a two-parent, well-to-do, suburban background charged with an identical offense. Or maybe justice requires that both receive the same sentence, a subject to which I turn in Chapters 5 and 6.

Patterns of crime by members of different groups may not tell us all we need or want to know in order to decide whether group patterns of punishment are appropriate, but those patterns are a good starting point. Arrests are the official data that come closest to criminal events, and, as Table 2-2 shows at three-year intervals since 1976, black and white arrest percentages have essentially

Table 2-2. Percentage of Black and White Arrests for Index I Offenses, 1976–91 (three-year intervals)[a]

	1976		1979		1982		1985		1988		1991		1992	
	White	Black	White	Black	White	Black	White	Black	White	Black	White	Black	White	Black
Murder and nonnegligent manslaughter	45.0	53.5	49.4	47.7	48.8	49.7	50.1	48.4	45.0	53.5	43.4	54.8	43.5	55.1
Forcible Rape	51.2	46.6	50.2	47.7	48.7	49.7	52.2	46.5	52.7	45.8	54.8	43.5	55.5	42.8
Robbery	38.9	59.2	41.0	56.9	38.2	60.7	37.4	61.7	36.3	62.6	37.6	61.1	37.7	60.9
Aggravated assault	56.8	41.0	60.9	37.0	59.8	38.8	58.0	40.4	57.6	40.7	60.0	38.3	59.5	38.8
Burglary	69.0	29.2	69.5	28.7	67.0	31.7	69.7	28.9	67.0	31.3	68.8	29.3	67.8	30.4
Larceny-theft	65.7	32.1	67.2	30.2	64.7	33.4	67.2	30.6	65.6	32.2	66.6	30.9	66.2	31.4
Motor vehicle theft	71.1	26.2	70.0	27.2	66.9	31.4	65.8	32.4	58.7	39.5	58.5	39.3	58.4	39.4
Arson	-		78.9	19.2	74.0	24.7	75.7	22.8	73.5	25.0	76.7	21.5	76.4	21.9
Violent crime[b]	50.4	47.5	53.7	44.1	51.9	46.7	51.5	47.1	51.7	46.8	53.6	44.8	53.6	44.8
Property crime[c]	67.0	30.9	68.2	29.4	65.5	32.7	67.7	30.3	65.3	32.6	66.4	31.3	65.8	31.8
Total crime index	64.1	33.8	65.3	32.4	62.7	35.6	64.5	33.7	62.4	35.7	63.2	34.6	62.7	35.2

[a] Because of rounding, the percentages may not add to total.
[b] Violent crimes are offenses of murder, forcible rape, robbery, and aggravated assault.
[c] Property crimes are offenses of burglary, larceny-theft, motor vehicle theft, and arson.

Sources: Bureau of Justice Statistics, Sourcebook of Criminal Justice Statistics (Washington, D.C.: U.S. Department of Justice, various years); Federal Bureau of Investigation, Uniform Crime Reports for the United States—1992 (Washington, D.C.: U.S. Government Printing Office, 1993), Table 43.

been stable, showing for many offenses a slight decline in black arrests. In 1976, for example, of all persons arrested for violent crimes, 47.5 percent were black, a figure that fell slightly to 44.8 percent by 1992. Blacks made up 53.5 percent of homicide arrestees in 1976 (up to 55.1 percent in 1992), 46.6 percent of rape arrestees (down to 42.8 percent in 1992), 59.2 percent of robbery arrestees (up to 60.9 percent in 1992), and 41 percent of aggravated assault arrestees (down to 38.8 percent in 1992).

The arrest data reveal two patterns. First, at least since 1976, the proportion of blacks among persons arrested for imprisonable crimes has greatly exceeded their 12 to 13 percent share of the general population. This is consistent with the notion that disproportionate black criminality has something to do with disproportionate incarceration of blacks. Second, however, the relative proportions of blacks and whites among persons arrested for imprisonable crimes have held steady for nearly two decades. This is not consistent with the increases since the early 1980s, shown in Figures 2-1 to 2-3, in the proportions of blacks among prison admissions and prison and jail populations.

Alfred Blumstein of Carnegie–Mellon's Heinz School of Public Policy and Management analyzed racial arrest and imprisonment patterns more carefully than anyone else and concluded that a large amount of the racial disproportion in prison populations can be explained by differential involvement in arrests. He did this by means of a much more sophisticated comparison between prison populations and arrests for imprisonable crimes than that offered in the preceding two paragraphs. Table 2-3 presents his four-step analysis and his findings.

First, using Bureau of Justice Statistics data on state prisoners in 1979, Blumstein divided the prison population into eleven categories on the basis of the offenses of which prisoners had been convicted and for which they had been sentenced to imprisonment. Thus the first column shows that 17.7 and 4.2 percent of prisoners had been convicted, respectively, of homicide and rape.

Second, within each category, Blumstein determined what percentage of sentenced prisoners was black. Thus the second column shows that 52.3 percent of prisoners convicted of homicide were black, as were 56.3 percent of those convicted of rape and 61.2 percent of those convicted of robbery.

Table 2-3. Comparison of Crime Type–Specific Percentages of Blacks in Prison and in Arrests

| Crime type | Crime-Type Distribution in Prison | Black Percentage | | Percentage of Disproportionality Unexplained[a] |
		Among Prisoners	Among Arrests	
Homicide	17.7%	52.3%	51.6%	2.8%
Forcible rape	4.2	56.3	48.7	26.3
Robbery	25.2	61.2	57.1	15.6
Aggravated assault	8.2	42.3	41.0	5.2
Other violent	2.3	46.9	39.1	27.3
Burglary	18.1	42.3	32.9	33.1
Larceny/auto theft	6.6	49.3	34.6	45.6
Other property	7.7	35.6	34.6	4.3
Drugs	5.7	39.5	25.0	48.9
Public Order	3.9	38.6	30.7	29.5
Other	.3	28.3	33.7	−28.7
Total		49.14	43.45	20.5

[a] The calculation on which "percent disproportionality unexplained" is described in Blumstein 1982.

Source: Alfred Blumstein, "On the Racial Disproportionality of United States' Prison Populations," *Journal of Criminal Law and Criminology* 73 (1982): 1259–81.

Third, using FBI data on arrests for 1978, Blumstein determined what proportions of persons arrested for the same eleven offense categories were black. Thus the third column shows that 51.6 percent of those arrested for homicide and 48.7 percent of those arrested for rape were black.

Fourth, assuming that in a nonbiased system, racial proportions in arrests would be mirrored in racial proportions imprisoned, he compared the arrest and imprisonment percentages. Thus when he compared the 52.3 percent blacks among persons imprisoned for homicide with the 51.6 percent blacks among persons arrested for homicide, Blumstein found that 97.2 percent of racial disproportion for that offense could be explained as the result of black homicide arrests. Put the other way around, only 2.8 percent of the racial disproportion for homicide remained unexplained. He made similar calculations for each offense category, shown in column 4, and concluded that overall in a nonbiased world, arrests would explain 80 percent of racial disproportions in prison in 1979.

One additional pattern stands out from Table 2-3. The amount of disproportionality left unexplained by Blumstein's analysis varies with the seriousness of the crimes. For the most serious crime of homicide, virtually all the disproportionate incarceration of blacks can be explained by arrests, as can 95 percent of their presence in prison for aggravated assault and 84 percent of their presence for robbery. For less serious crimes like burglary, drug offenses, nonserious assaults ("other violent"), and public-order offenses, the unexplained variation is much larger.

The pattern Blumstein found fits with one consistent research finding and with commonsense understanding of how discrimination is likely to operate. The research finding, recognized by the 1983 report of the National Academy of Sciences Panel on Sentencing Research and reiterated dozens of times by individual researchers, is that the seriousness of the current offense is, by a wide margin, the best predictor of which offenders are sent to prison and for how long, with the offender's prior record a distant second and other considerations trailing behind. For the most serious crimes, accordingly, imprisonment patterns should correspond to arrest patterns (assuming the latter to be nondiscriminatory), and this is very nearly what Blumstein's data show. For less serious crimes, however, a variety of considerations might make arrests less predictive of punishments. Some might be legitimate, like prior criminal records or the effects of penalties on the offender's family. Some might be illegitimate, like conscious racial bias or unconscious reliance on stereotypes detrimental to blacks. Some might result from idiosyncracies of individual judges.

Blumstein's basic finding that differential racial arrest patterns appear to explain much of the disproportionate incarceration of blacks has been replicated and confirmed by other research, which is discussed below. First, though, some of the limitations of Blumstein's analysis need mention, for, although the analysis is suggestive, it cannot be said to prove its conclusion. Even if Blumstein's assumption that racial arrest patterns reflect offending is right, his conclusion that "eighty percent of the disproportionality in prison was explained just by the differential involvement in arrest" is likely to be true only in a narrow statistical sense. There are a number of problems. First, since he relies on national data, he risks the overaggregation problem of relying on mean averages illustrated by the sad story of the statistician who drowned in a lake on average only three inches deep. Averages can hide major differences, and in theory Blumstein's aggregate analysis could hide polar differences between some states in which arrests explain 100 percent of disproportionality and others in which arrests explain only 60 percent. A major problem of racial bias in sentencing in only half the country would be a very large problem, whatever the national averages.

Similarly, Blumstein's analysis could hide offsetting forms of discrimination that are equally objectionable but not observable in the aggregate. If, for example, black offenders with white victims were punished more harshly than white offenders with white victims, and black offenders with black victims less harshly, the former would reflect bias against black offenders and the latter bias against black victims, and aggregate imprisonment data might reveal neither pattern.

Is Sentencing Racially Biased?

A sizable body of other research evidence, principally consisting of dozens of statistical studies of sentencing in individual jurisdictions, suggests that the overaggregation problems, though they exist, are not likely to undermine Blumstein's analysis fatally. Most modern empirical analyses of sentencing conclude that when legitimate differences among individual cases are taken into account, comparatively little systematic difference in contemporary sentencing outcomes appears to be attributable to race. The National Academy of Sciences Panel on Sentencing Research in 1983, for example, concluded:

> Our overall assessment of the available research suggests that factors other than racial discrimination in the sentencing process account for most of the disproportionate representation of black males in U.S. prisons, although discrimination in sentencing may play a more important role in some regions, jurisdictions, crime types, or the decisions of individual participants.

Other major surveys of sentencing research by University of Toronto sociologist John Hagan, Florida State University criminologist Gary Kleck, and Florida International University criminologist William Wilbanks reach similar conclusions, as is revealed in the title of Wilbanks's book *The Myth of a Racist Criminal Justice System* (1987).

Even minority scholars who believe discrimination is extensive implicitly concede the research findings. Coramae Richey Mann's 1993 book, *Unequal Justice—A Question of Color,* which expresses its viewpoint in its title, asserts that "racial minority suspects disproportionately become defendants and as defendants are disproportionately sent to prison or disproportionately executed. These are facts most peoples of color are aware of and that most criminologists and other social scientists should be aware of." Her criticisms of reviews of sentencing research do not, however, directly challenge their conclusions:

> The [research reviews like Kleck's] are especially disconcerting when the far-reaching effects of such a sensitive issue as mistreatment of minorities in any institutional or organizational analysis are addressed. Even a single verified case of unequal sentencing because of racial status serves to illuminate flaws in the criminal justice system, and indeed ample research demonstrates that there are thousands of such cases.

Her real point—and of course she is right—is that any discrimination on racial grounds is morally and ethically wrong, but to prove that some discrimination exists, which it incontrovertibly does, is not the same as proving that substantial intentional racial bias pervades the system and is *a,* or *the,* primary reason that disproportionate numbers of blacks are in prison, which the best evidence indicates it is not.

Although the research on discrimination in sentencing suggests that Blumstein's aggregation of data is not camouflaging evidence of wholesale, cross-cutting forms of racial bias, his analysis must overcome a set of problems related to timing. By comparing arrest patterns in 1978 with prison populations in 1979, he risked comparing apples and oranges. This year's prisoners were arrested in earlier years, which means that Blumstein may be comparing the wrong things. Table 2-2, showing relative stability in the racial composition of arrests, suggests that this is unlikely to be a serious problem.

A more significant timing problem is that prison populations vary with both admission patterns and length-of-stay patterns, and Blumstein's analysis confounds the two. Because average sentences for different crimes vary widely from many years in most jurisdictions for homicide to less than a year in many for auto theft, timing factors could distort Blumstein's overall analysis. It should not, however, significantly distort his analysis for particular kinds of crimes. Whether more convicted black robbers are sent to prison or those sent receive longer sentences, either pattern would increase the proportion of black robbers in prison relative to arrests compared with white robbers.

Taken together, these limitations of Blumstein's analysis caution a too-quick reliance on it as a definitive refutation of claims that the criminal justice system's discrimination against blacks is a serious problem. Blumstein himself does not claim to have disproved the existence of discriminatory decision making, but only that it is not the primary basis for the disproportion.

Although Blumstein's claim that his analysis explains 80 percent of black disproportion in prison thus may claim too much, it does demonstrate that a very large, if not precisely quantifiable, proportion does result from differential involvement in crime. That conclusion has held up fairly well, as is demonstrated by three different kinds of research. The reviews of many dozens of studies on disparity and discrimination in sentencing have already been mentioned. In addition, the largest and most sophisticated analysis of discrimination in a single state—a RAND Corporation study by Stephen Klein and Joan Petersilia of 11,553 California offenders convicted in 1980 of assault, robbery, burglary, theft, forgery, or drug crimes—determined that race had no independent effect on predictions of who went to prison or of lengths of prison sentences. The second kind of confirmatory research tests Blumstein's assumption that racial patterns in arrests are a reasonable reflection of racial patterns in offending. The third kind of confirmatory research consists of efforts to replicate his analysis using different or later data sets.

Are Arrests Racially Biased?

Blumstein's assumption about the reliability of arrests as a measure of racial crime patterns is essential to his analysis. If, for example, blacks who commit rapes were twice as likely to be arrested for rape as were whites who commit rapes, racial arrest patterns could not be taken as a reliable indicator of racial offending patterns, and Blumstein's analysis would be based on a false premise. This turns out not to be a serious problem.

Most reviews of research on racial discrimination by police in making arrests conclude that few or no reliable, systematic data are available that demonstrate systematic discrimination. Again, analogous to research on sentencing decisions, the claim is not that no discrimination occurs in individual cases or that there are no biased police officers but that overall the much higher arrest rates of blacks for serious crimes are not substantially the result of bias. In his 1987 survey, Wilbanks concludes that "there is little evidence that white police officers make different decisions with respect to arrests than black ones" and that the evidence supporting claims of systematic discrimination against blacks by the police "is sparse, inconsistent, and contradictory to the discrimination thesis." Coramae Richey Mann's *Unequal Justice* (1993) observes that "the few available studies of this issue offer support to both sides of the question." The police chapter in the 1991 *Race and Criminal Justice* by Michael J. Lynch and E. Britt Patterson observes that "race appears to have little effect on the probability that police will take disputants into custody" and that "neither the race of the disputing parties nor the racial composition of the neighborhood . . . has a significant impact on whether police take at least one of the disputants into custody." On a narrower question in the police chapter of an earlier book surveying research on race and crime, R. L. McNeely and Carl E. Pope's *Race, Crime, and Criminal Justice* (1981), James J. Fyfe concludes of police use of force against minority citizens that "there is nothing in these analyses to support the contention that the disproportion of Blacks among New York City shooting opponents is reflective of police misconduct or racial discrimination." The editors and authors of all these books, except possibly Wilbanks, are predisposed to look for and to find evidence of racial bias in police contacts with blacks. That the evidence in these books of systematic bias is absent or weak and contradictory makes it doubtful that such evidence exists. Arrests can by and large be taken as reasonable reflections of the involvement in serious crime of members of different racial groups.

Another body of evidence, data on crime victims' identifications of the race of their assailants, demonstrates more directly that arrests broadly reflect offending. As confirmation of his assumption that arrests reflect behavior, Blumstein cited the early victimization data analyses by the late Michael Hindelang. Using data from a survey of victimization in eight cities, Hindelang compared victims' descriptions of their assailants with arrest records from the FBI's *Uniform Crime Reports* and found no evidence of bias against blacks: "Overall the correspondence between the victim survey and the UCR percentages is striking." In his second analysis, relying on 1974 data from the National Crime Victimization Survey, Hindelang compared rape, robbery, and assault victims' descriptions of their assailants with UCR arrest data. He found that racial percentages among robbery arrestees were identical to the percentages in victims' descriptions, that for the other crimes blacks made up slightly larger percentages in arrest data than in victim identification data, but that "by far, most of the arrest percentage appears to be attributable to the substantially greater involvement of blacks than whites in these crimes." These studies deal with a period in which racially-biased police practices were far more prevalent than they are today, both because police departments then employed many fewer black officers and because police managers were much less concerned with community and race relations.

More recent data show a similar pattern. Figure 2-4 shows data from the National Crime Victimization Survey for the years 1980 to 1991 on victims' identifications of blacks as their assailant in robberies and aggravated assaults involving only one offender. The figure also shows the percentages of blacks among arrestees for those crimes in each year. Although the victim data on perceived race of assailants were reported slightly differently from 1980 to 1984 (whites and "blacks and other races") and afterward ("blacks" and "whites"), the pattern is clear. The black percentages among victim descriptions are stable year after year and closely parallel the black percentages among arrests. For example, 54.8 percent of robbery assailants were reported in 1980 to be of "black or other [nonwhite] race"; the percentages for identified black assailants in 1985 and 1990 were 55.5 and 51.5 percent. The percentages of blacks among persons arrested for robbery in 1980, 1985, and 1990 were 57.7 percent, 61.7 percent, and 61.2 percent.

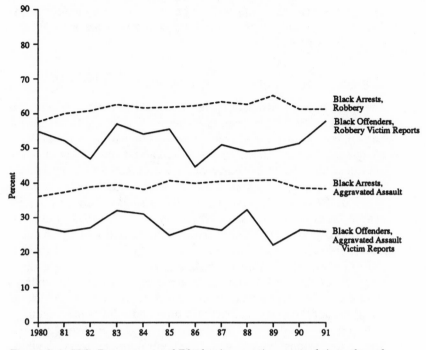

Figure 2-4. U.S. Percentages of Blacks Among Aggravated Assault and Robbery Arrestees and Among Lone Offenders for Those Offenses as Perceived by Victims, 1980–91

Note: After 1984, the "black and other races" category was changed to "black."

Source: Bureau of Justice Statistics, *Sourcebook of Criminal Justice Statistics* (Washington, D.C.: U.S. Department of Justice, various years and tables).

The black arrest percentages are somewhat higher than the victim identificaton percentages, but the two are not fully comparable. Figure 2-4 pertains only to single-offender crimes, whereas arrests include offenders involved in multiple-offender crimes. Thus one multiple-offender crime might result in two or more arrests. A closer comparison would compare arrests for blacks and whites, weighted to account for multiple arrests for single crimes, with victim identifications that combine single- and multiple-offender crimes. I do not have those data and doubt that anyone has worked out the appropriate weightings to make that comparison. In any case, the comparison of arrest and victim identification data does not suggest that racial arrest patterns are substantially out-of-line with behavior.

Can Blumstein's Findings Be Replicated?

The final major analysis of crimes and punishments of blacks was completed in 1985 by Bureau of Justice Statistics statistician Patrick Langan in an effort to build on the earlier Blumstein and Hindelang analyses. Whereas Hindelang compared arrest statistics with victim identifications from very early victimization surveys, Langan used national victimization survey data for the years 1973 to 1982. Whereas Blumstein's analysis was for a single year, Langan repeated his analysis for each of three years—1973, 1979, and 1982. Whereas Blumstein compared arrests with the national prison population, looking to victimization data to justify the use of arrests, Langan compared victimization data directly with prison use, stepping over any possible racial bias in arrest patterns. Finally, whereas Blumstein compared arrests with the prison population—which, as noted earlier, lags behind arrests in time and reflects prison admission patterns and time-served patterns—Langan used data on prison admissions, which avoids the confounding effects of admissions and length of sentence in Blumstein's data.

Langan's findings offer even less support for claims of wholesale racial discrimination in sentencing and punishment than did Blumstein's. Langan's analysis involved two steps. First, he obtained data on victims' identifications of assailants for ten years, both for all victimizations and for those more important events that are reported to the police, and showed that the black percentages for serious crimes were essentially stable from 1973 to 1982 (consistent with the arrest trends for 1976 to 1992 shown in Table 2-2). His data for robbery, aggravated assault, assault, theft, and burglary are shown in Table 2-4. For each year and for each offense, the percentages of cases in which blacks are identified by victims as their assailants are nearly the same for all crimes and for those that were reported to the police.

Second, for each of the years 1973, 1979, and 1982, Langan compared the percentages of racially identified offenders in the victimization data for the same years. Table 2-5 shows the data for

Table 2-4. Crime Victims' Descriptions of Their Assailants' Race: Percentage of Black Adult Offenders in All Incidents Experienced by Victims and Percentage of Black Adult Offenders in Incidents Reported to the Police

										Percentage of Black Adult Offenders

Year	Robbery		Aggravated Assault		Simple Assault		Burglary		Larceny	
	All	Reported	All	Reported	All	Reported	All	Reported	All	Reported
1973	67	67	30	29	23	21	42	40	40	36
1974	63	66	26	21	28	22	36	33	43	50
1975	66	66	32	30	23	21	31	35	44	42
1976	65	64	28	25	23	22	33	39	44	49
1977	57	60	25	27	21	21	23	15	43	47
1978	51	55	26	25	18	16	35	38	44	45
1979	61	60	26	28	20	17	29	34	43	49
1980	62	64	19	19	19	20	31	34	45	48
1981	61	64	29	30	21	21	37	35	47	53
1982	63	63	28	24	20	21	34	34	45	53

Note: Table data are based on NCS victimization surveys sponsored by the Bureau of Justice Statistics. Table figures were calculated from data on white adults and black adults only.

Source: Patrick A. Langan, "Racism on Trial: New Evidence to Explain the Racial Composition of Prisons in the United States," *Journal of Criminal Law and Criminology* 76 (1985): 666–83.

Table 2-5. Black Offenders According to Victims and Prison Population: Percentage of Black Adult Offenders in Crimes Reported to Police (Victim Survey) Compared with Percentage of Black Admissions to State Prisons According to National Prisoner Statistics (Prison Data)

| | Percentage of Black Adult Offenders | | | | | | | | | |
| | Robbery | | Aggravated Assault | | Simple Assault | | Burglary | | Larceny | |
Year	Victim Survey	Prison Data	Victim Survey	Prison Data	Victim Survey	Prison Data	Victim Survey	Prison Data	Victim Survey	Prison Data
1973	67	65	29	52	21	44	40	36	36	45
1979	60	58	28	47	17	49	34	41	49	49
1982	63	60	22	50	-	-	34	42	53	48

Source: Patrick A. Langan, "Racism on Trial: New Evidence to Explain the Racial Composition of Prisons in the United States," *Journal of Criminal Law and Criminology* 76 (1985): 666–83.

five offenses. For robbery, the most serious, and for larceny, the percentages are almost identical. They are more divergent for the other three offenses, but this may be misleading because of small numbers and random variation. Of the fourteen year/offense combinations shown, the difference in offending and admission percentages was statistically significant in each year only for aggravated assault. In general, however, Langan concluded that rather than suggest that prison disproportion resulted from racial bias, "test results generally support the differential involvement [in crime] hypothesis."

Third and most important, Langan compared prison admissions for blacks and whites relative to the victimization data on offenders' race and confirmed Blumstein's basic findings. Langan calculated white prison admissions relative to victimization data on white offending. Then he compared the two, assuming that black offenders in a racially nonbiased system should be incarcerated at the same rates relative to black offending as are whites relative to white offending. For 1973, he found that if admitted to prison in the same patterns as whites were, blacks would have numbered 19,344; the actual number was 19,953, a statistically nonsignificant difference. For 1979, if they were imprisoned at white rates, blacks should have made up 43.8 percent of admissions; the actual number was 48.1 percent. For 1982, the expected percentage was 44.9 percent, and the actual percentage was 48.9 percent.

Langan's analysis does not prove that racial bias is absent from the criminal justice system in individual cases or in general. Like Blumstein's analysis, Langan's leaves about 20 percent of the racial disproportion unexplained. Also like Blumstein's analysis, but more powerfully, it suggests that, as Langan put it, "the overrepresentation of blacks among offenders admitted to state prisons occurs because blacks commit a disproportionate number of imprisonable crimes" and that racism in the criminal justice system "might explain only a small part of the gap between the 11 percent black representation in the United states adult population and the now nearly 50 percent black representation among persons entering state prisons each year in the United States."

There the matter rests. In a more recent analysis using 1991 data, Blumstein replicated his earlier study and concluded that the percentage of the disproportionate black presence in prisons that could be explained by black offending patterns had fallen from 80 percent to 76 percent overall. Although arrest patterns explained a higher proportion of the confinement of blacks for homicide and robbery in 1991 than in 1979, they explained a considerably lower proportion of the confinement of blacks for drug and other less serious crimes.

A final postscript concerns one last, unsuccessful challenge to claims that arrests and victim identification data present a reasonably accurate picture of black offending. A number of commentators have argued that self-report studies, in which people are asked to provide information on their own offending, present a very different picture of racial offending patterns than do arrests or victim data. In their *Race, Crime, and Criminal Justice* (1981), for example, R. L. McNeely and Carl E. Pope observe, "When asked to self disclose their own criminal involvement, black and white respondents [in self-report surveys] reveal either zero or minimal differences." This is at best a speculative argument because there are no large, national representative self-report studies of offending that can be compared with arrest and victimization data. Most self-report studies involve either teenagers or convicted adult offenders. The teenager studies typically show few or no differences between blacks and whites but also, because they usually survey high school students (thereby missing drop-outs and truants), include few serious crimes. The prisoner surveys reveal few racial differences in offending, but the subjects are known serious offenders and so are characterized by the racial disproportions in prison that this chapter attempts to explain. Neither sort of study supports generalizations about the general adult population.

This speculative argument has, however, been undermined by recent publications from the National Youth Survey, a national (if small) representative self-report survey conducted since 1976 by researchers at the University of Colorado. The people surveyed are now in their thirties, and the findings over time bridge the gap between the teenager self-report studies and adult arrest and victim data. "Participation rates," that is, the percentage of persons admitting the commission of particular offenses, were calculated for blacks and whites. Through the teenage years, the National Youth Survey data reveal participation rates for serious violent offending (robbery, forcible rape, aggravated assault) that are generally comparable for blacks and whites. At ages 11 and 12, the ratio of black-to-white participation rates is 1:1. Through adolescence, the ratio is 1.5:1. By the late twenties, however, according to Delbert Elliot, the study's director, the ratio climbs to 4:1, which is "very similar to the differences observed in the *Uniform Crime Reports* of arrests for violent offenses at this age," unlike the adolescent years when the self-report ratio is 1.5:1 and the arrest ratio is 4:1.

The difference in participation rate ratios results not from a difference in the likelihood that blacks and whites will commit serious violent crimes, according to Elliott's analyses. By age thirty, the percentages of blacks and whites who had *ever* committed serious violent crimes were nearly identical. The differences were that those blacks who did commit violent acts began to do so at earlier ages and continued doing so for longer times. The best statistical predictors of *desistance* from offending for blacks and whites were employment and marriage, a pattern that fits well, if depressingly, with William Julius Wilson's research on the declining percentages of employed men ("marriageable males") available as partners for black women.

Thus the answer to the question, "Is racial bias in the criminal justice system the principal reason that proportionately so many more blacks than whites are in prison?" is no, with one important caveat, discussed in the next chapter concerning drugs. From every available data source, discounted to take account of their measurement and methodological limits, the evidence seems clear that the main reason that black incarceration rates are substantially higher than those for whites is that black crime rates for imprisonable crimes are substantially higher than those for whites. This conclusion is the beginning, not the end, of the policy problems, and it is to those problems that I turn in Chapters 4 to 7, after exploring the effects of the War on Drugs on black Americans.

Since socioeconomic conditions affecting black Americans are the reason for their high offending rates, how do we change those conditions? In the here and now, knowing that black offending rates are higher than whites', how can we change criminal justice policies so that they will become less destructive of the lives of black Americans and more restorative of the life chances of disadvantaged blacks? None of these are easy questions, but they are better and, in the long run, more socially constructive questions than those that are asked in efforts to ferret out a willful and pervasive racial bias in a criminal justice system in which most officials and participants believe in racial equality and worry about the racial patterns they see every day.

3

Race and the War on Drugs

Three effects of the War on Drugs stand out. First, it was a failure. The street price of cocaine, the war's signature drug, should have risen if dealing were becoming riskier and drugs less available; prices fell. Massive arrests and street-sweep tactics in many cities, backed up by harsh mandatory prison sentences, should have cleared out the drug dealers and made drugs harder to find; they did not. Most analysts and many police officials believe that arrested street dealers are nearly always replaced by others willing to take the risks and that drug sales are merely moved to other locations. Finally, there is no evidence that crime control efforts lowered levels of drug use in the United States. Drug use was declining years before the war was declared, and the war can claim no credit for the continuation of preexisting trends. There are reasons to believe that mass media and public education initiatives reduced drug use, especially among school-age people, but that is a different matter.

Second, although the war accomplished few if any of its ostensible goals, it did so at great cost. The doubling of arrests in the 1980s, combined with harsher penalties, more than doubled police, jail, prosecution, and court case flows and costs associated with drugs.

The war's effects on prisons and correctional programs were greater. Drug-offense sentences are the single most important cause of the trebling of the prison population in the United States since 1980. In the federal prisons, for example, drug offenders constituted 22 percent of admissions in 1980, 39 percent in 1988, and 42 percent in 1990. In 1980, 25 percent (4,912) of federal prisoners were drug offenders; by 1991, 56 percent (30,754) were drug offenders; and by 1992, 58 percent. Guarding, housing, feeding, and caring for all these prisoners cost a great deal. Typical estimates of the average annual cost of holding one prisoner range from $20,000 to $30,000. Typical estimates of the costs of building new prisons range, depending on climate and security level, from $50,000 to $200,000 per prisoner. Construction costs often are paid with borrowed money, to be repaid with interest in future years. Operating costs are paid from current revenues; the future burden will come from debt service and the need to continue year after year to pay to house drug offenders sentenced to ten, twenty, and thirty years in prison.

Third, as if ineffectiveness and immense, avoidable cost were not indictment enough, they pale before the most fundamental objection. The War on Drugs forseeably and unnecessarily blighted the lives of hundreds of thousands of young disadvantaged black Americans and undermined decades of effort to improve the life chances of members of the urban black underclass. The war was fought largely from partisan political motives to show that the Bush and Reagan administrations were concerned about public safety, crime prevention, and the needs of victims (as if Democrats, or any responsible mainstream political figure, were not). The bodies counted in this war, as they lay in their prison beds, however, are even more disproportionately black than prisoners already were. War or no war, most people are saddened to learn that for many years 30 to 40 percent of those admitted to prison were black. The War on Drugs was a calculated effort foreordained to increase those percentages, and this is what happened.

This chapter presents the evidence on which the preceding observations are based and explains why on both ethical and policy grounds, because of its implications for black Americans, the War on Drugs should never have been launched. I first examine whether on substantive, as opposed to ideological, grounds there was any reason to start the War on Drugs. I then trace the effects of the drug wars and show that blacks particularly were ensnared. Although disadvantaged young people of all races and ethnicities have been affected by the drug wars, the greatest attention has been on Hispanics and blacks. Black Americans in particular have been caught, and because of the heavy burdens borne by the war's black victims, the emphasis of this chapter is on them. I consider why so many young disadvantaged blacks were willing to risk injury, death, or prison in order to sell drugs and why policymakers should have known that and taken it into account in formulating policy. Finally, I show why the war's architects should be held accountable for what they have done to damage young black Americans.

Why the War Should Not Have Been Declared

The Reagan administration's declaration of a war on drugs resembles Argentina's declaration of war against Nazi Germany in March 1945. It was late and beside the point. Just as it was clear in 1945 that Germany was in military decline, so in 1987 and 1988 when the drug war was begun, it was clear that drug use was in decline and had been since the early 1980s.

There was no need in the late 1980s for a War on Drugs. Cases could be made for continuing support for efforts to target major importers, distributors, and traffickers, and for increasing support for drug education programs in school and for drug treatment for those who wanted it, but not for vastly more emphasis on law enforcement directed at users, user-dealers, and street-level trafficking. The ostensible goal of the drug war was to diminish drug abuse, and that goal, evidenced by a continuing decline in drug use, had been achieved before the drug war began. By all available measures of drug use in the general population, use of the major illicit substances, except cocaine, began to fall in the early 1980s, and the use of cocaine dropped from the mid-1980s onward.

By some disingenuous measures, the War on Drugs was bound to succeed, and President Bush made the disingenuous claims. Thus in December 1990, citing data on long-term drug use trends showing a 44 percent decline since 1985 in the number of people who used illegal drugs monthly, President Bush announced, "I am pleased to say that the news we have today suggests that our work is paying off, and that our national strategy is having an effect." The first drug czar and director of the White House Office on National Drug Control Policy, William Bennett, and Louis Sullivan, Secretary of Health and Human Services, made similar claims.

Because of the long-term decline in drug use, any comparison of levels of use in, say, 1985, before the war was launched, with levels of use in, say, 1989 and 1990, would appear to demonstrate that toughened drug laws and enforcement practices had deterred people from buying and using drugs and, accordingly, that the war had succeeded. This is a mistake commonly made when attempting to understand the effects of legal or policy changes. A simple comparison of conditions before and after the change will be misleading if there is a long-term trend of which both years are a part, in which case the change may have had nothing to do with events in the world. A homely example: A healthy ten-year-old child, if given cucumber sandwiches for lunch every day for a year, will be taller and heavier at year's end; a claim that the cucumbers caused the child to grow would be incorrect. The child might have grown more or less or in different ways on a different diet, but figuring that out requires more sensitive research designs than a simple before-and-after comparison. And so it is with drug use; year-to-year changes are meaningless except in the context of known long-term trends.

Figures 3-1 to 3-6, all based on surveys of large representative samples of the U.S. population conducted for or by the National Institute on Drug Abuse (NIDA), show steady downward trends in the use of dangerous substances over long periods for different age groups. All are based on surveys in which sample members are asked, in confidence, to answer questions about their use and frequency of use of different substances.

Figure 3-1 provides data for the period 1975 to 1991 from a series of annual surveys on drug use by high school seniors. The samples are huge, ranging from 15,000 to 18,000 students per year. Figure 3-1 shows the percentages admitting to any use of marijuana, cocaine (any form), heroin, or alcohol during the preceding twelve months. "Any use" includes just once, so this is the broadest measure of use and includes casual one-time experimenters. For each substance, reported use dropped. Reported heroin use was low at all times and fell throughout the period. The percentage reporting any marijuana use began at 40 percent in 1975, climbed to 51 percent in 1979, and fell continuously thereafter to 24 percent in 1991. For cocaine, the pattern is similar but with a later peak and a steeper drop. Fewer than 6 percent reported use in 1975, followed by a rise to 12 percent

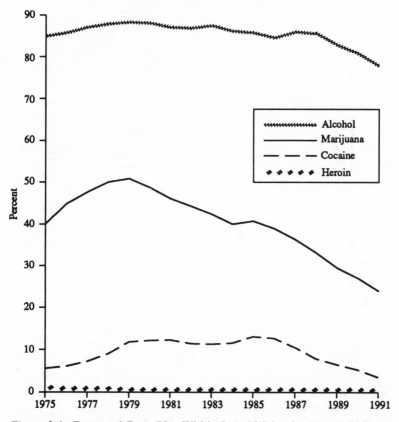

Figure 3-1. Reported Drug Use Within Last 12 Months Among U.S. High School Seniors, 1975–91

Sources: Bureau of Justice Statistics, *Sourcebook of Criminal Justice Statistics—1987* (Washington, D.C.: U.S. Department of Justice, 1988), Table 3.66; Bureau of Justice Statistics, *Sourcebook of Criminal Justice Statistics—1991* (Washington, D.C.: U.S. Department of Justice, 1992), Table 3.92.

in 1979; reported levels of use fluctuated around 12 percent, reaching a 13 percent peak in 1985 after which there was a precipitate drop to 3.5 percent in 1991. Even alcohol followed the same pattern, rising to a modern high of reported use in 1979 and falling steadily thereafter to a level in 1991 below the starting point.

It is possible, of course, that casual use of drugs might have been falling while regular use by smaller numbers of people was increas-

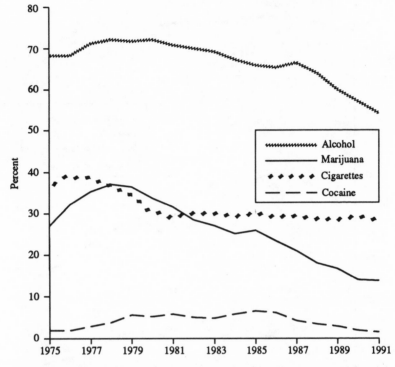

Figure 3-2. Reported Drug Use Within Last 30 Days Among U.S. High
School Seniors, 1975–91

Sources: Bureau of Justice Statistics, *Sourcebook of Criminal Justice Statistics—1987*
(Washington, D.C.: U.S. Department of Justice, 1991), Table 3.67; Bureau of Justice
Statistics, *Sourcebook of Criminal Justice Statistics—1991* (Washington, D.C.: U.S.
Department of Justice, 1992), Table 3.93.

ing. If so, the decline in drug use shown in Figure 3-1 might be
misleading. Figure 3-2 shows that the number of frequent users
was also declining. Figure 3-2 shows data from the same source on
the percentages of high school seniors reporting use of marijuana,
cocaine, alcohol, or cigarettes within the preceding thirty days.
Heroin is omitted because the use levels are so low (since 1976,
usually two-tenths of 1 percent), and cigarettes are included because they confirm the general trend toward decreasing use of
addictive substances by young people.

Those reporting drug use in the thirty-day period covered in

Figure 3-2 include some one- or few-time experimenters who just happened to conduct their experiments immediately before the survey was conducted. Most reporting such contemporaneous use are likely to be occasional or regular users. The ratio of experimental to regular users may change over time, with experimentation falling but steady users persisting. If that were true, the trend lines in Figure 3-2 should be very different from those in Figure 3-1. They are not. It thus appears that both experimental and regular use were falling.

The trend lines in Figure 3-2 closely resemble those in Figure 3-1. The cigarette pattern is striking because it anticipates those for alcohol and illicit drugs. The percentage reporting cigarette use within the preceding thirty days climbed to 39 percent in 1976, fell steeply to 30 percent, around which it fluctuated from 1980 to 1985, thereafter dropping to 28 percent in 1991.

To show that the patterns in the high school surveys are real and believable, Figures 3-3, 3-4, 3-5, and 3-6, encumbered with less textual summary and description, present data from the other major long-term surveys of Americans' drug use. Figure 3-3 shows trends in self-reported use within the preceding thirty days of marijuana, cocaine, alcohol, and cigarettes by full-time American college students one to four years beyond high school. Heroin is omitted because the reported use levels are generally below one-tenth of 1 percent.

Because of self-selection and economic and social background considerations that lead only some young people to college, the college survey represents a different and less heterogeneous population than the high school surveys. Nonetheless, the trends are the same as those for high school students. Marijuana and alcohol use fell steadily from the early 1980s onward: cigarette use declined somewhat; and the drop in cocaine use came later (in 1986) for college than for high school students, but it was steeper.

Figures 3-4 to 3-6, based on the National Household Surveys on Drug Abuse, summarize data on drug use among the American household population aged twelve and over. The surveys have been conducted periodically since 1972 for the National Institute on Drug Abuse and the National Institute on Alcohol Abuse and Alcoholism. The 1990 survey, the tenth conducted, included 9,259 interviews.

Figures 3-4, 3-5, and 3-6 show the percentages of survey respon-

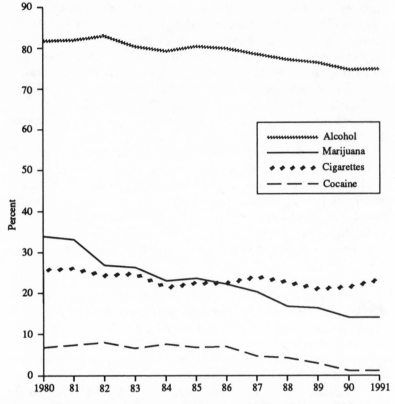

Figure 3-3. Reported Drug Use Within Last 30 Days Among U.S.
College Students, 1980–91

Source: Bureau of Justice Statistics, *Sourcebook of Criminal Justice Statistics—1991*
(Washington, D.C.: U.S. Department of Justice, 1992), Table 3.95.

dents reporting use during the preceding year of marijuana, cocaine, and alcohol. Data are presented separately for respondents
12 to 17 years old, those 18 to 25, and those over 25. For the two
younger age groups, the trends for each substance resemble those
from the high school and college-student surveys. Only among the
oldest age group, those over 25, are the patterns different. Most
initiation of drug use occurs in the teenage years or the early
twenties. People over 25 who report drug use are likely to be
committed users, and for both marijuana (Figure 3-4) and cocaine

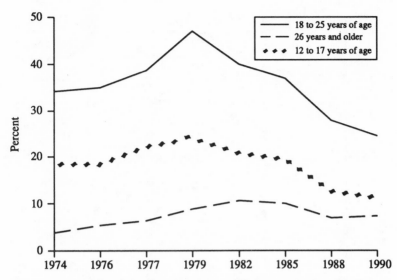

Figure 3-4. Estimated Prevalence of U.S. Marijuana Use by Age Group Within Last 12 Months, Selected Years, 1974–90

Source: Bureau of Justice Statistics, *Sourcebook of Criminal Justice Statistics—1991* (Washington, D.C.: U.S. Department of Justice, 1992), Table 3.101.

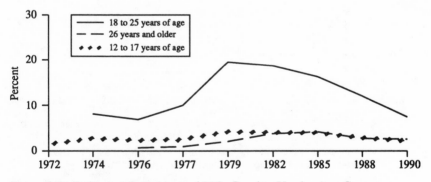

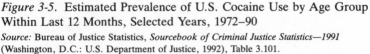

Figure 3-5. Estimated Prevalence of U.S. Cocaine Use by Age Group Within Last 12 Months, Selected Years, 1972–90

Source: Bureau of Justice Statistics, *Sourcebook of Criminal Justice Statistics—1991* (Washington, D.C.: U.S. Department of Justice, 1992), Table 3.101.

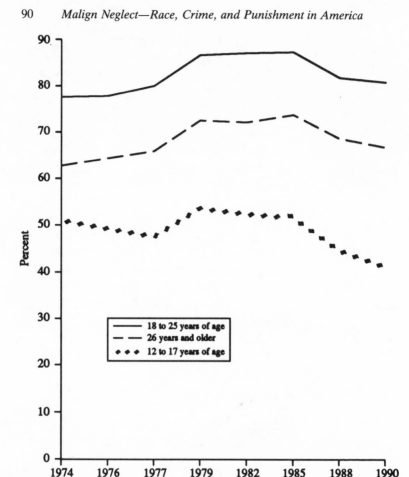

Figure 3-6. Estimated Prevalence of U.S. Alcohol Use by Age Group Within Last 12 Months, Selected Years, 1974–90

Source: Bureau of Justice Statistics, *Sourcebook of Criminal Justice Statistics—1991* (Washington, D.C.: U.S. Department of Justice, 1992), Table 3.101.

(Figure 3-5) the curves were essentially flat during the 1980s. For the younger groups, however, as in the high school and college surveys, marijuana use peaked in the late 1970s and fell sharply thereafter. For 18 to 25 year olds, cocaine use peaked around 1979 and declined thereafter. Finally, Figure 3-6 shows, for comparison purposes, that self-reported use of alcohol, a licit drug (except for underage drinkers) peaked in the 1980s for each age group and fell sharply after the mid-1980s.

Something was changing American attitudes toward drugs in the 1970s and 1980s, long before the politics of crime control produced a state of war. We can only speculate why that was happening. It is too soon for social histories to be written, and so explanations inevitably fall into the realm of pop sociology. The cigarette and alcohol trends are important because they signal a broadly based and widely shared change in American attitudes toward the ingestion of dangerous or unhealthy substances that can have little to do with the deterrent effects of law enforcement strategies or criminal sanctions. If NIDA had surveyed Americans on their use of caffeinated coffee since the 1970s, the use trends would resemble those for cigarettes and alcohol. The Department of Agriculture does measure food consumption per capita over time. Coffee consumption in the United States fell by a fifth between 1970 and 1991, from 33.4 gallons per person to 26.8, and the consumption of most fatty and high cholesterol foods fell sharply, including beef (from 79.6 pounds per capita in 1970 to 72.1 pounds in 1980 and to 63.1 pounds in 1991), whole milk (214 pounds per person in 1970, 142 in 1980, and 85 in 1990), and lard (4.6 pounds per person in 1970, 1.7 in 1991). No doubt for a variety of reasons—a reaction to the hedonism of the 1970s, the growing concern for personal health and fitness, a resurgence of social puritanism—Americans in the late 1970s became less enamored of drugs of most sorts and less inclined to use them. Only cocaine followed a somewhat different trajectory, with its use peaking later (but still before the declaration of war) and then falling more steeply.

By September 1989 when the Office of National Drug Control Policy issued its first National Drug Control Strategy, it was well known among public officials and drug policy scholars that drug use was in steep decline. Although specialized statistical reports like those published by the National Institute on Drug Abuse are seldom seen or read by lay people or journalists, they are well known among professionals. Only the willfully blind could have failed to know that no war was needed.

Something else was known about American drug policy that should have made government officials especially hesitant to start a war. Well-documented historical experience shows that policy-makers overreact in formulating and executing antidrug policies at times when social mores are becoming less accepting of drug use and their use is falling. David Musto, the leading historian of American drug policies, notes that

> in the decline phase of drug use . . . we tend to have an overkill, that is to say people become so righteous and so zealous that we can have excesses in the name of fighting drugs. There is very little opposition to draconian policies because no one wants to stand up for using drugs.

Musto has described a cyclical pattern of American tolerance and intolerance of alcohol and drugs. At least three times since the beginning of the nineteenth century, the United States has moved from periods of widespread, tolerated, even approved recreational use of alcohol and drugs to puritanical periods of uncompromising prohibition. The first period of intolerance began in the 1820s and culminated in the prohibition of alcohol in a dozen states by the 1850s. The temperance movement of the late nineteenth century led to national Prohibition; more generalized intolerance of drug use and users produced the first major federal narcotics legislation, the Harrison Act of 1914, and the first federal marijuana law, the Marijuana Tax Act of 1937. The contemporary period of intolerance began around 1970, a transition year when the U.S. Congress repealed most mandatory sentencing laws, many concerned with drug crimes, because they were too harsh, too rigid, and as a result were too often evaded by judges and lawyers uncomfortable imposing what they saw as unjust sentences. Also by 1970, however, the Nixon administration had declared its war on drugs. Within a few years, New York was widely portrayed as suffering a heroin epidemic, which was followed in the 1980s by successive cocaine and crack epidemics in various parts of the country.

Public tolerance of drug use has fallen. Mandatory penalties for drug crimes have proliferated and are now the harshest in the nation's history: Mandatory prison terms of ten, twenty, and thirty years and life without possibility of parole now face many drug traffickers, especially in the federal system and often in cases in which only tiny amounts are involved. In 1991, in *Harmelin v. Michigan,* 111 S. Ct. 2680, the Supreme Court upheld the constitutionality of life sentences without possibility of parole for drug traffickers. Drug testing of an extent and intrusiveness that would have been unthinkable twenty years ago is now commonplace.

The important thing is not the details of drug policy history, for which readers should consult the several good histories available, but the idea of cycles and movements between them. According to Musto, live-and-let-live attitudes prevail in periods of tolerance, like the 1890s and 1960s. In the late nineteenth century, for example, cocaine and opium (and their derivatives) were widely used in patent medicines; most addicts were conventional, law-abiding people, predominantly women; and cocaine was widely seen as a harmless recreational drug. In the 1960s, marijuana was widely and openly used; it and many hallucinogens were regarded by many as recreational drugs that were less harmful than alcohol.

During such periods of relative tolerance, traditional American notions of individualism and personal autonomy allow individuals to make their own choices about drug use; drug use is widely seen as only mildly deviant or not deviant at all; and people feel able to argue on the merits for the benefits and pleasures of drug use, for individuals' moral rights to make those choices. In periods of intolerance, drug use is widely seen as deviant, and few people feel comfortable risking moral disapproval or stigmatization by arguing in favor of drug use or tolerance of drug users.

The most intrusive laws and the cruelest penalties tend to be enacted *after* intolerance has reached its peak and when drug use is already falling. That is when self-righteousness is most uncompromising and voices in favor of tolerance are most muted. People with reservations, particularly elected officials, are reluctant to speak out for fear of being disparaged as "soft on drugs." And that is where the danger lies.

We all know this from personal experience. There are times when we are overwrought and our better judgment tells us that we are likely to act rashly or unfairly. Anger and emotion sometimes result in angry words that are later regretted or outraged letters that, our cooler self knows, should be put aside and reread tomorrow. When tomorrow comes, our cooler selves often win out and no letter, or a different one, is sent. Similarly, parents know that their own anger or tiredness or frustration can lead to overreaction to their children's behavior; we know we should listen to our doppelgänger's warning to get hold of ourselves and not to take out our frustrations on our children. When we are angry and vindictive, we tend to overreact. In private life we try to restrain these impulses. In public life, another doppelgänger is talking, but policymakers too seldom listen. Musto has described the dynamic that characterizes a period of declining tolerance:

> Soon the trend reverses; drug use starts to decline faster and faster. Public opinion turns against drugs and their acceptability begins to evaporate. Gradually, drug use becomes associated, truthfully or not, with the lower ranks of society, and often with racial and ethnic groups that are feared or despised by the middle class. Drugs begin to be seen as deviant and dangerous and become a potent symbol of evil.

The key words are "drug use becomes . . . associated with the lower ranks of society, and often with racial and ethnic groups that are feared or despised by the middle class." Throughout this century in periods of high intolerance of drug use, minority group stereotypes have been associated with deviant drug use. Early in this century, even though mainstream women were the modal category of opiate users, Chinese opium smokers and opium dens were among the images invoked by opponents of drug use and were part of the backdrop to the Harrison Act. In the 1920s, it was blacks and cocaine. In the 1930s, images of Mexicans and marijuana were prominent in the antimarijuana movements that culminated in the Marijuana Tax Act of 1937 and in many state laws prohibiting marijuana use. In the antidrug hysteria of the 1980s, crack cocaine, the emblematic drug of the latest "war," is associated in public imagery with disadvantaged minority residents of the inner cities.

Given what we know about past periods of intolerance of drug use and their tendencies to scapegoat minority groups, and that disadvantaged urban blacks are the archetypal users of crack cocaine—and therefore are the principal possessors, sellers, and low-level distributors—anyone who knew the history of American drug policy could have foreseen that this war on drugs would target and mostly engage young disadvantaged members of minority groups as the enemy. And it has.

A policy that foreseeably would damage many young blacks and

Hispanics was bad enough, but this one was worse than it appeared, because the damage to minority-group members would be inflicted primarily for the benefit of the great mass of, mostly white, nondisadvantaged Americans. Explaining why requires some discussion of how laws influence behavior and a look back at our knowledge from NIDA surveys of drug use patterns since 1975.

Politicians proposing new, tougher laws tend to argue that longer sentences will deter or incapacitate prospective offenders. As noted in Chapter 1, research evidence on the deterrent and incapacitative effects of penalties is ambiguous and inconclusive at best, but for many kinds of crimes there is no basis for believing that altering penalties will significantly affect behavior. This is especially true of many drug crimes. Falling cocaine prices and the common experience that arrested dealers are replaced on the streets within days suggest that traditional law enforcement strategies are an ineffective way to diminish drug use.

There is, however, a broader way to think about how criminal laws operate that goes back at least to Emile Durkheim, one of the nineteenth-century pioneers of modern sociology. Durkheim argued that laws operate in diffuse ways to define and reinforce social norms. The criminal laws define the outer limits of acceptable behavior. These limits change over time and as different groups holding different values achieve greater or lesser influence. In thinking about the effects of criminal laws, we should therefore look not simply to their direct short-term effects but also to what modern philosophers like the Norwegian Johannes Andenaes call their moral-educative effects. The announcement, application, and enforcement of laws have dramaturgical properties that are part of the process by which people's values and beliefs are shaped and sustained. Watching or knowing the processes by which wrongdoers are apprehended and tried and punished helps bring home the inappropriateness of their behavior. Social learning occurs in part by example. Most people abstain from crime and drug use not because of the immediate threat of penalties but because they are socialized to believe the behaviors are wrong; they are not the kind of people who are tempted (or tempted enough) to do such things. Thus, at least in part, criminal law shapes behavior not only through the short-term effects of legal threats but also dramaturgically by helping reinforce values and norms that make people less likely to commit crimes.

The hypothesis that law affects behavior indirectly no doubt is right, although at best it is only a partial explanation of why people obey laws. However, it has the problem that it is amoral. If laws exist to underscore norms concerning the boundaries of legitimate behavior, legitimacy and hence criminality depend on what groups' values are ascendent. In Nazi Germany, for example, Goebbels might have argued that laws forbidding political dissent and authorizing the denial of Jews' legal and human rights should be vigorously enforced, not only to achieve short-term instrumental objectives, but also to help shape German mass public opinion to support the policies and credos of National Socialism.

Marxists argue that the class interests of those who control capital dominate government and the laws that governments pronounce and so laws are biased in favor of the wealthy and their values. Hence, Anatole France's aphorism that the law in its majestic equality forbids the rich as well as the poor to sleep under bridges, to beg in the streets, and to steal bread. Similarly, feminists believe that many laws reflect traditional male domination of society and government and express "patriarchal" values and male interests. Members of minority groups contend that many laws reflect traditional white domination of society and government. The contrasts between aggressive enforcement and strict penalties associated with violent and common-law property crimes, which blacks disproportionately commit, and alleged half-hearted enforcement and trifling penalties associated with white-collar financial and environmental crimes, which whites disproportionately commit, are often cited as evidence that criminal law is biased in favor of whites.

Laws, including criminal laws, are not disembodied, timeless statements of eternal values. In the United States it would be difficult to deny that politicians and officials respond to and represent the interests of the great mass of the population whose behavior is captured in the NIDA surveys. Thus it might be argued that the goal of the War on Drugs in an era when drug use is dropping is to reinforce values and norms that are influencing the decline and through dramas of crime and punishment to affirm repeatedly that drug use is immoral and wrong. This argument assumes, however, that there are no competing values violated by using the law to shape norms. There are.

The problem with the rationale of the War on Drugs as an exercise in moral education is that it destroyed lives of young, principally minority people in order to reinforce existing norms of young, mostly majority people. Put crudely if explicitly, the lives of black and Hispanic ghetto kids were destroyed in order to reinforce white kids' norms against drug use. Reference back to the NIDA surveys will show why this is so.

At the same time that the NIDA surveys were showing broad-based declines in drug use throughout the 1980s, two other drug use indicators, drug-related admissions to hospital emergency rooms and urinalyses of felony defendants across the country, were implying stable or rising levels of drug use. Figure 3-7, based on a NIDA-sponsored reporting program called the Drug Abuse Warning Network (DAWN), shows the drugs involved in drug-related emergency room admissions to hospitals in metropolitan areas from 1980 to 1990. Contrary to the patterns shown in the NIDA surveys, the DAWN data show that mentions of cocaine, heroin, and marijuana increased slowly but steadily through mid-decade and rapidly thereafter.

The differences between the NIDA and DAWN data series may be less than initially appears. People admitted to hospital emergency wards are, after all, likely to be the heaviest abusers of drugs. Data from a number of sources suggest that three to five years typically separate the initiation of drug use from the onset of acute medical disorders. If that is so, the peak of cocaine emergency room admissions in 1988 followed by a drop in 1989 is consistent with peaks in self-reported use in 1985, with declines afterward.

An even greater contrast with the findings of the NIDA surveys is revealed by urinalyses of felony arrestees that have been conducted in American cities since 1987 as part of the U.S. Department of Justice's Drug Use Forecasting program (DUF). The DUF data show astonishingly high levels of drug use. Sixty, 70, and even 80 percent of male arrestees test positive in some cities. Table 3-1 shows the 1991 findings on positive urinalysis for male arrestees in twenty-three cities in 1991 for any drug, for cocaine, for marijuana, and for heroin. Positive test results for any drug ranged from a high in San Diego of 75 percent to a low in Omaha of 36

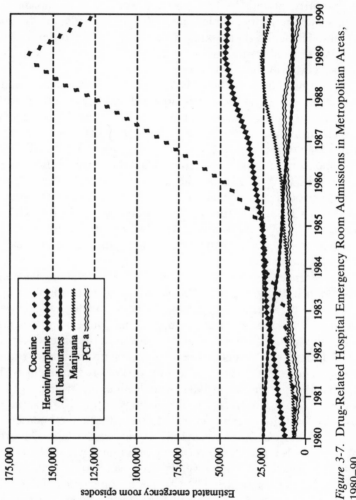

Figure 3-7. Drug-Related Hospital Emergency Room Admissions in Metropolitan Areas, 1980–90

^a PCP and PCP combinations.

Source: Bureau of Justice Statistics, *Drugs, Crime, and the Justice System* (Washington, D.C.: U.S. Department of Justice, 1992), p. 11.

Table 3-1. Percentage of Male Arrestees Testing Positive by Urinalysis for Any Drug, Cocaine, Marijuana, and Heroin, 1991

City	Any Drug	Cocaine	Marijuana	Heroin
Atlanta, GA	63	57	12	3
Birmingham, AL	63	52	16	5
Chicago, IL	74	61	23	21
Cleveland, OH	56	48	12	3
Dallas, TX	56	43	19	4
Denver, CO	50	30	25	2
Detroit, MI	55	41	18	8
Fort Lauderdale, FL	61	44	28	1
Houston, TX	65	56	17	3
Indianapolis, IN	45	22	23	3
Kansas City, MO	53	37	18	1
Los Angeles, CA	62	44	19	10
Manhattan, NYC	73	62	18	14
Miami, FL	68	61	23	2
New Orleans, LA	59	50	16	4
Omaha, NE	36	14	26	2
Philadelphia, PA	74	62	18	11
Phoenix, AZ	42	20	22	5
Portland, OR	61	30	33	9
St. Louis, MO	59	48	16	6
San Antonio, TX	49	31	20	16
San Diego, CA	75	45	33	17
San Jose, CA	58	33	25	8
Washington, DC	59	49	11	10

Note: Drugs tested for include cocaine, opiates, PCP, marijuana, amphetamines, methadone, methaqualone, benzodiazepines, barbiturates, and propoxyphene.

Source: National Institute of Justice, *Drug Use Forecasting* (1991 annual report) (Washington, D.C.: U.S. Department of Justice, 1992).

percent, and for cocaine ranged downward from highs of 62 percent in Manhattan and Philadelphia.

The patterns shown by the 1991 DUF data are remarkably stable. Figure 3-8 shows the positive drug urinalysis test results for booked arrestees in Dallas, Kansas City, Manhattan, San Diego, Portland, Oregon, and Washington, D.C. These six cities were chosen because they represent all regions of the country. Although the proportions of positive test results among arrestees varied

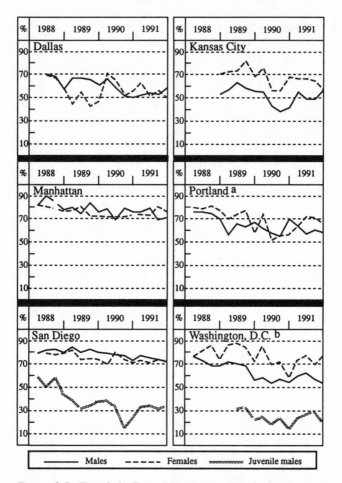

Figure 3-8. Trends in Drug Use Among Booked Arrestees

Notes: Positive by urinalysis. Drugs tested for include cocaine, opiates, PCP, marijuana, amphetamines, methadone, methaqualone, benzodiazepines, barbiturates, and propoxyphene. Gaps on graph represent periods when data were not collected.

[a] Before 1991, site did not test for all 10 drugs listed.

[b] 1988 Washington, D.C., data based on arrestees tested by D.C. Pretrial Services Agency. Drugs that the agency tests for include cocaine, opiates, PCP, amphetamines, and methadone. Data collected after 1988 are from the DUF program.

Source: National Institute of Justice, *Drug Use Forecasting* (1991 annual report) (Washington, D.C.: U.S. Department of Justice, Office of Justice Programs, 1992).

among cities—around 80 percent in Manhattan, 60 percent in Portland and Dallas, and 50 percent in San Antonio—in any single city they fell slightly but were essentially stable.

Whatever their race, most felony defendants are poor, badly educated, un- or underemployed, and not part of a stable household. Disproportionately, they are black. In 1990, for example, 29 percent of all felony arrests were of blacks, as were 45 percent of persons arrested for violent index offenses and 58 percent of persons arrested for the three most serious crimes—murder, rape, and robbery. Among the arrestees included in the DUF program, similar patterns hold. Table 3-2 shows the positive test results, by race, for males in the twenty-three DUF cities in 1991 for any drug and for cocaine. In no city was the percentage of whites testing positive for "any drug" or cocaine higher than the black percentage (though they were equal or close in some sites) and whites in many cities tested higher than blacks for marijuana and heroin.

If such large percentages of arrestees in the DUF program test positive for drugs, and nearly half of those arrested for the most serious crimes in the United States are black, it must mean that drug use among some black groups has remained high. How can that be reconciled with the NIDA surveys? We now know the answer: It cannot.

It is now well understood that the NIDA surveys, although they are a reasonably reliable indicator of drug use by most Americans, are not based on a representative sample of the American population. Like the decennial population counts of the U.S. Bureau of the Census and the ongoing National Crime Victimization Survey conducted for the U.S. Department of Justice—both conceived as representative samples of the U.S. population—the NIDA surveys undercount young, mobile, inner-city people. This means that all three purportedly representative surveys miss large numbers of minority men and women living in American cities. The nature of the NIDA surveys probably exacerbates this problem. The high school surveys are of high school seniors, and so they miss those young people who leave school before their senior year. Even among registered students, truancy rates are high among disadvantaged students. Students absent when surveys are adminstered are disproportionately likely to include disadvantaged minority youth.

Table 3-2. Percentage of Male Arrestees, by Race, Testing Positive by Urinalysis for Any Drug or Cocaine

City	Any Drug				Cocaine			
	Black	White	Hispanic	Other	Black	White	Hispanic	Other
Atlanta, GA	65	48	-	-	59	33	-	-
Birmingham, AL	66	55	-	-	59	27	-	-
Chicago, IL	75	72	72	-	63	60	53	-
Cleveland, OH	61	41	44	-	56	21	38	-
Dallas, TX	59	55	45	-	50	35	30	-
Denver, CO	61	41	49	25	47	16	25	3
Detroit, MI	56	49	-	-	41	40	-	-
Fort Lauderdale, FL	71	53	41	-	58	32	26	-
Houston, TX	77	59	41	-	70	49	29	-
Indianapolis, IN	45	44	-	-	30	10	-	-
Kansas City, MO	56	41	-	-	43	16	-	-
Los Angeles, CA	77	65	51	20	63	27	38	10
Manhattan, NYC	77	74	68	-	68	59	54	-
Miami, FL	76	57	56	-	70	44	40	-
New Orleans, LA	60	51	-	-	54	28	-	-
Omaha, NE	44	32	31	18	23	6	10	0
Philadelphia, PA	75	65	76	-	66	41	68	-
Phoenix, AZ	53	43	37	19	41	17	15	8
Portland, OR	66	58	73	44	46	18	64	19
St. Louis, MO	60	54	-	-	53	26	-	-
San Antonio, TX	55	48	48	-	45	18	30	-
San Diego, CA	79	74	75	58	59	22	54	31
San Jose, CA	72	59	56	37	54	25	33	19
Washington, DC	60	49	-	-	51	26	-	-

Notes: Drugs tested for include cocaine, opiates, PCP, marijuana, amphetamines, methadone, methaqualone, benzodiazepines, barbiturates, and propoxyphene.
- = fewer than 20 cases.

Source: National Institute of Justice, *Drug Use Forecasting* (1991 annual report) (Washington, D.C.: U.S. Department of Justice, 1992).

The broadest survey, the National Household Survey on Drug Abuse, carefully describes itself as an effort "to measure the prevalence of drug use among the American *household* population aged twelve and over." It therefore excludes the homeless, people with no permanent residence, and people institutionalized in jails and prisons. The homeless include higher than normal percentages of drug users. Those without permanent residences or in jails or prisons are disproportionately young, poor, and members of minority groups.

The NIDA surveys and other indicators of drug use like DAWN and DUF are not inconsistent; they simply measure different things. In 1990, Senator Joseph Biden, Democratic chairman of the U.S. Senate Judiciary Committee, and William Bennett, then head of the White House Office of National Drug Control Policy, fought a drug policy duel using little-read government reports as weapons. Bennett, using NIDA data in the 1990 report of the Office of National Drug Control Policy, claimed that the Bush administration was winning its drug war. Biden riposted, citing DAWN and DUF data in a Senate Judiciary Committee report, and claimed that drug abuse was as bad as ever or worse.

Biden and Bennett both were right. Among the 95+ percent of the population who were reliably represented in the NIDA surveys, drug use in the 1980s was declining. Among disadvantaged young people in the inner cities, especially in minority areas of highly concentrated poverty, drug use was not declining, and this was captured by the DUF and DAWN data.

The drug use indicators measure different phenomena, not unlike the way that oceanographic instruments measure deep currents and surface perturbations. In the deep currents of evolving values and norms, Americans in the 1980s were moving away from use of drugs and other substances perceived as harmful, ranging from cholesterol and caffeine to quaalude and cocaine. At the surface, fierce storms were raging. By a variety of measures, including the concentration of urban poverty, labor force participation, illegitimate births, single-parent households, and general deterioration of neighborhoods, things were getting worse in the inner city in the late 1980s. Increased drug abuse and drug-related crimes were not unexpected correlates and consequences.

In the longer term, the deeper currents will likely affect most segments of the population. The social traumas affecting minority underclass areas buffered those attitudinal changes for a while, but eventually they should show up in less drug use. Already there are slight indications in the DUF urinalysis data (see Figure 3-8) of a downturn in positive drug tests among arrestees. Newspapers like the *New York Times* and the *Washington Post* have recently begun carrying stories reporting that drug use is falling out of favor among disadvantaged members of minority groups. A May 31, 1993, *Washington Post* story, for example, was entitled "Crack Epidemic Appears to Wane; Seeing Drug's Destructiveness, Younger People Are Turning Away."

The white-shirted-and-suspendered officials of the Office of National Drug Control Policy understood the arcane intricacies of NIDA surveys, DUF, and DAWN better than anyone else in the United States. They knew that drug use was falling among the vast majority of the population. They knew that drug use was not declining among disadvantaged members of the urban underclass. They knew that the War on Drugs would be fought mainly in the minority areas of American cities and that those arrested and imprisoned would disproportionately be young blacks and Hispanics. Senator Daniel Patrick Moynihan, for example, in a 1993 article in the *American Scholar,* made the same point: "It is essential that we understand that by choosing prohibition [of drugs] we are choosing to have an intense crime problem concentrated among minorities." If the criminal law's mens rea equivalence between purpose and knowledge were applied to the decision to launch the war, knowing its likely effects on black Americans, the indictments would be unanswerable: The war's planners knew exactly what they were doing.

The Foreseeable Disparate Impact on Blacks

The crucial question is whether the architects of the War on Drugs should be held morally accountable for the havoc they have wrought among disadvantaged members of minority groups. The answer is that they should, and this section explains why. Three sets of issues arise. First, were the disparate impacts on black Americans forseeable? The only possible answer, as the data presented in the following sections demonstrate beyond peradventure of doubt, is yes, they knew what they were doing. Second, putting aside its disparate impact implications, were there valid grounds for believing that the war's prohibitionistic approach would diminish drug trafficking and drug use? Third, is there any arguable basis for justifying the war's forseeable effects on black Americans? In particular, what should be made of the standard defense of the war's racial effects—almost a confession in avoidance—that most crime is intraracial and that the war's strategies were devised not to damage blacks but to protect black victims and communities? The answers to these questions are that there were no valid bases for believing that the war would accomplish its ostensible objectives, that the claim to protect black victims was disingenuous, and that there is no arguable basis for justifying the war's malign neglect of its implications for black Americans.

Urban black Americans have borne the brunt of the War on Drugs. They have been arrested, prosecuted, convicted, and imprisoned at increasing rates since the early 1980s, and grossly out of proportion to their numbers in the general population or among drug users. By every standard, the war has been harder on blacks than on whites; that this was predictable makes it no less regrettable.

Cocaine and, more recently, crack have been the drugs primarily targeted, and they, particularly crack, are notoriously used and distributed in the inner city. The political symbolism of cocaine has been high since the mid-1980s. The United States invaded Panama in part because Manuel Noriega was believed to be cooperating with Colombian drug lords. In the United States, the Medellín and Cali cartels were for many years among the best-known foreign business enterprises. Newspapers, television, and movies regularly portray trafficking in cocaine and crack as characteristic of inner-city minority neighborhoods. Any mildly informed person in the late 1980s knew that the major fronts in the drug wars were located in minority neighborhoods.

The institutional character of urban police departments led to a tactical focus on disadvantaged minority neighborhoods. For a variety of reasons it is easier to make arrests in socially disorganized neighborhoods, as contrasted with urban blue-collar and urban or suburban white-collar neighborhoods. First, more of the routine activities of life, including retail drug dealing, occur on the streets and alleys in poor neighborhoods. In working-class and middle-class neighborhoods, many activities, including drug deals, are likelier to occur indoors. This makes it much easier to find dealers from whom to make an undercover buy in a disadvantaged urban neighborhood than elsewhere.

Second, it is easier for undercover narcotics officers to penetrate networks of friends and acquaintances in poor urban minority neighborhoods than in more stable and closely knit working-class and middle-class neighborhoods. The stranger buying drugs on the urban street corner or in an alley or overcoming local suspicions by hanging around for a few days and then buying drugs, is commonplace. The substantial increases in the numbers of black and Hispanic police officers in recent decades make undercover narcotics work in such neighborhoods easier. An undercover policeman of Irish or Polish descent in the 1960s was much less likely to be successful working undercover in a minority neighborhood than is a black policeman today in Chicago's Woodlawn or an Hispanic policeman in South-Central Los Angeles.

A stranger trying to buy drugs in the working-class Highland Park neighborhood around the Ford plant in St. Paul, Minnesota, or in Highland Park, Illinois, a middle-class suburb of Chicago, is likely to have much less success. Drugs are used and sold in both places, but rarely in the streets and not to strangers. Police undercover operations can succeed in such places but they take longer, cost more, and are less likely to succeed.

Both these differences between socially disorganized urban neighborhoods and other neighborhoods make extensive drug-law enforcement operations in the inner city more likely and, by police standards, more successful. Because urban drug dealing is often visible, individual citizens, the media, and elected officials more often pressure police to take action against drugs in poor urban neighborhoods than in other kinds of neighborhoods. Although wholesale drug arrests are seldom strategically successful in reducing drug use or trafficking, they briefly disrupt the drug markets and so win media and public approval.

There is another more powerful reason that the police focus their attention on the inner city. Both for individual officers and for departments, numbers of arrests made have long been a measure of productivity and effectiveness. If it takes more work and longer to make a single drug arrest in either Highland Park than in Woodlawn, the trade-off may be between two arrests per month of an officer's time in Highland Park and six arrests per month in

Woodlawn. From the perspectives of the individual officer's personnel record and the department's year-to-year statistical comparisons, arrests are fungible, and six arrests count for more than two.

Thus, a major reason that relatively more drug arrests are made in minority communities than elsewhere is that they are easier to make. Somewhat surprisingly, I am told by leading drug policy experts that there is no literature that confirms or contradicts this analysis or that considers why police target drug-law enforcement on minority communities. There are ethnographic and economic literatures on urban drug markets, and there are police and policy literatures on the tactics of street-level law enforcement and undercover narcotics work. The ethnographic literature documents the porousness of urban drug markets, and it and the economic literature explain why arrested dealers are nearly always quickly replaced by successors willing to accept the risks, but neither sheds light on police tactics. The police and policy literatures explain how and why narcotics enforcement operates but shed no light on why the emphasis is so much more often on the Woodlawns than on the Highland Parks.

Experienced police officials and prosecutors confirm my analysis. Former Kansas City prosecutor Albert Riederer, for example, is one person who offered this analysis to me. The police chief in Charlottesville, Virginia, justifying police targeting of casual drug dealing in University of Virginia fraternities, observed that "local civil rights advocates had a good point when they argued that anti-drug efforts were directed mainly toward the poor and members of minorities." In a 1993 article on drug policy in *Criminology,* Alfred Blumstein offers a similar analysis and, because of the absence of a literature, cites "personal communication with several individuals involved in drug-related police work."

No matter why it happens, the police emphasis on disorganized minority neighborhoods produces racial proportions in arrests that do not mirror racial proportions in drug use. Figure 3-9 shows the percentages of blacks and whites among drug arrestees reported in the FBI's *Uniform Crime Reports* for the years 1976 to 1992. The black percentage climbed steadily throughout the period and by two-fifths—from 30 to 42 percent—between 1985 and 1989. Since the absolute number of arrests was also rising, the number of arrests of blacks grew even faster. As Table 3-3 shows, between

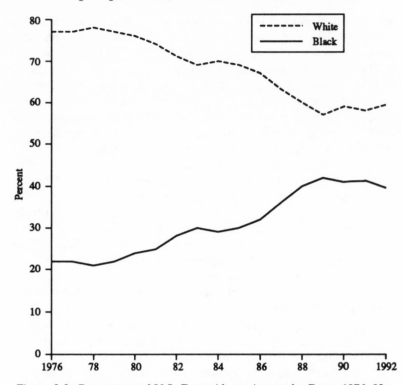

Figure 3-9. Percentage of U.S. Drug Abuse Arrests by Race, 1976–92
Sources: Bureau of Justice Statistics, *Sourcebook of Criminal Justice Statistics* (Washington, D.C.: U.S. Department of Justice, various years from 1978 to 1992), various tables; Federal Bureau of Investigation, *Crime in America—1992* (Washington, D.C.: U.S. Government Printing Office, 1993), Table 43, p. 235.

1985 and 1989 the number of black arrests more than doubled, from 210,298 to 452, 574. The number of white arrests grew only by 27 percent.

The arrest percentages by race bear no relation to drug use percentages, as Table 3-4 shows. Black Americans are less likely to have used drugs than whites are, for all major drugs of abuse except heroin. In 1990, for example, a year in which 41 percent of drug arrestees were black, NIDA's national household survey on drug abuse indicated that only 10 percent of blacks reported that

Table 3-3. U.S. Drug Abuse Violations by Race, 1976–92

Year	Total Violations	White	White (%)	Black	Black (%)
1976	475,209	366,081	77	103,615	22
1977	565,371	434,471	77	122,594	22
1978	592,168	462,728	78	127,277	21
1979	516,142	396,065	77	112,748	22
1980	531,953	401,979	76	125,607	24
1981	584,776	432,556	74	146,858	25
1982	562,390	400,683	71	156,369	28
1983	615,081	423,151	69	185,601	30
1984	560,729	392,904	70	162,979	29
1985	700,009	482,486	69	210,298	30
1986	688,815	463,457	67	219,159	32
1987	809,157	511,278	63	291,177	36
1988	844,300	503,125	60	334,015	40
1989	1,074,345	613,800	57	452,574	42
1990	860,016	503,315	59	349,965	41
1991	763,340	443,596	58	312,997	41
1992	919,561	546,430	59	364,546	40

Sources: Federal Bureau of Investigation, *Uniform Crime Reports for the United States—1992* (Washington, D.C.: U.S. Government Printing Office, 1993), Table 43; Bureau of Justice Statistics, *Sourcebook of Criminal Justice Statistics* (Washington, D.C.: U.S. Department of Justice, 1978–92), various tables.

they had *ever* used cocaine (compared with 11.7 percent of whites and 11.5 percent of Hispanics), 1.7 percent reported *ever* using heroin (compared with 0.7 percent whites and 1.2 percent Hispanics), 31.7 percent reported *ever* using marijuana (34.2 percent whites, 29.6 percent Hispanics), 3.0 percent reported *ever* using hallucinogens (8.7 percent whites, 5.2 percent Hispanics), and 76.6 percent reported *ever* using alcohol (85.2 percent whites, 78.6 percent Hispanics).

As Table 3-4 also shows, whether the questions concerned drug use within the previous year or within the previous month, the comparative black, white, and Hispanic patterns were much the same. The only data in Table 3-4 showing higher levels of black drug use are for marijuana and cocaine use in the last 30 days and the "ever used" data on heroin. Although in percentage terms, blacks' reports of cocaine use in the preceding 30 days or heroin

Table 3-4. U.S. Percentage of Drug Use by Race, 1990

Drug	White	Black	Hispanic
Alcohol			
Ever Used	85.2	76.6	78.6
Most recent use			
Within last year	68.3	55.6	64.5
Within last 30 days	53.1	43.7	47.1
Marijuana			
Ever used	34.2	31.7	29.6
Most recent use			
Within last year	10.1	11.2	10.9
Within last 30 days	5.0	6.7	4.7
Cocaine			
Ever used	11.7	10.0	11.5
Most recent use			
Within last year	2.8	4.0	5.2
Within last 30 days	0.6	1.7	1.9
Hallucinogens			
Ever used	8.7	3.0	5.2
Heroine			
Ever used	0.7	1.7	1.2

Source: Bureau of Justice Statistics, *Sourcebook of Criminal Justice Statistics* (Washington, D.C.: U.S. Department of Justice, 1991), Tables 3.103, 3.104, 3.105.

use ever are three times the white levels (1.7 to 0.7), in absolute terms these differences are insignificant. There were, after all, 213 million white Americans in 1991, compared with 30 million blacks.

Drug arrests are a principal reason that the proportions of blacks in prison and more generally under criminal justice system control have risen rapidly in recent years to the extraordinary levels indicated in Figures 2-1, 2-2, and 2-3 in Chapter 2, which show the percentages of blacks and whites among persons admitted to prisons and in prison and jail on survey dates over extended periods. The black percentages climbed slowly for several decades but rapidly after 1980.

The pattern of increasing black percentages is apparent in the aggregate national data on arrests and in state data. Figure 3-10 shows the national arrest rates per 100,000 population for whites

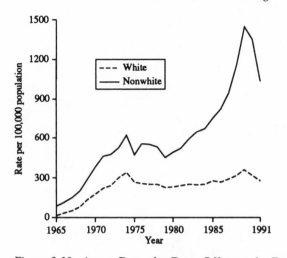

Figure 3-10. Arrest Rates for Drug Offenses, by Race, 1965–91
Source: Alfred Blumstein, "Making Rationality Relevant: The American Society of Criminology 1992 Presidential Address," *Criminology,* January 1993, Fig. 1.

and nonwhites from 1965 to 1991. Nonwhite rates were higher than white rates, usually at least double, throughout that period. From the early 1970s onward, white drug arrest rates were basically stable, fluctuating around 300 per 100,000. After 1980, nonwhite rates rose steadily and then skyrocketed: By 1988 they were five times higher than white rates.

A more striking pattern of racial difference is revealed when juvenile drug arrests by race are examined. Alfred Blumstein, longtime dean of the Heinz School of Public Policy and Management, and America's leading authority on racial trends in criminal justice statistics, presented Figure 3-11 as part of his 1992 presidential address to the American Society of Criminology. White arrest rates for juvenile drug offenses were higher than those for black juveniles from the late 1960s to the early 1980s, though both rates fell sharply after 1974. After the early 1980s, white arrest rates continued to drop. Black rates shot up until the late 1980s when they were four to five times higher than white rates. Blumstein's "our kids, their kids" explanation for those trends is that drug use in the 1970s was a middle-income, principally white, phenomenon, which is why en-

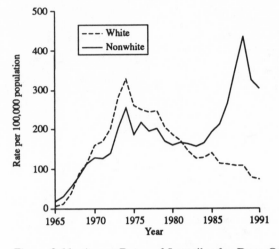

Figure 3-11. Arrest Rates of Juveniles for Drug Offenses, by Race, 1965–91

Source: Alfred Blumstein, "Making Rationality Relevant: The American Society of Criminology 1992 Presidential Address," *Criminology,* January 1993, Fig. 2.

forcement severity dropped, whereas in the late 1980s, drug use was a low-income, principally minority, phenomenon, which is why enforcement was uncompromisingly aggressive:

> The decline after the 1974 peak was undoubtedly a consequence of the general trend toward decriminalization of marihuana in the United States. A major factor contributing to that decriminalization was undoubtedly a realization that the arrestees were much too often the children of individuals, mostly white, in positions of power and influence. These parents certainly did not want the consequences of a drug arrest to be visited on their children, and so they used their leverage to achieve a significant degree of decriminalization.

One irony attending the data on arrests is their juxtaposition with drug use patterns. They are out of synch. During the late 1970s and early 1980s when arrests were falling or essentially stable, as Figures 3-1 to 3-6 show, drug use climbed to its modern peaks and began falling, well before arrests and arrest rates began their steep climb.

Blumstein's analysis of national drug arrest trends by race is mirrored in the states. Stephens Clarke of the Institute of Government of the University of North Carolina at Chapel Hill, the pre-eminent scholar of North Carolina's criminal justice trends, reports that drug arrests of nonwhites in that state climbed five times faster than white rates between 1984 and 1989. Nonwhite drug arrests increased from 5,021 in 1984 to 14,192 in 1989, a 183 percent increase. White drug arrests increased from 10,269 in 1984, twice the nonwhite number, to 14,007 in 1989, less than the non-white number and an increase of only 36 percent. Similar patterns can be found in other states, as of course they must, since the respective increases nationally in black and white arrests between 1985 and 1989 were 115 and 27 percent. In Minnesota, drug arrests of blacks grew by 500 percent during the 1980s, compared with 22 percent for whites, according to Debra Dailey, director of the Minnesota Sentencing Guidelines Commission.

The drug war's effect on prison populations has been substantial, and since the mid-1980s it has been the single most important cause of population increases. Twenty-five percent of state prisoners in 1991 had been convicted of drug charges, as had 56 percent of those in federal prisons. Twelve years earlier, in 1979, a year for which a special population profile makes detailed state data available, 6.4 percent of state and 25 percent of federal inmates had been convicted of drug crimes.

At every level of the criminal justice system, empirical analyses demonstrate that an increasing black disproportion has resulted from the War on Drugs—in jails, state and federal prisons, and juvenile institutions. The title of a 1990 publication of the Department of Justice's Office of Juvenile Justice and Delinquency Prevention captures the juvenile story: "Growth in Minority Detentions Attributed to Drug Law Violators." The experience in several state prison systems is illustrative. Figure 3-12 shows nonwhite and white admissions per 100,000 same-race population to North Carolina prisons from 1970 to 1990. White rates held steady during the entire period. Nonwhite rates doubled between 1980 and 1990 from a higher starting point, growing most rapidly after 1987, the period when nonwhite drug arrests more than doubled.

Figure 3-13 shows increases in prison commitments in Pennsylvania between 1980 and 1990 for drug and other offenses by race and

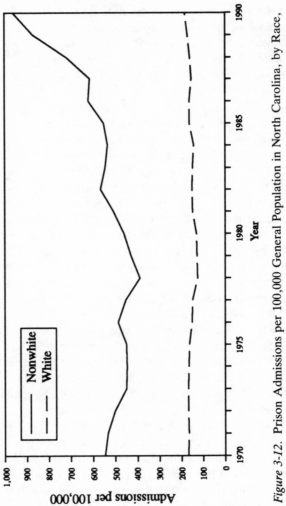

Figure 3-12. Prison Admissions per 100,000 General Population in North Carolina, by Race, 1970—90

Source: Stevens H. Clarke, "North Carolina Prisons Growing." *Overcrowded Times* 3(4)(1992): 1, 11–13.

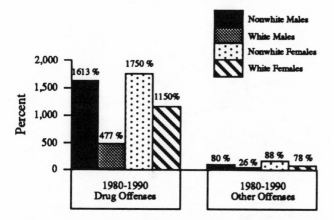

Figure 3-13. Percentage of Growth in Prison Commitments in Pennsylvania by Race, Sex, and Offense, 1980–90

Source: Stover Clark, "Pennsylvania Corrections in Context," *Overcrowded Times* 3(4)(1992): 4–5.

sex. Drug commitments of nonwhite males rose by 1613 percent during the decade; white males by 477 percent. The pattern for females was similar, though the differences were less dramatic. In 1990, 11 percent of Pennsylvanians were white; 58 percent of state prisoners were nonwhite.

Figure 3-14 shows white and nonwhite drug commitments to Virginia prisons from 1983 to 1989. Sixty-two percent of drug offenders committed in 1983 were white, and 38 percent were nonwhite. By 1989, those percentages had more than reversed; 65 percent of drug commitments were nonwhite, and 35 percent were white. Drug commitments have continued to rise since 1989; current data would show worse racial disproportion.

These figures are illustrative of prison admission and population trends across the country. Phrased most charitably to the officials who launched and conducted America's latest War on Drugs, worsening of racial incarceration patterns was a foreseen but not an intended consequence. Less charitably, the recent blackening of America's prison population is the product of malign neglect of the war's effects on black Americans.

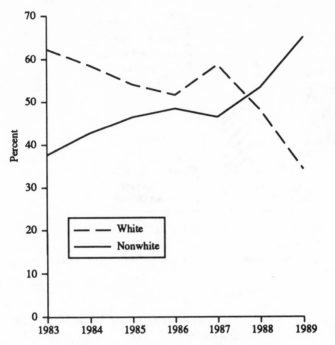

Figure 3-14. Percentage of New Drug Commitments in Virginia by Race, Fiscal Years 1983–89

Source: James Austin and Aaron D. McVey, *The Impact of the War on Drugs* (San Francisco: National Council on Crime and Delinquency, 1989).

The Case for the War

There was no basis on which policymakers could have believed in good faith that the key strategies of the War on Drugs would be so successful as to justify the burdens they would impose on minority citizens. By trying to reduce the supply of drugs, rather than demand for them, by adopting a prohibitionistic crime control approach, rather than a harm-reduction approach, policymakers chose strategies that had little prospect of succeeding but a high likelihood of worsening racial disproportions in the criminal justice system. The argument has two strands. The first concerns the evidence for the effectiveness of drug-law enforcement per se. The second concerns the evidence on effectiveness of harsh crime control approaches generally.

There is no reason to doubt that drug-law enforcement has some modest dampening effect on drug use and trafficking, but there is no reason to believe that substantial increases or decreases in the scale of drug-law enforcement would substantially increase or decrease drug use or trafficking.

A prefatory glossary may be helpful. Although it is an oversimplified distinction, discussions of drug policy typically distinguish between supply reduction and demand reduction. Supply-reduction strategies aim to reduce the availability of drugs and, by reducing supplies and increasing risks, to increase their prices. The major supply-reduction approaches are source-country programs (crop eradication, financial support to other countries' drug-law enforcement agencies, extraterritorial assignment of American military and law enforcement personnel), interdiction programs (border patrols, air and marine surveillance and apprehension of importers, baggage inspection at entry points), and law enforcement efforts at local, state, and federal levels to arrest and punish people involved in drug trafficking.

Demand-reduction strategies try to persuade people not to use drugs and not to buy them. The major demand-reduction approaches are mass-media public education programs, drug education programs in elementary and secondary schools, drug abuse treatment programs, and law enforcement efforts aimed at possession of drugs. In addition—and this is why the broad distinction is oversimplified—supply-reduction efforts have collateral demand-reduction effects if their very existence and occurrence serve to create or reinforce social norms antithetical to drug use.

A second conventional distinction is between prohibitionistic and harm-reduction strategies. Prohibitionistic strategies forbid the use or distribution of drugs and attempt to enforce those prohibitions by means of legal threats backed up by the criminal justice system. Drug use and users are stigmatized as deviant and immoral. The principal reliance is placed on legal sanctions, and particularly in the United States, when the legal threats prove ineffective, the tendency has been to threaten harsher and yet again harsher penalties.

The logic of prohibitionistic approaches implies primary emphasis on supply-reduction strategies and on the criminalization of use, possession, and distribution of proscribed substances. That is why drug-law enforcement has been the principal cause of rapid prison population increases, and it is why the U.S. Congress and state legislatures in the 1980s repeatedly passed sentencing laws calling for mandatory minimum sentences for drug crimes.

Harm-reduction strategies, by contrast, treat drug abuse as a social problem with undesirable effects for drug users and for society and so attempt to minimize their aggregate adverse effects. By adopting the public health perspective on health problems—that it is more important to alleviate suffering and loss of health, life, and property than to render moral judgments on individual behavior—the main reliance is not placed on criminal processes and legal threats. In the Netherlands, for example, although law enforcement targets the importation and manufacture of drugs and high-level trafficking, harm-reduction approaches guide policy for handling social users, addicts, and user-dealers. Needle exchange and maintenance programs exist, serviced from mobile medical units and clinics. Addicts participate fully in the Dutch social welfare system and are entitled to both income support and health care. Drug abuse treatment is available on demand through the national health system. In certain areas of some cities, police turn a blind eye to street-level trafficking, and coffee houses sell small amounts of marijuana to customers. The effects are to weaken the illicit drug markets, to reduce drug market–related violence, to cut down on the health problems of drug users, and to retard the spread of AIDS. Dutch authorities also claim that their approach reduces crime generally by eliminating addicts' need to steal to support their habits. And they claim their approach lessens drug use by making it less beguiling to experimenting young people; addicts are seen for what they are, inadequate welfare-state clients, rather than countercultural outlaws symbolizing resistance to bourgeois values.

No doubt drug warriors would challenge some or all of my description of the Dutch experience, which is based on research conducted by the research division of the Dutch Ministry of Justice. Although I believe it is substantially accurate, my view is less important than that a picture of a harm-reduction approach has been sketched. Any imaginable country will simultaneously pursue elements of both prohibitionistic and harm-reduction strategies, as the Dutch do and as the United States does. The question is one of balance. In recent years, American policy has tilted heavily toward prohibition, exemplified by a long-standing 70/30 federal funding split between law enforcement programs and treatment and education programs. Too many people in prison and too few people in treatment are among the results.

Every element of the supply-reduction approach has been shown to be ineffective. To quote Senator Moynihan again, a sometime supporter of the drug wars, "Interdiction and 'drug busts' are probably necessary symbolic acts, but nothing more." After surveying research and experience through 1990, James Q. Wilson, for two decades the country's leading conservative scholar of crime control policy and research, concluded that "significant reductions in drug abuse will come only from reducing demand for those drugs . . . the marginal product of further investment in supply reduction is likely to be small." He reports "that I know of no serious law-enforcement official who disagrees with this conclusion. Typically, police officials tell interviewers that they are fighting a losing war or, at best, a holding action."

Interdiction and source-country efforts have long been known by policy analysts and evaluators to be ineffective, but because they have had relatively little effect on racial trends in prosecution and incarceration, little about them is said here. The problem with interdiction efforts is that the boundaries of the United States are so long and so porous, and the volume of legitimate movement across borders so large, that it is impossible to intercept more than a small percentage of incoming drugs. A series of RAND Corporation analyses and evaluations commissioned by the Department of Defense so advised. In addition, the cost of imported drugs to U.S. distributors accounts for less than 10 percent of their street price. A RAND analysis estimated that doubling the volume of intercepted drugs would increase street prices by only 10 percent.

Knowledge of the effectiveness of source-country programs is even less encouraging. With the notable exception of reductions in Turkey's production of opium in the early 1970s that temporarily interrupted the flow of heroin into the United States, source-country programs have been ineffective. Partly this is because conditions for growing cocaine, opium, and marijuana are suitable in many countries, and so production can easily shift from less to more hospitable places. Many of these places—in the Andes, in the "Golden Triangle" of Thailand, Burma, and Laos, in the mountainous regions of Southwest Asia—are outside the effective control of any government. Partly the ineffectiveness of source-country programs results from the unavailability of alternative cash crops for peasant farmers and of the economic infrastructure for marketing them. Again quoting James Q. Wilson's summary, "We should not expect much gain from even sharply increased [source-country efforts]. It is a view shared by many top federal law-enforcement officials."

Domestic law enforcement is the remaining supply-side strategy, and the demonstrated success has been no greater. The ultimate measure of the effectiveness of drug control efforts at reducing the availability of drugs is their price. If drugs are becoming scarcer, simple economic theory tells us they should become more costly. If the risks of arrest and incarceration associated with drug sales are rising, simple economic theory tells us that those increased costs should be passed along and drugs should become more costly. To the contrary, since the early 1980s, as Drug Enforcement Agency and RAND Corporation data demonstrate, prices of cocaine have fallen steadily, and prices of heroin have alternated between stability and decline.

There are at least two other places to look for evidence of positive effects of supply-side efforts. One is to look at the literature on the effects of efforts to achieve deterrence effects by increasing penalties. The most deliberate and publicized increase of drug penalties in this country occurred in the early 1970s in New York when the "Rockefeller Drug Laws" mandated harsh prison terms for traffickers and forbade plea bargaining that would avoid the mandatories. A massive multi-year evaluation concluded that implementation of the laws had no effect on drug trafficking, drug use, or drug-related health problems.

Another approach is to look at the effects of street sweeps, in which police saturate an area in order to clean it. This tactic is highly popular with the public and with some drug policy scholars, but the best evidence is that sweeps move the drug markets around and, at least for a time, make drugs harder to find for some buyers, but that overall they have no effect on the volume of drug trafficking in a city or metropolitan area. Arrested dealers are quickly replaced by others willing to accept the risks in order to win the rewards.

One last approach is to look at the evidence on the use, in general, of harsh penalties and war-against ideology in reducing crime. The War on Drugs was after all but one front in a series of wars against crime waged by the Reagan and Bush administrations. If vigorous enforcement and harsher and tougher penalties can be shown to lower crime generally, perhaps the War on Drugs can be justified as a specific application of that general proposition.

Here, too, the evidence is no more convincing. Although Reagan and Bush administration crime bills year after year increased penalties and extended mandatory minimum sentences to additional drug crimes, a conservative U.S. Sentencing Commission toughened penalties even more and insisted on their application, prison populations tripled from 1980 onward, and similar developments occurred in many states, there is little reason to believe that crime was much diminished. On mandatory penalties, a considerable literature instructs that they have had no, little, or transient effects. More generally, it has long been established—most authoritatively in this country by the 1978 report of the National Academy of Sciences Panel on Research on Deterrent and Incapacitative Effects—that imaginable increases in penalties are likely at most to achieve modest crime reduction through deterrence or incapacitation.

The last twenty years have provided a natural laboratory for assessing the effects of harsher penalties on behavior. Along with the trebled prison population since 1980, the 1993 report of the National Academy of Sciences Panel on the Understanding and Control of Violence observed that

> while average prison time served per violent crime roughly tripled between 1975 and 1989, reported levels of serious violent crime varied around the level of 2.9 million a year. . . . If tripling the average length of incarceration per crime has a strong preventative effect, then violent crime rates should have declined.

That experience, said the panel, "is not compatible with any substantial deterrence effect."

Appropriate skepticism about punitive crime control policies in general or about supply-side drug control strategy in particular does not mean that drugs should be legalized or that there are no social benefits from law enforcement efforts. Drug-law enforcement, for example, through its clear message that drug trafficking is illegal and wrong, may help reinforce social norms against drug use. As long as private drug sales remain illegal, no one can disagree with enforcement targeted at the distributors, manufacturers, importers, and organizations that perform these functions. Similarly, few would argue that it is inappropriate to try to stop the flow of drugs through airports, tollbooths, and seaports or that police should not make arrests in drug-ridden neighborhoods to protect the right of residents to live in a safe and congenial environment. Even source-country and extraterritorial interdiction programs may be justifiable, albeit largely for dramaturgical reasons.

Much less need be said about demand-side tactics because the evidence is so much more positive. A sizable literature now documents the effectiveness of school-based drug education at reducing drug experimentation and use among young people. Recent work by Phyllis Ellickson of the RAND Corporation and Gilbert Botvin of the Cornell Medical Center are the most prominent among many demonstrations of the effectiveness of drug abuse education. Another sizable literature, recently summarized by Douglas Anglin and Yih-Ing Hser in *Crime and Justice,* and also by the General Accounting Office and the National Institute of Medicine, documents the capacity of drug abuse treatment programs to reduce drug use and drug-related crime. Late in 1993, the President's Commission on Model State Drug Laws, appointed by President Bush following a congressional mandate, categorically concluded, "Treatment works." There is no credible literature that can document the effects of mass-media campaigns on drug use, but a judge could take judicial notice of their ubiquity, and it is not unreasonable to believe that such campaigns have reinforced changing social norms that have led to across-the-board falls in drug use in the United States since 1980.

Supply-side strategy has a role, but so does demand-side strategy. The choice between them is a false one. Rather, the question is one of balance, and, in setting that balance, the likely effects of alternative choices on members of minority groups are ethically an inexorably relevant consideration. It is hard to imagine any legitimate rationale for the decision by the drug war's designers to adopt policies that were unlikely to achieve their ostensible goals and that were foreordained to affect disadvantaged black Americans disproportionately. At the end of Chapter 1, I summarized the unpersuasive arguments offered by Bush administration spokesmen to justify the disproportionate impact on blacks of cynical crime control policies. The same unpersuasive arguments have been offered to justify the drug war's disproportionate effects on blacks. They are no more persuasive in this specific context than in general.

The willingness of the drug war's planners to sacrifice young black Americans cannot be justified. Crime and drug abuse do disproportionately affect disadvantaged minority communities. Amelioration of their effects should be a paramount policy priority. So much is clear. Racially sensitive policies would, however, take account of any foreseeable racially disparate impacts as well as the policy's likely instrumental effects. By those twin criteria, neither today nor in 1987 could anyone claim that supply-side methods were likely to be more successful than demand-side methods. What was clear both then and now is that a program built around education, drug abuse treatment, and social programs designed to address the structural social and economic conditions that lead to crime and drug abuse would have much less destructive impact on disadvantaged young blacks than would a program whose primary tactics were the arrest, prosecution, and lengthy incarceration of street-level sellers who are disproportionately black and Hispanic.

All that is left is politics. The War on Drugs and the set of harsh crime-control policies in which it was enmeshed were launched to achieve political, not policy, objectives, and it is the adoption for political purposes of policies with foreseeable disparate impacts, the use of disadvantaged black Americans as a means to the achievement of politicians' electoral ends, that must in the end be justified, and cannot.

4

Social Adversity and the Criminal Law

The conditions of disadvantage that shape the lives of too many black Americans are the reason why so many are involved in crime. The question is how, if at all, the criminal law and the criminal justice system should take account of that reality. At one pole are those—mainly political conservatives and the more rigid social theorists—who see crime solely as a failure of character and who argue that environmental and developmental influences have nothing to do with moral responsibility and should have nothing to do with legal responsibility.

There is no other pole. No one argues that disadvantaged offenders should be given a license to attack, rape, or steal from others. Because most violent crime is intraracial, the absolution of disadvantaged black offenders would require a fatalistic acceptance of the suffering of black victims. And as moral philosophers have long instructed, to deny that human beings are responsible for their voluntary acts is tantamount to denying that they are human beings. Animals and children and incompetents are not legally responsible—animals because they are not human beings, and children and incompetents because they lack maturity or capacity. No one would argue for policies that imply that minority offenders are more like children or animals than like morally autonomous adults.

There are, however, middle positions. Some judges, for example, try to give the benefit of the doubt to "worthy" disadvantaged offenders by "giving them another chance" and imposing a less severe sentence than would otherwise be called for. This is inevitably idiosyncratic and depends on the personality of the judge and on stereotypes of worthiness. Similarly, many prosecutors' offices operate diversion and suspended prosecution programs. Some minority offenders benefit, but again, the process is serendipitous.

The better middle ground is to give the benefit of the doubt to all disadvantaged offenders, whatever their race, by eliminating sentencing laws that require judges to impose minimum sentences and by permitting judges to lower sentences in particular cases to take account of the offender's circumstances. In criminal-law jargon, informal mitigation should be encouraged.

Analyses of the criminal law typically distinguish among three types of defenses: justifications, excuses, and mitigations. Justifications involve circumstances, like killings in self-defense, in which the defendant did the right thing. It may be regrettable that the attacker died but few would disagree that the killing was justifiable. Excuses involve circumstances, like crimes committed while the perpetrator was insane, in which it would be unjust to impose legal responsibility because the actor lacked the capacity to do anything else. Mitigations involve circumstances, like assaults or killings by people who have been deeply provoked, are extremely emotionally disturbed, or lack normal mental capacities, in which the defendant's actions seem less culpable than do similar actions by others who are not so afflicted. When successful, excusing and justifying defenses result in acquittals. Mitigating defenses result in conviction of a lesser charge, often a form of manslaughter rather than murder.

Once a conviction has been entered, informal excuses, justifications, and mitigations influence the sentences that offenders receive. For example, even though an abused woman's experience may not have satisfied the legal criteria for an abused-spouse-syndrome claim to self-defense in killing her husband, a judge may take her victimization into account as informal partial justification and reduce her sentence. Even though assisted suicide may be criminal, and a surviving spouse's agonized motive to respect a partner's wishes and end his suffering no formal excuse, a judge may take into account the motive and sentence her to probation. And so it is with mitigations. Judges often impose reduced sentences because of special circumstances in the actors' lives that make them seem less blameworthy than others.

If the criminal justice system is to begin to diminish the racial disparities that characterize American prisons and jails, and the harms that those disparities inflict on black Americans, the system must be opened up to allow judges informally to mitigate the punishments suffered by disadvantaged offenders. This modest proposal is less modest than it may appear, however, because it involves fundamental changes in direction in American policies toward punishment and sentencing. It requires rejection and reversal of mandatory and habitual-offender ("three strikes and you're out") sentencing laws and ever-escalating calls for harshness. And it requires rejection of "just deserts" as an overriding rationale for sentencing and the systems of rigid sentencing guidelines based on that rationale. Both just-deserts theories and most American guidelines systems base sentences on the nature of the current offense and to varying degrees on the offender's prior record, and generally forbid judges to mitigate sentences to take account of the offender's background and personal circumstances.

Neither the initial modern proponents of just-deserts theories nor the designers of the original sentencing guidelines systems meant to do special harm to minority offenders. They meant to do good. In the 1970s when the Committee for the Study of Incarceration and Andrew von Hirsch produced *Doing Justice,* the initial modern statement of just-deserts theory, and the Minnesota Sentencing Guidelines Commission provided in America's first presumptive guidelines that employment, education, living arrangements, and marital status "should not be used as reasons for departing" from sentencing guidelines, they hoped to reduce racial and class disparities. By establishing new sentencing systems based only on the offender's current and past criminality, they hoped to keep judges from imposing less severe sentences on middle-class offenders and to ensure that all comparable offenders, whatever their race or social class, received the same punishment. In a time when indeterminate sentencing systems were all but ubiquitous and accorded immense and unreviewable discretion to judges and parole boards, when many of the great legal victories of the civil rights movement were less than a decade old, and when overt racial hostility was widespread, their concern for bias and their wish to narrow its ambit were understandable. Unfortunately, their proposals were widely adopted and they backfired, making things worse for minority offenders, not better.

Offending Patterns by Race

At least since the Federal Bureau of Investigation began collecting arrest data in the 1920s, blacks have constituted much larger percentages of persons arrested for serious crimes than of the general population. In recent decades, for example, approximately 45 percent of those arrested for the violent crimes of murder, rape, aggravated assault, and robbery have been black (declining from 47.5 percent in 1976 to 44.8 percent in 1992), compared with 12 to 13 percent of the general population. Victims' reports of the identities of their attackers suggest that the arrest data provide a reasonably accurate indicator of offending patterns.

Why these patterns exist is no mystery. For as long as crime statistics have been compiled, crime and poverty have marched together. Mountains of social welfare, health, employment, and educational data make it clear that black Americans experience material conditions of life that, on average, are far worse than those faced by white Americans. In 1990, for example, 65 percent of black babies were born to unwed mothers, compared with 20 percent of white babies. In 1991, using the U.S. Department of Labor's official poverty line, 30.4 percent of black families had incomes below the poverty level. Of children in black single-parent families headed by women, 67.9 percent lived in households with incomes below the poverty level.

A large majority of black children experience poverty. For example, according to David Ellwood, of Harvard's Kennedy School of Government, among people who are now young adults, those raised during the 1970s, five of ten black children were poor for four of their first ten years of life, compared with one in twelve whites. One black child in three, but only one white child in thirty-three, was poor for at least seven of their first ten years.

Criminogenic forces are strongest in inner-city areas of concentrated poverty, where incomes are low and families unstable, and unemployment and welfare dependence are high. Blacks are far more likely than whites to live in such neighborhoods. In 1980, for example, according to sociologists Robert Sampson and William Julius Wilson of the University of Chicago, fully 38 percent of poor blacks lived in areas of extreme poverty, compared with less than 7 percent of poor whites. Conversely, 70 percent of poor non-Hispanic whites in the ten largest cities lived in non-poverty areas; only 16 percent of poor blacks lived in nonpoverty areas.

Those data are from 1980. More recent research would show even larger racial contrasts. The 1990 census showed that poverty became even more concentrated in 1990 than in 1980, and Bureau of the Census analyses show that the proportion of people living in poverty in cities increased by one-third from 1978 to 1991 (from 15.4 percent of city residents to 20.2 percent).

By almost every imaginable statistical measure of collective well-being, blacks are less well off than whites. In 1991, the median income for a black American family was 59 percent of that of a white family. In 1992, the unemployment rate for black males was 15.2 percent, and for white males, 6.9 percent. And so on, through education, housing, infant mortality, and life expectancies; the litany is nearly endless.

The preceding comparative racial data, if anything, understate the relative disadvantage of poor blacks. This is because most of the data are averages and combine the experiences of the advantaged and the disadvantaged. Data on only the worst-off third of American blacks would be even more disturbing. For at least two decades, a sizable proportion of the American black population has been moving toward fuller social and economic integration into American society. Black women's incomes are very similar to white women's; younger, college-educated black women earn more than comparable white women. Blacks are moving into managerial and professional jobs in increasing numbers. Middle-class blacks are more and more likely to live in racially integrated areas. As these positive developments unfold, the characteristics of the affected subset of middle-and upper-class black Americans become indistinguishable from those of comparable white Americans.

University of Chicago law professor Norval Morris, the leading American criminologist, for example, has long argued that crime rates for middle-class blacks should be the same as those for middle-class whites, once we control for education, occupation and income, residence, and living arrangements. For college-educated married professional couples with children, living in middle- or upper-class suburban or urban residential neighborhoods, race should not be a good predictor of criminality.

Morris's argument, though speculative, was recently confirmed by research by Faith Peeples and Rolf Loeber in Pittsburgh. As part of the Pittsburgh Youth Study, a long-term project exploring the development of prosocial and antisocial behavior, Loeber and his colleagues wanted to learn whether blacks and whites of comparable backgrounds have similar delinquency experiences. To do this, they compared the self-reported delinquency of black and white boys living in underclass and all other Pittsburgh neighborhoods and found that "when African American youths did *not* live in underclass neighborhoods, their delinquent behavior was similar to that of the white youths" (emphasis in original). There were too few white boys living in underclass neighborhoods to compare racial patterns in offending among the disadvantaged. These findings are all the more striking because the blacks living in nonunderclass neighborhoods were on average less well off than the whites in the study (as is true generally in America). Their findings are "all the more remarkable," Peeples and Loeber note, "when one appreciates that the non-underclass-neighborhood African American youths nevertheless live in relatively poor neighborhoods."

If conditions of life are improving for a growing black middle class, and yet the relative differences between blacks and whites on many social indicators are as great as they are, imagine how difficult life must be for those black Americans who are not moving into the mainstream. Some of the prison and jail statistics presented in earlier chapters are illustrative. In 1990, for example, on the annual census dates, 1,860 per 100,000 resident blacks were in prison or jail. Differently stated, 1 of every 50 blacks was in confinement (not counting mental institutions, juvenile facilities, or military prisons). Women in 1990, however, made up 6 percent of the prison and jail population, but 51 percent of the general population. Once those gender differences are accounted for, it turns out that 1 in 23 black men was in prison or jail. Only tiny percentages of inmates are under eighteen (0.5 percent of state prisoners in 1986) or over fifty-five (2.4 percent in 1986). Once those age differences are taken into account, something like 1 in 12 black men aged eighteen to fifty-four was in jail or prison on the counting dates in 1990.

I stop there, but similar analyses taking account of occupation, residence, and living arrangements would generate an even larger fraction among unemployed eighteen- to fifty-four-year-old black men who are neither married nor part of a stable household. Once this kind of analysis is digested, some of the National Center on Institutions and Alternatives analyses discussed in Chapter 1 showing that 40 to 60 percent of young black men in some cities are under criminal justice system control seem less surprising.

These patterns are confirmed by research on offending, which shows that young black men in some urban areas have remarkably high chances of being arrested before they reach age eighteen. For example, in his longitudinal study of the lives of a birth cohort of boys born in Philadelphia in 1945, Marvin Wolfgang found that 52 percent of nonwhites and 29 percent of whites had been arrested by age eighteen. Crime and arrest rates were far lower in the 1950s and 1960s when Wolfgang's boys were growing up than in the 1970s, 1980s, and 1990s, and Wolfgang's data included all males, not just those living in disadvantaged homes.

How are we to understand these patterns? Some, including Attorneys General Richard Thornburgh and William Barr during the Bush administration, see criminality as no more than the moral failings of people of weak character. Some perceive a more complicated phenomenon. The *Chicago Tribune* columnist Mike Royko (reprinted in Judge David Bazelon's *Questioning Authority* [1988]) captured the problem in his musings about the daily choices made by two young men in Chicago:

> You take some teenager in an affluent suburb. He has just returned from playing tennis or football after school. . . . He walks into a seven- or eight-room house in which he has his own room, equipped with a stereo and maybe his own TV set, and a closet full of clothes.
>
> After having dinner with his father, who has a well-paying job, and his mother, who might work but also might be home every day, he goes in his room, looks in the mirror and asks himself: "What is in my heart? Do I want to join a gang and go out and mug somebody and pursue a life of violence and crime? Or do I want to go to college and become a CPA?": Goodness, thank goodness, usually prevails over evil. So the lad does not go out and join [a street gang].

A similar decision is made by a youth in one of the city's many slum areas. His home is a dismal flat or a congested housing project. Income is his mother's welfare check. School is a place where the most important thing you learn is not to turn your back on strangers. Security and social life are the other kids on the street—the gang.

So he looks in the cracked mirror and asks: "What is in my heart? Do I want to become a CPA, or a physician, or a lawyer? Do I want to go to Northwestern or Georgetown or maybe Yale? Hell no. I *want* to pursue the life of crime and violence. I *want* to go out and mug somebody. I *want* to wind up doing 10 to 20 in [prison] so I can be with my friends. I want this because it is in my heart and has been there since I was born."

We know why the inner-city youth does not plan to be an accountant and why the suburban youth is unlikely to participate in a gang fight. We also know a lot about the reasons why the inner-city youth's prospects are so bleak.

The explanations of conservatives, liberals, and radicals differ in detail, but they mostly agree that the inner-city youth's bleak prospects are not primarily the product of his own inherent moral failings. Conservatives like Charles Murray, George Gilder, and Lawrence Mead, among many others, claim that psychologically naive social welfare programs sap the initiative and self-respect of disadvantaged people and perversely induce them to live in the hedonistic present rather than to defer gratifications now in order to live more satisfying lives later.

Liberals like William Julius Wilson, again among many others, argue that the origins of the black urban underclass, from which many offenders come, lie in a combination of historical racism and denied opportunities, and contemporary social and economic structural changes. This is expressed in the title of Wilson's pioneering 1978 book, *The Declining Significance of Race.* The structural changes include the loss of unskilled and semiskilled manufacturing jobs in the cities, thereby removing economic opportunities for personal advancement, and the movement of middle-class blacks from racially homogeneous inner-city neighborhoods to socially homogeneous suburban ones, thereby removing from the inner city both role models and effective participants in organizations like churches, political organizations, and neighborhood associations.

Because Wilson's argument has often been misunderstood and he has sometimes, as a result, been described as a political conservative with views not unlike those of Murray and Meade, a bit of elaboration may be appropriate. Wilson questions neither the scale of historical racial discrimination nor its lingering long-term effects. But for discrimination by employers and labor unions, many more black families today would have middle-class incomes and lifestyles. But for segregated and substandard schools, many more blacks would have educations and skills that equip them for professional, managerial, and information-age jobs. But for housing segregation, many fewer blacks would live in racially homogeneous urban neighborhoods of concentrated poverty. These patterns, and others equally unfavorable to blacks, are exhaustively described and documented by Harvard sociologist Stanley Lieberson in *A Piece of the Pie—Blacks and White Immigrants Since 1880,* a classic 1980 book in which he attempts to understand why successive immigrant groups, including racial minorities like the Chinese and the Japanese, have fared better in America than have blacks.

Nor does Wilson deny the existence of contemporary discrimination. His argument, however, is that the disappearance overnight of racial discrimination would not be enough to achieve full social and economic integration. Poor blacks would continue to be concentrated in poverty-stricken urban areas with deteriorated public services and limited job opportunities, and they would continue to be afflicted by high rates of illegitimacy, single-parent households, welfare dependence, and unemployment.

Radicals like New York University law professor Derrick Bell, perhaps not among so many others, contend that barely submerged contemporary racism explains the conditions faced by disadvantaged black Americans. This is expressed in the title of Bell's 1992 book, *Faces at the Bottom of the Well—The Permanence of Racism.* Sometimes the racism argument invokes genocidal white conspiracies. University of North Carolina researcher Bernard Boxill, for example, believes that whites may use the black underclass "as an excuse to undo the legal, social, and economic advances made by the black middle class, plunge the country into a race war, and worst of all, be a pretext for genocide." More commonly, the argument is circular, asserting that allowing conditions to endure that result in racial disparities is "systemic racism," thereby using the evidence of disparity as proof of racism. In Chapter 7, I develop a positive version of such arguments to urge that in setting public policies, ethical policymakers should take into account foreseeable racial disparities in their implementation. The use of self-defining terms like systemic racism, however, neither helps us understand the conditions facing underclass blacks nor offers guidance on how to improve those conditions.

What all these explanations have in common is that they provide structural accounts that explain the conditions in inner cities that shape the development of disadvantaged young men. In other words, as Mike Royko's two boys illustrate, and as Peeples and Loeber's research documents, crime by young disadvantaged black men does not result primarily from their individual moral failures but from their misfortune of being born in places and times and under circumstances that make crime, drug use, and gang membership look like reasonable choices from a narrow range of not very attractive options.

There is no other defensible explanation for why crime, delinquency, and drug abuse are so extraordinarily more prevalent among disadvantaged minority youth than among other youth. Few inside the lunatic fringes of American society believe or are prepared to argue that genetic or biological factors explain disproportionate black offending. Some conservatives apparently still subscribe to "culture of poverty" explanations of black disadvantage, but because no one doubts that culture in the shorter or longer term is shaped by environmental conditions, this merely changes the contextual description of the forces that shape disadvantaged young men's choices.

In the end, every mainstream explanation of the inner-city underclass converges on an explanation of disproportionate minority offending that gives far greater explanatory power to the social forces that shape people's development and life chances than to the moral failures of individual persons. And it is this problem that analyses of the handling by the criminal law and the criminal justice system of minority offenders must address.

A Social Adversity Defense?

Suppose it is true that 80 percent of young black males in the worst neighborhoods of Chicago and New York are arrested for a nontrivial offense by age eighteen, compared with 5 percent of young males of diverse races in selected affluent suburbs. Unless invidious assumptions are make about constitutional differences between the two groups of men, it must be the case that the environments of the young urban men provide more temptations and fewer disincentives.

These different levels of criminality must exist because it is easier to avoid criminal temptation in the suburbs than in the inner city. That fewer suburban youth succumb, as an empirical matter, is not testament to their better character but to their lesser temptation. The financial benefits from selling drugs and stealing purses are less enticing to a well-off suburban youth with a part-time job, an adequate allowance, or both, a family that will be mortified by an arrest, and long-term college and career plans that will be jeopardized, than to an impoverished urban youth with no lawful job or allowance, no family or a dysfunctional one, and no realistic chances for material and professional success. Few would credit an affluent suburban youth with unusual strength of character for failing to sell drugs. Should the criminal law blame a disadvantaged youth for succumbing to all but overwhelming temptation?

Empirical realities such as those just described provoked a flurry of writing in the 1970s and 1980s on the merits of a "social adversity" defense, an "excuse" akin to the insanity defense. Norval Morris, arguing for the abolition of the insanity defense, may have precipitated the debate when he observed in 1968 that an "adverse social and subcultural background is statistically *more* criminogenic than is psychosis" (emphasis in original). His point, and few informed observers would disagree, is that future commission of serious crimes can more accurately be predicted from knowledge of a person's background and circumstances than from knowledge of his psychiatric diagnosis. Since the insanity defense is premised on the idea that people should not be held criminally liable for actions over which they lack control, Morris contended that the same deterministic insight applied at least equally powerfully to social disadvantage and would equally plausibly support a social disadvantage defense akin to the insanity defense.

Morris's proposition has been a taking-off point for a number of influential analyses of a social adversity defense, even though he was making the contrary argument: Because the law does not recognize a social adversity defense, it should not recognize an insanity defense.

With a few tentative exceptions, most analysts have agreed with Morris's view that recognition of such a defense is unwise, though often for the wrong reason. The wrong reason is the proposition that temptations, no matter how strong, are morally irrelevant and, as University of Pennsylvania law professor Stephen Morse put it, "Convicted offenders are punished because they have offended and thus deserve to be punished." The right reason is that, in principle and in practice, such a defense, however ethically appealing, is unworkable, for reasons that are set out below.

The fullest discussion of the case for a social adversity defense unfolded in a series of exchanges between the late federal court of appeals judge David L. Bazelon and Stephen Morse in the pages of the *University of Southern California Law Review* in the mid-1970s. Judge Bazelon started from the premises that a criminal conviction is a moral condemnation and that condemnation is not just unless the person "could reasonably have been expected to have conformed his behavior to the demands of the law." He urged adoption of a broad irresponsibility defense, encompassing both mental abnormality and the effects of extreme disadvantage: "A defendant is not responsible if at the time of his unlawful conduct his mental or emotional processes or behavior controls were impaired to such an extent that he cannot justly be held responsible for his act."

Bazelon's proposal was intended to open up criminal trials to "expert and lay testimony on the nature and extent of behavioral impairments and of physiological, psychological, environmental, cultural, educational, economic, and hereditary factors." It derived from several decades of frustration with various reforms of the insanity defense, including the broadest, *Durham,* for which Bazelon had written the opinion for the federal Court of Appeals for the District of Columbia Circuit, setting out a new insanity defense standard. Under *Durham,* the defendant could not be held criminally responsible if "his unlawful act was the product of mental disease or defect."

Durham and Bazelon's proposed broader irresponsibility defense were based on his belief that the traditional legal insanity defenses were too narrow and could easily result in the conviction of people whose characteristics or life circumstances in a meaningful sense made them incapable of controlling their behavior. In the classic formulation of the insanity defense, the *M'Naghten* test, a defendant was not entitled to aquittal on grounds of insanity if he understood the nature and quality of his acts and that they were (legally) wrong. This formulation and all others in use have been criticized because they are expressed in terms and concepts that cannot be reconciled with psychiatric diagnostic categories and as a result that expert testimony has often proved to be unhelpful. Bazelon's goal in *Durham* and with the later proposal was to allow a broad range of testimony to be presented and then to allow the jury to decide the ultimate question, in light of all the testimony, whether the defendant should justly be held responsible for his acts.

Bazelon doubted that the adoption of his irresponsibility proposal would alter decisions in many cases: "I strongly suspect that those who fear my emphasis on moral culpability would jeopardize our safety are unrealistic. . . . To believe that putting the question of culpability to juries will sharply increase the number of acquittals of dangerous defendants strikes me as unrealistic." After all, his proposal required the jury to find that the defendant's ability to control his behavior was so impaired that he "cannot justly be held accountable," a conclusion few juries are likely to reach, especially in cases involving violent and other serious crimes. Still, Bazelon argued, if juries were often to acquit on moral culpability grounds, the discovery that many juries believed social injustice to be so pervasive is so important that we would be better off knowing than not knowing it.

The two most sustained critiques of Bazelon's and similar proposals have come from Stephen Morse, a lawyer/psychologist, and his colleague at the University of Pennsylvania, Michael Moore, a lawyer/philosopher. Morse responded to Bazelon's original proposal, raising four main objections. First, Bazelon was empirically mistaken concerning the influence of deprivation on behavior: "The vast majority of persons faced with the hardest choices obey the law," and "most poor families do manage to convey to their children a sense of order, purpose, and self-esteem." Second, insofar as Bazelon was arguing that mentally competent disadvantaged offenders lack free will, he was wrong: "Even if obeying the law is harder for some persons than for others . . . the decision to offend is still a result of the actor's choice." Third, treating mentally competent human beings as less than fully responsible for their actions would imply that they were not "autonomous and capable of that most human capacity, the power to choose. To treat persons otherwise is to treat them as less than human." Fourth, as a practical and political matter, acquitted offenders who appeared dangerous and potentially violent would not be released, and the resulting "noncriminal" systems of preventive detention and compulsory treatment would "lead to disrespect for personal autonomy, to massive invasions of privacy, and to the 'tyranny of the normative.' "

The second and third points concerning free will and moral autonomy are the stuff of Michael Moore's critique and I defer discussion of them. The fourth is surely right. When Americans are frightened, and the dark side of our culture takes over, we do not allow concern for offenders' interests to impede the search for greater safety. This is demonstrated by the adoption of systems of pretrial preventive detention in this country since the mid-1970s that were then unimaginable to most criminal and constitutional lawyers, and the widespread movement to limit or eliminate the insanity defense in the aftermath to John Hinckley's acquittal on grounds of insanity after his attempted assassination of Ronald Reagan. Added demonstration comes from the proliferation of sentencing laws that permit or require decades-long or life sentences for people convicted of violent and sexual offenses and even some drug crimes and the recent enthusiasm for "Three Strikes and You're Out" laws. Inasmuch as I agree with Morse—though for different reasons—that a social adversity defense would be impracticable, I do not discuss his fourth point, except to acknowledge its force.

The empirical data concerning Morse's first point, however, are much more compelling than his view that "the majority of persons in the most criminogenic subculture are law-abiding" recognizes. No doubt the data known to Morse in 1975 when he wrote his article made his observation seem right. Sociologist Marvin Wolfgang's study of the criminality of a cohort of Philadelphians born in 1945, showing that more than half of black males had an arrest record by age eighteen, had been published in 1972, but it takes time for learning in one discipline to penetrate another. There were no other broad-based credible studies that shed light on the question. Both Bazelon and Morse were drawing on their impressions and intuition, and Morse's were not self-evidently wrong.

Today we know better. Many different sources of data show us that very large proportions of disadvantaged blacks are not "law-abiding." The studies of the proportions of black males under criminal justice system control—nationally in 1990, one in four black males aged 20 to 29; in New York State in 1990, 23 percent of black males aged 20 to 29; in Baltimore in 1991, 56 percent of black males aged 18 to 35—are one source. Ethnographic and other studies of drug dealing showing the large proportions of disadvantaged kids who participate are another. A 1989 Urban Institute study by Paul Brownstein and others, showing that one-sixth of ninth and tenth graders in inner-city Washington schools admitted selling drugs, is an example. The data presented in Chapter 3 on racial disproportions in prison and among drug arrestees are a third source.

As a probabilistic matter, therefore, the problem is much more complicated than Morse in 1975 realized. Once we disaggregate the general population into smaller and smaller groups, by race and gender and place of residence and concentration of poverty and household type, we now know that the hypothesis with which I began this discussion—that there are groups for which the probability of being arrested for a nontrivial crime by age eighteen is 80 percent or more and that there are other groups for which the chances are 5 percent or less—is not unreasonable.

When only one in twenty privileged suburban males succumbs to crime's allure and four of five disadvantaged urban minority males do, it becomes more than a bit glib to suggest that the pattern results simply from offenders' bad moral characters, that in Morse's terms, a decision to participate in crime is merely "a matter of harder choices and easier choices."

The sunny side of American culture celebrates fairness and compassion, and from that perspective it is not easy to be sanguine about a world in which some people have such harder choices to make. The title of John Rawls's early article, "Justice as Fairness," expresses this, as does nearly universal support across the American political spectrum for "equality of opportunity." Many liberals doubt that equal opportunity is enough in a world in which people begin life from vastly different starting points, but few challenge its appeal in principle.

Social welfare theorists use the concept of life chances to express the normative idea that, in a just world, every person at birth should have the same chances for a healthy, satisfying, and materially rewarding life. But as the comparative racial data on crime and punishment indicate, as also do the comparative racial data on social welfare, ours is not a country in which every child is born with equal life chances. Nor is inequality in life chances randomly distributed, but along lines of class and race.

It is sometimes argued that the existence of persons who, Horatio Alger–like, overcome the odds, complete their educations, and move on to successful mainstream lives disproves the claim that disadvantage leads to crime. Morse makes this argument when he observes, albeit mistakenly, that the majority of persons in the most criminogenic subcultures are law-abiding. The argument is a non sequitur. That Horatio succeeds shows that heroic efforts and luck can overcome enormous obstacles, but his success does not show that disadvantage does not lead to crime.

Participation in crime, like everything else, is probabilistic. Whether a person will commit crimes depends in part on the circumstances of his or her life. Statisticians use the term *base expectancy rate* to describe the rate at which members of defined groups experienced some phenomenon in the past and to predict the probability that they will experience it in the future. For a group of newly released parolees with a 45 percent base expectancy rate for rearrest within two years, we would predict that percentage of rearrests. When we say that one young man comes from a background in which people like him have an 80 percent chance of being arrested by age eighteen, and another from a group with a 5 percent chance, we are talking about base expectancy rates.

Being in a group with a high base expectancy rate for future crime does not mean that the conditions that define membership in the group *cause* crime. Rather, it means that the odds are high that people will commit crimes, but it also means that some knowable proportion will overcome the odds. The higher the base expectancy rate is, the longer the odds will be, and the more unusual the person will be who can overcome them. A small percentage of highly exceptional people can overcome the conditions that lead to an 80 percent base expectancy rate for predicted offending. A very large percentage of very ordinary people can overcome a 5 percent rate.

Horatio Alger examples do not prove that disadvantage does not cause crime; they prove that exceptional people, heroes, can beat the odds. However, the higher the odds are, the greater the required heroism will be. Thus the Horatio Alger example merely rephrases the question. Would a just system of criminal law distinguish among groups of people, in one of which most become offenders and a few heroes do not, and in another of which a few become offenders and most ordinary people do not? The right answer, I believe, is that a just system would draw those distinctions but not by means of a social adversity defense.

There are two sets of compelling reasons to reject a social adversity defense, one principled and one practical. The principled objections concern ideas of moral autonomy. Establishing as a matter of criminal-law doctrine that some people's bad acts do not count implies that those people are not responsible adults whose moral choices matter. Since recognition of moral autonomy entails acknowledgment of people's responsibility for their willed actions, a social adversity defense cutting that link would deny the actor's autonomy. This seems wrong in principle and doubly wrong in practice when many of the people whose autonomy would be denied are members of a racial minority group. The practical objection is that an adversity defense would have the perverse effect of removing disincentives to crime even from those people who would be deterred by them.

Principled Objections

The moral autonomy objection to a social adversity defense has power, but much less power than objectors claim. Because the most vigorous, subtle, and unqualified attack was launched by University of Pennsylvania philosopher Michael Moore, I focus on his analysis.

Moore offers two reasons that the law should not take account of "the sympathy we may feel for wrongdoers whose wrongdoing was caused by factors such as social adversity or psychological abuse during childhood." First, the sympathy is misplaced. Such "sympathetic judgments may simply have to be discarded" because they are incoherent. Moore offers the metaphor of the perception that a stick partly immersed in water is bent. If we know the stick is straight, we reject our contrary sensory perception as inaccurate. Likewise, says Moore, we should set aside "our sympathetic responses to disadvantaged criminals" because they are inconsistent with "the much larger set of judgments about responsibility that we make in daily life." If offenders are competent adults, they are by definition responsible for their actions and that, as far as the criminal law is concerned, should be that.

Second, Moore argues that such sympathy is ignoble. Although on the surface, compassion and generosity toward the disadvantaged may appear humane and virtuous, behind that appearance lie baser instincts. Observes Moore,

> There is an elitism and a condescension often (and perhaps invariably) connected with such feelings. To stand back and refuse to judge because one understands the causes of criminal behavior is to elevate one's self over the unhappy deviant. . . . This . . . betokens a refusal to acknowledge the equal moral dignity of others.

At first impression, there is a hauteur about such arguments, a whiff of the "Let them eat cake" attributed to Marie Antoinette on hearing that the poor of Paris were starving for want of bread. The bent-stick metaphor works only if we know that the stick is straight; otherwise we cannot reach a conclusion from simple observation. Once the metaphor is altered, it works against Moore's position. If the seemingly bent stick may indeed be bent, so the apparent environmental pressures toward offending may indeed be real.

Similarly, the argument to disregard our seemingly humane sympathies because our deepest motives may be suspect artificially stops a reductionist spiral. The inclination to smother sympathetic instinct may come not from respect for the other's moral autonomy but from hubris, a preference to distance oneself from the lives of lesser beings. And the hubris may mask a lack of a sense of self-worth, and so on. The spiral can be stopped at any point. The inferences that can be drawn will vary with the stopping point.

Finally, Moore's separate body of writings on punishment seems, again at first impression, dissonant with his writing on social disadvantage. Moore is the best-known modern proponent of retributive punishment theories derived from moral intuitions. He presents hypothetical cases of crimes, posits common reactions of outrage and a thirst for revenge on the wrongdoer, and contends that we should trust our intuitions that such offenders deserve to be punished. It seems inconsistent that he is prepared to trust punitive intuitions, and to invoke them as the basis for arguments about the justness of retributive punishment schemes, while distrusting sympathetic intuitions and rejecting them as the basis for arguments about the justness of empathetic punishment schemes. (His writings on excuses and punishment, however, are consistent concerning the significance of the offender's disadvantage; in both bodies of work he asserts that recognizing such defenses would be patronizing and disrespectful of the offender's moral autonomy.)

Moore's analysis of disadvantage and legal responsibility derives from sophisticated and exceedingly subtle analyses of the problem of free will. In his 1985 essay "Causation and the Excuses," Moore attempts to apply a formidable body of philosophical writing on free will to the criminal law's treatment of excusing and justifying defenses. His task is to explain and evaluate the traditional criminal law defenses according to the alternative assumptions that there is no free will and all actions are completely determined (what he calls *hard determinism*) and that there is free will and human choices and actions are not determined. If hard determinism is true, no one is morally responsible for anything, and so the defenses are sophistry. If nondeterminism is true, then acknowledgment of the individual's moral autonomy becomes a first principle for the criminal law, and so many traditional defenses warrant reconsideration. On neither assumption, hard determinism or free will, is there a place for a social adversity defense.

Moore considers and rejects a third, middle possibility, which he calls *partial determinism*. After describing writings on the effects of social adversity on crime by Norval Morris and David Bazelon, among others, and agreeing that we can make probabilistic statements about the effects of circumstances on behavior, Moore rejects the notion of partial determinism as incoherent: "It makes sense to say that we are determined or that we are free, but to speak of being partly determined or partly free makes as much sense as to speak of being partly pregnant." The law and lawyers are unlikely ever to resolve the free will/ determinism debate on principled grounds. The debate has been resolved, as a practical matter, by philosophically impure means. The late Herbert Packer explained the compromise:

> The idea of free will in relation to conduct is not, in the legal system, a statement of fact, but rather a value preference having very little to do with the metaphysics of determinism and free will. . . . Very simply, the law treats man's conduct as autonomous and willed, not because it is, but because it is desirable to proceed as if it were.

And so it should be with the problem of adversity and responsibility. In the same way that the law in general makes Packer's compromise, it may, without sacrificing important principles, simultaneously presume that people are responsible for their acts and acknowledge that disadvantaged offenders face temptations and pressures that are relevant to deciding how the state should respond to their crimes.

Michael Moore's is the most sophisticated analysis of the rationales for a social adversity defense and the most outspoken condemnation. His apparent lack of sympathy for disadvantaged offenders and rejection of the empathetic insight of "there but for the grace of God go I" turn out to be a philosopher's idealistic commitment to the conclusions to which his analysis leads. That the analysis and the conclusions lend little assistance to solution of the law's dilemmas is, perhaps regrettably, a not uncommon attribute of philosophical analyses of legal problems. However, in his offhand acknowledgment of our ability to make probabilistic statements about human behavior, Moore gives the game away. In the end, policymakers must decide whether the criminal law should take account of an offender's being in a group having a base expectancy rate for offending of 80 percent. It is the difference between the 80 percent probability for some disadvantaged inner-city youth and the 5 percent probability for some advantaged suburban youth that poses the policy dilemma. It is simply easier, much easier, for privileged Americans to live crime-free lives than it is for disadvantaged Americans to do so, and the question is whether a just criminal law would take that difference into account. The assumption of free will does not help.

Practical Objections

The practical objections are more prosaic and involve the mechanics of a social adversity defense. Would it apply to all offenses committed by an offender to which it applies? That seems doubly wrong because it would eliminate all incentives to be law-abiding and, as Stephen Morse argues, public safety concerns would inevitably lead to a system of preventive detention to protect the rest of us from offenders who cannot be held legally accountable for crimes. Would it apply only to first offenses? That would suggest that disadvantaged offenders get one free crime, which makes no sense from a deterrence perspective. How would the defense be expressed? The verbal formulas in which criminal-law doctrines are expressed are ambiguous and depend on subjective interpretation. The use of base expectancy rates might provide more concrete criteria, but reliable and timely data for all population groups for all states and cities are not available and likely never will be.

The overriding objection to a social adversity defense is that there are no groups for which the base expectancy rate for first offenses is 100 percent. No matter how conducive to criminality the circumstances are, there always are people who live law-abiding lives. The reason may be remarkable strength of character, religious convictions, nurturing parents, a friend or coach or employer who provides a positive role model, or sheer good luck. Whatever the reason, the general interests in public safety and in encouraging the development of law-abiding people argue powerfully against a social adversity defense.

The analogy between insanity and social adversity is only partial. In the paradigm case to which the insanity defense applies, there is little question that the defendant is not morally responsible. If we accept that the knife-wielding killer believed that he was slicing bread, that he was defending himself against Martian attackers, or that he is Czar Nicholas II and was defending himself and his family against Bolshevik kidnappers, few would argue that he was morally responsible for his actions. He may be dangerous, and we may want to take steps to assess that danger and to prevent future dangerous acts, but he is not responsible.

There is widespread opposition to the insanity defense, but it is not because of cases like those I described. It is because many people fear that sane offenders too often are wrongly acquitted on grounds of insanity and, fed by the imaginations of mystery writers, that calculating villains may plan murders in ways that will allow them to claim to have been insane and thereby to escape punishment. (The latter fear overlooks the facts that most people acquitted on grounds of insanity are committed to mental institutions and that many are held longer than if convicted of murder.)

There are no paradigm cases in which most people agree that a particular disadvantaged offender could not have done otherwise. And if we believe that there are individuals who in specific circumstances may or may not commit an offense, the idea of removing all threat of consequences for making the wrong choice is perverse. As James Fitzjames Stephen, the leading Nineteenth Century scholar of the English criminal law, observed, "it is at the moment when temptation is strongest that the law should speak most clearly and emphatically to the contrary." Put provocatively, a social adversity defense would authorize one or more "free crimes," a policy that public opinion would not tolerate.

There is another problem related to Moore's moral autonomy analysis. No doubt most if not all charged offenders would happily accept acquittal on grounds of adversity, without for a moment worrying about possible inferences concerning their moral autonomy. But this trivializes the point. Any society should be exceedingly reluctant to stigmatize some of its citizens as being less than fully responsible adults whose actions have consequences. All members of the high-risk group, however carefully delineated, will bear the stigma, even though some of them will not commit crimes. Labeling theory, one of the main theoretical perspectives in criminology, instructs that labeling people as deviants increases the likelihood that they themselves and others will think of them as deviant. The same problems of self-fulfilling prophecies and people living down to others' expectations bedevil our public schools. The bearers of those burdens in our society would disproportionately be members of racial and ethnic minority groups. A policy motivated to take account of the effects of disadvantage on minority offenders as a class would have the effect of harming minority citizens as a class.

Even if an adversity defense were politically feasible, and seemingly desirable, we would have great difficulty formulating it. Judge Bazelon's proposal that a defendant be acquitted if his "behavior controls were impaired to such an extent that he cannot justly be held responsible" was designed to authorize case-by-case gestalt decisions by juries. Most lawyers and legislators prefer legal rules whose application is predictable and whose correct application can be assessed on appeal. Otherwise it is nearly impossible to identify and correct bad decisions. Without establishing criteria concerning the nature of qualifying impairments, the degree of their extent, and the grounds for knowing when a defendant can and cannot "justly be held accountable," few predictions can be made. Even for the insanity defense, as to which paradigm cases exist, no generally satisfactory language has been developed in the century and a half since the English House of Lords decided the *M'Naghten* case. We are unlikely to do better with social adversity.

Statistical tests are not likely to prove any more satisfactory. For such a test to have moral authority, it would have to distinguish between otherwise comparable people who are and are not likely to succumb to crime's temptations. Even in a group with an 80 percent base expectancy rate, one in five in the past have not succumbed. The statistical criteria that produce the 80 percent prediction encompass the "successes," and so a test that reduced their incentives to conformity would not serve them and the rest of society.

Because disadvantaged underclass areas have the highest rates of offending, another possibility would be to permit the defense for people coming from the most devastated areas. This, too, would perversely reduce the incentives to conformity for those with the greatest chances of avoiding crimes, and it also reveals the inevitable arbitrariness of any social disadvantage test. To draw the necessary distinctions, we would need to develop base expectancy rates for states, cities within states, districts within cities, neighborhoods within districts, and streets within neighborhoods. Such research is expensive, time-consuming, and fraught with methodological issues and would quickly become obsolete as population shifts occurred. For example, whether data for a street at the margin between a deeply depressed neighborhood and a stable working- or middle-class neighborhood were included in the calculation of rates for the depressed neighborhood could reduce the predicted offending rates for that neighborhood below the threshold for the adversity defense, or, alternatively, if the depressed neighborhood qualified for the defense, offenders from the marginal street would benefit. In gentrifying areas of cities, disadvantaged people are replaced by middle-class "urban pioneers" who would then become entitled to benefit from the categorical defense available to neighborhood residents.

Sheldon Glueck, the most influential American criminologist of the 1930s and 1940s, made the most serious effort to work out a kindred scheme. To determine whether people were mentally responsible, he proposed using a scale ranging from free will to determinism. Depending on the presence and extent of intelligence, mental abnormality, and psychopathy, 10 or 50 or 90 percent free will would be attributed to individuals; somewhere along the continuum a line would separate those who were legally responsible from those who were not. Perhaps it is not surprising that nothing has come of Glueck's proposal.

5

Social Adversity
and Punishment

Disadvantaged offenders present formidable challenges to contemporary writers on the philosophy of punishment. Retributive views are predominant, and yet many writers are troubled by the reality that most offenders charged with violent crimes and serious property crimes are poor, disadvantaged, and often from minority groups. The final chapter in Andrew von Hirsch's *Doing Justice* (1976), the most influential modern statement of "just-deserts" views, is entitled "Just Deserts in an Unjust Society." From the beginning of the modern emphasis on retributive punishment theories, the problem of social disadvantage and punishment has been lurking just out of sight.

Most writers working in the retributive tradition believe that equality and proportionality are hallmarks of a just punishment system, equality in the sense that like cases are treated alike, proportionality in the sense that different cases are treated differently. For such writers, just sentences are scaled in proportion to the severity of different crimes, and differences in the characteristics and life histories of offenders are irrelevant. All who commit offense X with criminal history Y should receive the same punishment, and that is the end of the matter.

Before I explain why that view is mistaken, I need to sketch the intellectual backdrop to such analyses. Accepting a framework proposed by H. L. A. Hart, this century's leading writer on jurisprudence, most philosophers distinguish among three different punishment questions. The first, What is the general justification of the institution of punishment? is generally referred to as the question of justification. The second, Whom should we punish? is generally referred to as the question of liability. The third, How much should offenders be punished? is the question of amount. Sometimes the second and third questions together are referred to as questions of distribution.

Punishment writers' views fall along a continuum that has thoroughgoing retributivism at one end and vulgar consequentialism at the other. Thoroughgoing retributivism is the view that the answers to all three questions concern the offender's moral responsibility. Punishment is imposed because the state has a moral obligation to punish culpable wrongdoers, only morally culpable wrongdoers may be punished, and they should be punished in strict proportion to the moral wrongness of their acts. The eighteenth-century German idealist philosopher Immanuel Kant comes closest to being a thoroughgoing retributivist. Among modern writers, the views of Michael Moore, which I discussed earlier, are not inconsistent with thoroughgoing retributivism.

Vulgar consequentialism is the polar view that offenders' moral culpability is immaterial and that the only considerations relevant to punishment are the consequences of alternative possible decisions. Jeremy Bentham, the nineteenth-century English writer on utilitarianism, comes closest. He disparaged the notion of intrinsic human rights, for example, as "nonsense on stilts" and declared that the maximization of happiness and the minimization of suffering were the only appropriate goals of social policy. Barbara Wootton, an English writer on social policy, comes closest among modern writers. Wootton proposed that the only legal question to be decided concerning an apparent crime was whether the defendant had caused it. The criminal law's mens rea doctrines concerning mental states—whether the defendant's actions were willful or reckless or negligent or inadvertent—could be abandoned. After conviction, the decision what to do would be made. If the harm were inadvertent, nothing would happen. Depending on what had happened and why, rehabilitative, deterrent, incapacitative, or other preventive measures might be in order. The decision would have nothing to do with the defendant's moral culpability; the question would be how best to minimize whatever public safety threat the actor posed.

Twenty or fifty years ago, few writers on punishment would have had any principled objections to a proposal for mitigation of penalties for disadvantaged offenders. Most writing on the subject was consequentialist (although as that term has come into wide use only in recent years, most writers would have described themselves as utilitarians). Most people believed that the rehabilitation of offenders was a primary objective of punishment. Establishmentarian punishment views, as evidenced by the provisions of the American Law Institute's *Model Penal Code* (1962), favored use of the "least restrictive alternative."

Today, however, few writers on punishment admit to being utilitarians (Nigel Walker of Cambridge University is the leading exception). Most are retributivists of one sort or another, and mostly they write about the justification of punishment and not about liability or amount.

There are two major reasons why a just system of punishment would take account of offenders' disadvantaged backgrounds. First, from a consequentialist perspective, by mitigating disadvantaged offenders' punishments when feasible, we would do less harm to them as individuals and to disadvantaged black Americans as a class, without significantly diminishing public safety. Recent punishment policies, to the contrary, have destabilized disadvantaged inner-city communities, without significantly reducing crime or achieving their ostensible objectives. Second, from a retributive perspective, wrongdoers who give in to great pressure are less blameworthy than wrongdoers who face no pressure at all. In the eye of God—or as Nigel Walker would put it, in the log of the Recording Angel—Jean Valjean is far less blameworthy for stealing a loaf of bread than is Leona Helmsley for evading her income taxes. Most retributive writing on the distribution of punishment ignores the Recording Angel's perspective and argues for proportionality of sentences in relation only to the offense and the offender's past record of criminality.

Concern for the effects of sanctions on disadvantaged offenders poses a conflict between the conventional retributive principle of proportionality and the competing utilitarian principle of parsimony. Concern for proportionality calls for like treatment of like-situated offenders. Concern for parsimony, a Hippocratic criminal justice prescription to do the least harm and impose no unnecessary suffering, calls in every instance for imposing the least severe punishment that meets legitimate social purposes.

The tension between proportionality and parsimony became apparent when American jurisdictions began to develop sentencing guidelines for prison sentences. American sentencing guidelines set standards for prison sentences calibrated to measures of current and past criminality. Guidelines derive in part from concern to alleviate sentencing disparities; once offenses are scaled for severity, some proportionality among penalties for different offenses inexorably follows. In effect, sentencing guidelines for prison sentences prefer proportionality to parsimony. If some sentences are harsher than judges believe appropriate, the harshness is said to be justifiable because the punishment is no more or less severe than that suffered by "like-situated" offenders.

Neither classical utilitarian punishment theories in principle nor classical retributive theories in practice provide convincing explanations of why punishment should (or can) observe strict proportionality conditions.

Proportionality is presumably a value for utilitarians only to the extent that its nonobservance produces net unhappiness or dissatisfaction. For utilitarians, invoking Bentham, punishment itself is an evil and should be used as sparingly as possible: "Upon the principle of utility, if [punishment] ought at all to be admitted, it ought only to be admitted in as far as it promises to exclude some greater evil."

No doubt utilitarian concerns require some observance of proportionality in punishment. Punishments completely divorced from community notions of fairness—in our time, perhaps, to refuse to punish child abusers or to sentence two of three equally culpable participants in a crime to five years' imprisonment and the third to a $50 fine—would produce unacceptable levels of cynicism and dissatisfaction and indicate, on utility grounds, that some greater acknowledgment of the importance of violated community values is required. Short of such extreme cases, however, utilitarian concerns do not require that proportionality be assigned overriding importance.

Thoroughgoing retributivists might prefer a system of perfectly proportioned punishments, but in practice such a system cannot be realized. Kant's principle of equality, the right of retaliation, "the mode and measure of punishment which public justice takes as its principle and standard," has practical limits. It may be that "the principle of equality . . . may be rendered by saying that the undeserved evil which anyone commits on another is to be regarded as perpetrated on himself," but it is far from clear what that means. Generally it is construed to mean that the offender's punishment should closely match his offense. Capital punishment for murder, a $500 penalty for a $500 theft, perhaps (squeamishly) a beating for an assault; these crimes and punishments satisfy the test. But how to punish an attempted murder, a rape, emotional abuse of the elderly, securities fraud, environmental crimes? No doubt systems of scaled punishment could be devised, but only with a formidable working out of details. Does Kant's principle of equality require punishment scaled to the offender's culpability, to the offender's benefit, to the victim's harm? What about villainous attempted crimes that serendipitously produce no harm? What about venial crimes that unexpectedly produce great harm? Is the offender's evildoing to be assessed as the Recording Angel would, taking account of his weaknesses, the pressures to which he was subject, and his motives, or primarily as measured by the objective evil that his offense embodies?

There are three major positions among writers who argue that proportionality should be only a minor consideration in punishment. First, writing in a utilitarian framework and positing that punishment has mainly preventive purposes, H. L. A. Hart writes of "the somewhat hazy requirement that 'like cases be treated alike.' " Hart's argument for this modest recognition of proportionality is not retributively premised but derives from concern for the adverse social effects of divorcing punishment too greatly from common morality: "For where the legal gradation of crime expressed in the relative severity of penalties diverges sharply from this rough scale, there is a risk of confusing common morality or flouting it and bringing the law into contempt."

Second, proponents of hybrid punishment theories that combine retributive and consequentialist elements, including Norval Morris and the Australian philosopher C. L. Ten, contend that principled systems of punishment must take account of both preventive and retributive considerations. Morris, for example, in *The Future of Imprisonment* (1974), calls for a system of "limiting retributivism" in which punishment's primary purposes are seen as preventive but subject to the just-desert constraint that punish-

ments be "not undeserved" and, within the range of not undeserved punishments, the parsimonious constraint that no punishment be imposed that is more severe than is necessary to achieve
legitimate social purposes.

Third, proponents of a variety of retributive punishment theories reject their policy implications on "just deserts in an unjust
world" grounds but presumably would allow room for distributive
echoes of their ideal rationales. The Scottish philosopher Antony
Duff, for example, argues in *Trials and Punishments* (1986) that a
principled punishment system would include both retributive and
expressive elements and, accordingly, that proportionality in punishment would be given great importance. However, in a world in
which the vast preponderance of offenders are poor, badly educated, often mentally subnormal, and often from minority groups,
for social injustice reasons he sets aside his own ideal theory in
favor of preventive (utilitarian) approaches.

Efforts to apply philosophers' distinctions to policymakers' decisions necessarily raise different concerns than do disagreements
among philosophers. There are at least three difficulties. First,
punishment systems based on proportionality require objectification of categories of offenders and offenses that are oversimplified
and overinclusive. Second, proportionality arguments are often
premised on objective legal measures of desert, typically current
and past crimes, rather than on the subjective degree of moral
culpability expressed by the offender's behavior, under particular
circumstances and conditions. Third, proportionality arguments
run head-on into "just deserts in an unjust society."

The Illusion of "Like-Situated Offenders"

"Like-situated offenders" is nested in quotation marks to express
the artificiality of notions of like-situated offfenders, comparable
crimes, and generic punishments. A strong proportionality-in-
punishment argument insists on equal treatment of like-situated
offenders and proportionately different treatment of differently
situated offenders. A fundamental difficulty is that this assumes
that offenders can conveniently and justly be placed into a manage-
able number of more or less just-desert categories and that stan-

dard punishments can be prescribed for each category. Unfortunately, neither side of the crime-and-punishment equation lends itself to standardization.

Neither offenders nor punishments come in standard cases. The practice of dividing offenders and punishments into generic categories produces much unnecessary suffering and provides only illusory proportionality. A look at Minnesota's original sentencing guidelines shows why.

Figure 5-1 shows the 1980 Minnesota sentencing guidelines grid, which was expressly premised on "modified just deserts." Offenses are divided on the vertical axis into ten categories and criminal history on the horizontal axis into seven categories. An offender's presumptive sentence is determined by consulting the cell at which the row containing the conviction offense meets the column expressing criminal history. Cases falling in cells below the bold black line are presumed bound for state prison for a term of months within the narrow range specified. Cases falling above the line are presumed not bound for prison (the number in the above-the-line cells represents the prison sentence to be imposed if the offender fails satisfactorily to complete a nonprison sentence).

Because the guidelines attach high value to proportionality, "departures" are discouraged. Either party may appeal a departure that, to be upheld, must be found to have been based on "substantial and compelling" reasons. Rules offer illustrative bases for departures and forbid some, including consideration of an offender's education, employment prospects, marital status, or living arrangements.

The *original* Minnesota guidelines allowed little play for noncriminal-record factors to influence penalties. (I stress *original* because case law on "amenability to probation" now authorizes some, limited consideration of personal circumstances.) Consider a minority offender charged with theft who grew up in a single-parent, welfare-supported household, who has several siblings in prison, and who was formerly drug dependent, but who has been living in a common-law marriage for five years, has two children whom he supports, and has worked steadily for three years at a service station—first as an attendant, then an assistant mechanic, and now a mechanic. None of these personal characteristics was supposed to influence the sentencing decision, and certainly not

Severity Levels of Conviction Offense		Criminal History Score						
		0	1	2	3	4	5	6
Unauthorized use of motor vehicle, possession of marijuana	I	12 [a]	12 [a]	12 [a]	15	18	21	24
Theft-related crimes ($150-2,500), sale of marijuana	II	12 [a]	12 [a]	14	17	20	23	27 *25-29*
Theft crimes ($150-2,500)	III	12 [a]	13	16	19	22 *21-23*	27 *25-29*	32 *30-34*
Burglary—felony intent, receiving stolen goods ($150-2,500)	IV	12 [a]	15	18	21	25 *24-26*	32 *30-34*	41 *37-45*
Simple robbery	V	18	23	27	30 *29-31*	38 *36-40*	46 *43-49*	54 *50-58*
Assault, second degree	VI	21	26	30	34 *33-35*	44 *42-46*	54 *50-58*	65 *60-70*
Aggravated robbery	VII	24 *23-25*	32 *30-34*	41 *38-44*	49 *45-53*	65 *60-70*	81 *75-87*	97 *90-104*
Assault, first degree, criminal sexual conduct, first degree	VIII	43 *41-45*	54 *50-58*	65 *60-70*	76 *71-81*	95 *89-101*	113 *106-120*	132 *124-140*
Murder, third degree	IX	97 *94-100*	119 *116-122*	127 *124-130*	149 *143-155*	176 *168-184*	205 *195-215*	230 *218-242*
Murder, second degree	X	116 *111-121*	140 *133-147*	162 *153-171*	203 *192-214*	243 *231-255*	284 *270-298*	324 *309-339*

Figure 5-1. Minnesota Sentencing Guidelines Grid (presumptive sentence lengths in months)

[a] One year and one day.

Italicized numbers in the grid denote the range within which a judge may sentence without the sentence being deemed a departure. First-degree murder is excluded from the guidelines by law and continues to carry a mandatory life sentence.

Source: Minnesota Sentencing Guidelines Commission, *Report to the Legislature—1990* (St. Paul: Minnesota Sentencing Guidelines Commission, 1990).

to justify imposing a noncustodial sentence on a presumed prison-bound offender.

Minnesota attached no significance to the collateral effects of a prison sentence on the offender or on the offender's family or children. Incarceration for a drug crime for a woman raising children by herself may result in the breakup of her family and the placement of her children in foster homes or institutions or in homes of relatives who will not be responsible care providers. Incarceration of an employed father and husband may mean loss of the family's home and car, perhaps the breakup of a marriage, perhaps the creation of welfare dependency by the wife and children. To ignore that collateral effects of punishments vary widely among seemingly like-situated offenders is to ignore things that most people find important.

A similar analysis could be offered of the punishment side of the crime-and-punishment equation. Objectively, punishments valued in the generic coin of imprisonment can be very different. In most American jurisdictions, a prison sentence means "placed in the custody of the department of corrections," which in turn can mean anything from placement in a fear-ridden, gang-dominated maximum security prison under lockup twenty-three hours a day, through placement in a minimum security camp or campus, to home confinement. Objectively, a sentence to twenty-four months' probation can mean anything from living normally and mailing a bimonthly postcard to the probation office to being contacted ten to twenty-five times a month, reporting to the probation office three times a week, observing a curfew, paying restitution, doing community service, wearing electronic monitoring equipment, and being subject to frequent unannounced urinalyses.

Subjectively, three years' imprisonment may mean very different things to a twenty-three-year-old gang member, for whom it may be a rite of passage; a forty-year-old employed husband and father, for whom it will likely destroy the material conditions of his and his family's lives; a frightened, effeminate twenty-year-old middle-class student, for whom it may result in sexual victimization; or a seventy-five-year old, for whom it may be life imprisonment.

Retributive theories are premised on notions of individual blameworthiness, which seem inherently linked to particularized judgments about moral culpability. Objective measures of harm are seldom sufficient for conviction in the criminal law, which is why doctrines of competency, mens rea, and affirmative defense exist and why doctrines like strict liability and felony-murder are disfavored. If individualized moral judgments are germane to conviction, it is not obvious why they are not also germane to punishment.

If punishment is principally about blaming, it is relevant whether the offender was mentally impaired, socially disadvantaged, a reluctant participant, or moved by humane motives. Surely it is morally relevant, whatever the path to conviction, what the offender did, with what mens rea, and under what circumstances. Surely it is morally relevant whether a particular punishment will be more intensely experienced by one person than by another. In other words, the three subjective considerations that Minnesota's guidelines ignore—what did he really do and why, what will the conditions of his sanction really be, will be suffer more intensely than others—are relevant to moral judgments of blameworthiness and proportionate punishments. Nigel Walker expresses this when he observes: "Retributive reasoning would lead" not to standardized lists of crimes and punishments but "instead to a 'personal price list' which would take into account not only gradations of harm but offenders' culpability and sensibility."

An Unjust Society

The problem of "just deserts in an unjust world" is a fundamental problem for retributive punishment theories that attach much importance to proportionality. Some theories are based on an idea of "benefits and burdens"—offenders benefit from others' acceptance of the burdens of law-abidingness, and so it is unfair if the offenders themselves refuse to accept the same burden. Some theories are based on ideas of social equilibrium—an offender's wrong throws the social equilibrium out of balance, and punishment restores the balance. Some theories are based on ideas of blaming— the actor's wrong is blameworthy, and his punishment is a way to attribute blame. Some theories are based on ideas of offenders' moral autonomy—punishment signifies that the offender is a morally responsible person whose actions have consequences. Some theories are based on ideas of moral expression—punishment is a way in which the state communicates with the offender and others about the moral quality of the offender's acts.

Whatever the rationale, all retributive theories presume equal opportunities for all to participate in society. When some are prevented from full participation by discrimination, disability, or exclusion, by denial of access to public goods, or by the burdens of social and economic disadvantage, it is difficult to claim that they enjoy the benefits of autonomy that produce obligation. To take just one example, proponents of benefits and burdens theories are hard pressed to explain how a deeply disadvantaged person who enjoys few of society's benefits deserves to be burdened by social obligation.

Many writing on the philosophy of punishment recognize this problem. After developing an expressive theory of punishment based on social condemnation and individual penance, Scottish philosopher Antony Duff rejected his own proposals in favor of a deterrence-premised system: "Punishment is not justifiable within our present legal system; it will not be justifiable unless and until we have brought about deep and far-reaching social, political, legal, and moral changes in ourselves and our society."

After developing a punishment theory deriving from a social contract theory analysis of benefits and burdens, University of Arizona philosopher Jeffrey Murphy rejected it on the grounds that it could not deliver justice until "we have restructured society in such a way that criminals genuinely do correspond to the only model that will render punishment permissible—i.e., make sure that they are autonomous and that they do benefit in the requisite sense."

Even Andrew von Hirsch, arguing that a just deserts–based system of punishment will produce less additional disadvantage to the disadvantaged than a utilitarian system, concluded nonetheless: "As long as a substantial segment of the population is denied adequate opportunities for a livelihood, any scheme for punishing must be morally flawed."

Not surprisingly, proponents of utilitarian and mixed-punishment theories acknowledge the same problem. For example, in explaining the role of excusing defenses in the criminal law, H. L. A. Hart noted in regard to deeply disadvantaged people, "The admission that the excusing condition may be of no value to those who are below a minimum level of economic prosperity may mean, of course, that we should incorporate as a further excusing condition the pressure of gross forms of economic necessity."

English philosopher Ted Honderich, who subscribes to a hybrid punishment theory, observed: "There is nothing that can be called the question of [punishment's] moral justification which is left to be considered if one puts aside the great question of the distribution of goods in society."

In the United States, while giving lip service to concern for offenders from disadvantaged backgrounds, most sentencing commissions have forbidden judges to "depart" from sentencing guidelines on grounds of the offenders' personal circumstances. The perversity of such policies is that they forbid special treatment of offenders from deprived backgrounds who have achieved some personal successes. The minority offender from a broken home and a devastated neighborhood who has nonetheless managed a reasonably stable domestic life, achieved some educational success, and found secure employment is as unentitled to a mitigated sentence as is a middle-class offender. Thus, policies designed to prevent unfair treatment of disadvantaged offenders as a class operate to treat many disadvantaged offenders unfairly as individuals.

A proponent of proportionality might respond by noting that loosening proportionality restraints to permit the mitigation of sentences for "deserving" disadvantaged offenders also permits the aggravation of sentences for the "undeserving," especially those who appear most apt to offend again. This is a different problem and is discussed later in Chapters 6 and 7. By using presumptive sentencing guidelines, it is possible to reduce greatly the risk of aggravated sentences for disadvantaged offenders. We now know that strict proportionate limits on maximum sentences can be established and that judges will follow them.

Sorting out Principles

Disagreements about just punishments, like disagreements about the death penalty or abortion, are often in the end disagreements about powerful intuitions or deeply bedded values. It may be that differences in view between those who give primacy to proportionality and those who give primacy to parsimony cannot be bridged.

The burden of persuasion should rest, however, on those who reject English political philosopher Isaiah Berlin's observations that "not all good things are compatible, still less all the ideals of mankind" and that "the necessity of choosing between absolute claims is then an inescapable characteristic of the human condition."

Punishment raises at least two important conflicts between ideals: between the principles of proportionality and parsimony, and between the quests for criminal justice and social justice.

Punishment is not unique in this respect. *Justice, Equal Opportunity and the Family* (1983) by James Fishkin identifies similar irreconcilable conflicts in ideals that are posed by family policy. Even in ideal theory, he points out, values inherent in support for equal opportunity conflict with values inherent in support for family autonomy. Notions of equal opportunity, he argues, must include a "principle of merit," that "there should be a fair competition among individuals for unequal positions in society," and a "principle of equal life chances specifying roughly equal expectations for everyone regardless of the conditions into which they are born." Without equal life chances, both common experience and modern sociology demonstrate, scarce social goods will not be distributed according to merit. As Fishkin observes, "If I can predict the outcomes achieved by an individual merely by knowing his or her race, sex, ethnic origin, or family background, then equality of life chances has not been realized."

If we were single-mindedly devoted to equal opportunity, then, we should view equalization of life chances as an overriding goal of social policy. However, Fishkin observes, efforts to equalize life chances run head-on into another powerful principle, that the value of autonomy in a private sphere of liberty encompasses a principle of family autonomy, of nonintrusion by the state into the family's sphere of private liberty.

In other words, equal opportunity and family autonomy conflict fundamentally. Full respect for equal opportunity would involve intrusion into the family that would widely be seen as objectionably intrusive. Full respect for family autonomy would widely be seen as cruel disregard for children's basic needs.

And so it may be with punishment. Principles of proportionality and parsimony may simply conflict. The need to deliver just punishments in an unjust world requires that judges be authorized to mitigate sentences of disadvantaged offenders whenever possible.

6

Social Adversity and Sentencing Policy

Rejection of social adversity as a complete defense does not require that it be rejected as a mitigating consideration in a just sentencing system. To say to an offender that it was he who decided to burglarize a home and that he is responsible for his act and will be convicted does not mean that we cannot sympathize with the pressures he was under and try, for his sake and ours, to help him resist temptation next time and to fashion a sentence as constructive and as little destructive as possible. We must do so if we are to lessen the disproportionate numbers of blacks in our jails and prisons, and the damage that those disproportions do to the lives of black Americans.

The resources of the criminal justice system are few. The answers to poverty, underemployment, and racial bias must be sought elsewhere, in schools and social welfare programs and broad-based social policies. To look to the criminal justice system to solve fundamental social problems would be foolish and doomed to fail. The criminal justice system can, however, resolve not to exacerbate fundamental social problems and to do as little harm as possible.

We need to reverse course in sentencing policy and reject arbitrary laws and guidelines that make the offender's crime and criminal history the only legitimate considerations in sentencing. Recognizing that most offenders of all races coming before our courts are the products of disadvantage, we need to invest in programs that attempt to enhance their modest life chances, not to solve the problems of illiteracy, education, job training, or drug abuse in

America, but to make it more likely that offenders will be able to live satisfying, law-abiding lives.

The shifts toward sentencing guidelines and just deserts as the rationale of sentencing beginning in the mid-1970s set the right course then and the wrong course now. Then the perceived problems were judges' unfettered discretion and the appearance and prospect of unwarranted disparities and racial and class discrimination in sentencing. Now the problems in many jurisdictions are overly rigid sentencing standards, the inability of judges to take account of offenders' personal circumstances at sentencing, and the racial disproportions that characterize American prisons and jails.

The last thing that proponents of sentencing reform wanted or envisioned in the 1960s and 1970s was that the reforms they proposed, when implemented, would adversely affect members of minority groups. Amelioration of racial disparities and discrimination was a major objective of proponents of constraints on judicial discretion. Civil rights litigation on many subjects had heightened concern for racial bias and made it appear amenable to legal controls. The proceduralist movement, exemplified by *Goldberg v. Kelly,* 397 U.S. 254 (1970), a landmark welfare-law decision holding that individuals could not be denied benefits without the observance of minimum procedures like hearings, provision of reasons for unfavorable decisions, and rights of appeal, made control of criminal justice officials' discretion appear to be a realistic objective. The prisoners' rights movement focused attention on racial biases and abuses of officials' discretion and led to calls to narrow the scope of their authority.

Some of the earliest proposals for a radical overhaul of sentencing policies, like the American Friends Service Committee's *Struggle for Justice* (1971), David Fogel's *We Are the Living Proof* (1975), the Twentieth Century Fund's *Fair and Certain Punishment* (1976), and Andrew von Hirsch's *Doing Justice* (1976), came from points distinctly on the left of the American political spectrum. Most of these writers believed that racial discrimination in the criminal justice system was epidemic, that judges, parole boards, and corrections officials could not be trusted, and that tight controls on officials'discretion offered the only way to limit racial disparities.

Apprehension about racial bias was not unrealistic. National concern about civil rights was at or near its height. Then, as now, there were disproportionate numbers of blacks in prison (disproportions are, however, much worse in the 1990s than in the 1960s and 1970s). In many parts of the country, rearguard actions against the civil rights movement were under way. Many judges and officials were racist, or at least appeared to be. And "indeterminate sentencing," the ubiquitous American system, by design accorded great discretionary powers to judges and others to tailor sentences to offenders' individualized rehabilitative needs and the public safety dangers they posed. With so much power, racist officials could do great harm.

Not only from the left did calls come for changes in sentencing. From the right came books such as Ernst van den Haag's *Punishing Criminals* (1975) and James Q. Wilson's *Thinking About Crime* (1975), calling for greater certainty in sentencing and less coddling of criminals by liberal judges and parole boards.

In many states, with odd-couple supporters on the left and right, sentencing laws were changed. Parole release was abolished in some states, thereby eliminating entirely the risk of discrimination in those decisions. Some, and eventually all, states adopted mandatory sentencing laws for some offenses that required judges to impose prison sentences of specified lengths. A few, and eventually many, states adopted systems of sentencing guidelines that established criteria to guide judges' sentencing decisions. The federal government did it all, abolishing parole release, enacting many mandatory penalties, and creating a system of sentencing guidelines.

With the benefit of two decades' hindsight, two stategic choices have operated to harm black offenders and to contribute to racial disproportions. First, liberal reformers vastly underestimated the electorate's susceptibility to law-and-order appeals, and the resulting likelihood that penalties would be made substantially harsher. Under indeterminate sentencing, judges typically imposed a minimum prison term and a maximum that was three times as long; for example, three to nine years. Prisoners were generally eligible for time off for good behavior that, if fully earned, might reduce both the minimum and maximum sentences by a third, making the sentence two to six years. A parole board could release a prisoner at any time after serving the net minimum sentence and often did so at the earliest opportunity. Thus a sentence that the newspapers might report as nine years would result in release after two years.

That was how indeterminate sentencing was supposed to work. It was sometimes called "bark and bite" sentencing. A nine-year maximum sentence (the "bark") meant the possibility of release after two years (the "bite"). All corrections and parole officials understood the system, as did most judges, some journalists, and virtually no members of the general public. Some liberal reformers worried that new systems of "truth in sentencing," in which there was no parole release and the judge would announce the sentence to be served, would be seen by laymen as unduly lenient. They were right, as Franklin Zimring, a law professor at the University of California at Berkeley, warned in 1976. A public accustomed to reading about nine-year sentences was easily convinced by conservative politicians that two years were too few.

Since the 1970s, sentencing in the United States has become progressively harsher. Between 1980 and 1994, while crime rates were either falling (according to the National Crime Victimization Survey based on interviews of victims) or little changed (according to the FBI's *Uniform Crime Reports* based on police records), the number of inmates in American prisons and jails tripled. According to the 1993 Panel on the Understanding and Control of Violence of the National Academy of Sciences, the average time served per violent crime also tripled between 1975 and 1989. In effect, time served in America for run-of-the-mill offenders has crept up from the indeterminate sentencing levels of the 1970s to what were then the maximum sentences that would be served only by the most dangerous offenders who were not released by the parole board and who were so intractable in prison that they were denied all possible time off for good behavior.

Toughened sentences have had a disastrous impact on American blacks. Of course, a rising tide lifts all boats, and all offenders have faced steadily harsher penalties. However, blacks have made up at least 40 percent of the prison population during the last twenty years; necessarily at least 40 percent of offenders who have suffered longer separations from their families and communities have been black. But, it is worse that that because, as Chapter 2 showed, the absolute numbers of blacks and the black proportions among those admitted to prisons and jails and held there have steadily increased (at risk of undue repetition, readers should recall that, by contrast, the proportion of blacks among persons arrested for violent crimes has been steady or slightly declining). Thus the effects of harsher penalties on blacks have been compounded: Absolutely and proportionately, more blacks are going to prison, and when they get there, they are being held for longer times.

The second strategic mistake was empirical and conceptual, not political. The conceptual element—thinking that moral culpability must be calibrated only to the offender's crime—was discussed in Chapter 5. By trying to eliminate considerations from sentencing that appeared to favor middle-class offenders, policymakers put judges in straitjackets that make it difficult to impossible to make allowances for disadvantaged offenders.

If the diminution of racial disparities were a sentencing reform goal and judges were not to be trusted to be unbiased, obviously judges shoud be forbidden to take race into account in sentencing. It seemed equally obvious that factors that were strongly correlated with race, like educational attainment or occupation or living arrangements, should also be forbidden. Otherwise, college-educated or highly skilled or stably married offenders, predominantly white, would be given lighter sentences; disadvantaged offenders would not; and class- and race-linked disparities would result. Most American sentencing guidelines expressly forbid judges to base mitigated departures on education, employment, or family status.

Policies of "class neutrality," however, are based on the false empirical premise that there are middle-class offenders in felony courts. They are, to the contrary, chimerical beings, conspicuous by their absence, as anyone who has spent time in an urban felony court can attest. The fulcrum on which Tom Wolfe's *Bonfire of the Vanities* (1987) balances is the improbability that an affluent defendant like Sherman McCoy would appear in a New York felony court and the rare opportunity that his appearance gave politicians to show that they could be tough on a middle-class white defendant.

The reality is different. Very few defendants in urban felony courts resemble Sherman McCoy. Most come from deeply disadvantaged backgrounds. Of inmates in American prisons in 1991, for example, 65 percent had less than a high school education, 62 percent were regular drug users, 67 percent were employed at the time of their arrests (55 percent full time), and only 18 percent were married. Of persons admitted to prisons in thirty-five states in 1988, only 8 percent had any education beyong high school. Of jail inmates in 1989, 19 percent were married, 13 percent had any education beyond high school (median eleventh grade), and only 38 percent were employed when arrested.

The false premise has had three unhappy consequences. First, because there are so few middle-class offenders to be favored, those who are denied the possibility of a mitigated sentence on account of the adverse effects of a sentence on their job or their family's well-being or because their skills or education gave them a reasonable chance at achieving a stable, law-abiding life are the 85 to 95 percent of felony offenders who came from disadvantaged backgrounds. These policies in practice distinguish not between privileged and disadvantaged offenders but between disadvantaged and slightly less disadvantaged offenders.

Second, the effort to root out seemingly class-biased sentencing factors sent policymakers down a slippery slope that had no bottom. Because crime is powerfully correlated with disadvantage and because proportionately so many more blacks than whites are disadvantaged, almost any factor turns out to be class and race biased. The experience of the U.S. Parole Commission offers an illustration. In the late 1960s and the early 1970s, the commission developed parole guidelines based in part on the "salient factor score." The salient factor score, based on research on the recidivism of parolees, was a device to predict the future criminality of prospective parolees. The guidelines thus permitted the commission to hold longest those prisoners who represented the highest risks. Three of the items in the salient factor score were measures of education, employment, and residential pattern that were known to be correlated with recidivism. When their potential race-through-class bias was challenged, they were deleted.

Another of the most predictive factors, age at first arrest, was soon challenged on the basis that it too was correlated with race. Whether because police are more likely to arrest young blacks, because they are more likely to live and offend in places where their offenses become known, or because they commit their first offenses at earlier ages—whatever the reason—blacks on average are younger at first arrest than whites are. But even without age at first arrest, other criminal history factors are correlated with arrest, and unless they are omitted altogether, they will skew the results of any guidelines system.

Third, the adoption of a policy that most of an offender's personal circumstances are irrelevant to sentencing narrows down the set of allowable circumstances to nothing more than the crime and some aspects of the offender's criminal record. If those are the only or the main "legitimate" considerations at sentencing, zealous policymakers will go to extreme lengths to ensure that their policies are followed. This is what happened with the U.S. Sentencing Commission's guidelines.

The Sentencing Reform Act of 1984 provided that the guidelines shall, "in recommending a term of imprisonment or length of a term of imprisonment, reflect the general inappropriateness of considering the education, vocational skills, employment record, family ties and responsibilities, and community ties of the defendant," which the commission construed as forbidding for all practical purposes any consideration of such matters. The commission's guidelines manual states, for example, that "family ties and responsibilities . . . are not ordinarily relevant in determining whether a sentence should be outside the applicable guideline range" and nearly identical provisions apply to age, employment skills, emotional conditions, and drug and alcohol dependence. The commission has been vigorous in its efforts to achieve compliance with its guidelines, and these policies have received particular attention. Whenever courts have attempted on humanitarian grounds to take into account individual defendants' special circumstances and appellate courts have upheld the trial court's decisions, the commission has revised its rules expressly to eliminate the use of that rationale for future departures from the guidelines. This is unusual. Ordinarily, administrative agencies do not have the authority to overrule judicial interpretations of their enabling legislation or of the rules they have issued. In *Braxton v. U.S.,* 111 S. Ct. 1854 (1991), however, the Supreme Court gave the sentencing commission those powers. Thus when the sentencing commission says none, it means none, and it has the power to enforce it.

The victims of these "loophole closings" have largely been offenders from modest circumstances who have to some degree overcome dismal life chances. Thus, after the Eighth Circuit Court of Appeals in *U.S. v. Big Crow,* 898 F2d. 1326 (1990), approved a sentence reduction for a Native American who had overcome severe childhood adversity and had an exemplary work record, the commission amended its policy statements to forbid reductions for "employment-related contributions and similar prior good works." When the Ninth Circuit in *U.S. v. Lopez,* 945 F.2d 1096 (1991), approved a reduction on the grounds of a defendant's lack of guidance as a youth, the commission amended its policy statements to forbid reductions for "lack of guidance as a youth and similar circumstances indicating a disadvantaged upbringing." The burden of the commission's efforts to root out all consideration of offenders' personal circumstances has not been borne by middle-class offenders; it has been borne mostly by disadvantaged offenders. Kate Stith and Steve Yoh, in a 1993 article on the federal guidelines in the *Wake Forest Law Review,* concluded "denying judges the opportunity to mitigate sentences on the basis of social disadvantage has worked *against* poor and minority defendants." (emphasis in original)

Thus, it appears that a first step toward reducing racial disproportion is to loosen up sentencing laws and guidelines in order to let judges more often mitigate sentences to take account of offenders' personal circumstances. Two additional important sets of issues, however, need to be considered before the wisdom of that course becomes clear. First, is it not likely that looser sentencing standards will be applied so as to benefit more privileged and white offenders and that disadvantaged and minority offenders will be punished more harshly? Second, are there not important countervailing concerns, notably more effective crime control, to be achieved from rigid sentencing laws?

Invidious Sentences

In the 1980s when policymakers decided to prevent favoritism toward affluent offenders by forbidding consideration of personal information at sentencing, they did so in a context in which their concerns were justified. In indeterminate sentencing systems, judges often had the discretion to impose any sentence ranging from probation to a ten- or twenty-year prison term, and the power to mitigate was matched by a power to aggravate. If the normal sentence for a particular offense were two to four years, a worthy defendant might receive a sentence of probation, and an unworthy one might receive ten years. This is why punishment theorist Andrew von Hirsch has often argued against allowing judges the discretion to mitigate sentences because of offenders' special circumstances: "Under the commensurate-deserts principle, an impoverished defendant would be punished no more severely than an affluent individual convicted of an equally serious crime. . . . Utilitarian allocation theories, by contrast, have much greater potential for bias. They support taking sterner measures against the poor expressly because of their poverty."

In the 1960s and 1970s, von Hirsch's concerns were well taken. No American jurisdiction then had a meaningful system of appellate sentence review (few do now). The parole boards had the power to release defendants after they became eligible, but often the judge could set the eligibility date by specifying a minimum sentence. If the judge were racially biased, members of minority groups might be sentenced to harsher terms; and a defendant who received an aggravated sentence had no recourse. Thus, against that backdrop, limiting the judge's power to mitigate sentences in exchange for limiting the judge's power to aggravate was a reasonable trade. Sentencing standards that confined judges to consideration of the offender's crime and his past criminal record provided a way to prevent both merciful mitigation of penalties and invidious aggravation.

The context of sentencing has changed, and in the 1990s the risk of invidious harshness has diminished greatly. There is no longer an equal chance that sentences will be more or less harsh than the norm. The single most robust finding from evaluations of sentencing guidelines is that judges seldom impose sentences more severe than the applicable guidelines specify. Table 6-1 presents data from selected jurisdictions for recent selected years on "departures" from sentencing guidelines. The jurisdictions' guidelines vary widely. In the federal system, the standards are highly specific, and the legal presumption against departures is great. In Minnesota and Washington, the standards are specific, and the presumptions against departures are less strong. In Pennsylvania, the standards

Table 6-1. Departure Rates, American Guidelines Systems, Recent Years (in %)

	Ad hoc Aggravated Departures	Approved Aggravated Sentences	Standard Sentences	Approved Mitigated Sentences	Ad hoc Mitigated Sentences
Federal (1991)	1.7	—	80.6	11.9	5.8
Minnesota (1989)[a]	6.4	—	80.9	—	12.7
Minnesota (1989)[b]	6.8	—	75.3	—	17.9
Oregon (1991)	3	—	94	—	3
Pennsylvania (1991)	2	2	74	8	13
Washington (1991)	1.6	—	80.7	15.4	1.7

[a]Dispositional departures only (state incarceration or not).
[b]Durational departures (length of sentence).

Sources: Kathryn Ashford and Craig Mosbaek, *First Year Report on Implementation of Sentencing Guidelines* (Portland, Oregon: Oregon Criminal Justice Council, 1991); Minnesota Sentencing Guidelines Commission, *Summary of 1989 Sentencing Practices for Convicted Felons* (St. Paul: Minnesota Sentencing Guidelines Commission, 1991); Pennsylvania Commission on Sentencing, *Sentencing in Pennsylvania—1991* (Harrisburg: Pennsylvania Commission on Sentencing, 1993); U.S. Sentencing Commission, *Annual Report—1991* (Washington, D.C.: U.S. Sentencing Commission); Washington State Sentencing Guidelines Commission, *A Statistical Summary of Adult Felony Sentencing* (Olympia: Washington State Sentencing Guidelines Commission, 1992).

are broad, and there is little pressure against departures. Yet in every system, "aggravated departures" are rare and are much less frequent than mitigated departures.

The rarity of aggravated sentences is not a coincidence. Judges are under asymmetrical pressures to reduce sentences. By temperament and ethos, judges are inclined to enforce the law. In a guidelines jurisdiction, the enabling legislation makes it clear that judges are supposed in most cases to impose a sentence no harsher than the applicable guidelines authorize. In addition, most criminal convictions result from guilty pleas. Few defendants would plead guilty without the assurance that their sentence will be reduced or, at the very least, not increased above the level that the guidelines specify. Finally, if judges impose a sentence above the applicable guideline, written reasons must be given, and the adequacy of those reasons may be appealed by the defendant. This is a hassle that most judges would prefer to avoid.

There is another reason why the dangers of invidious use of

increased powers of mitigation are less today than in earlier times. Judges are much less likely to be racially biased than in the 1960s and 1970s when opposition to the civil rights movement was widespread and openly segregationist candidates were still running for office and winning. Many judges were or appeared to be racist. In the 1990s, my impression from working with state and federal judges around the country is that most judges are extremely sensitive to the racial implications of their decisions and are reluctant to do anything that might provoke a charge of racism. This is one reason that more than half the states in recent years have appointed judicial task forces to study racial disparities in their judicial systems and to offer recommendations for their amelioration. Thus the concern that judges will use their greater powers of mitigation to lighten sentences for white offenders and to increase them for blacks no longer seems as warranted as in earlier times.

Crime Control

The final objection is that strengthening judges' mitigation powers will make sentences less certain, thereby making them less effective deterrents, and that crime will rise as a result. This argument raises political and policy issues. On the unrealistic premise that public policies toward crime should be based on rational analysis and examination of the best available evidence of the likely effects of alternate policy choices, I begin with the evidence.

There is no credible basis for believing that allowing judges to mitigate sentences will have any discernible effect on crime rates. The belief that more certain or harsher penalties will reduce the rates for serious crimes is not supported by evidence on the effects of recent increases in punishment severity, the scientific literature on deterrence, or research on the effects of mandatory penalties. This is ironic, because the proponents of harsher or mandatory penalties generally claim that their enactment will make our streets safer.

Since the mid-1970s, American prison populations have surged and sentences have become longer, but there is no evidence that crime rates have fallen as a result. Between December 31, 1975, and June 30, 1993, the number of federal and state prisoners nearly quadrupled, rising from 240,593 to 925,247. Between 1975 and 1989, the average time served in prisons per violent crime tripled. To establish what we know about the causes and prevention of violence, the Reagan administration's Department of Justice asked the National Academy of Sciences to appoint an expert panel to survey existing knowledge. The Bush administration's Department of Justice provided additional funding to support the four-year effort. I mention sponsorship to make the point that the panel's work was supported by Attorneys General Edwin Meese and Richard Thornburgh, both outspoken supporters of harsh crime control policies. This was not an ad hoc effort sponsored by liberal foundations or the American Civil Liberties Union. A question and answer in the final report of the Panel on the Understanding and Control of Violence say it all: "What effect has increasing the prison population had on levels of violent crime? Apparently very little. If tripling the average length of sentence of incarceration per crime had a strong preventive effect," reasoned the panel,"then violent crime rates should have declined." They have not.

The findings are consistent with other, equally authoritative examinations of our knowledge of the effects of criminal sanctions. An earlier National Academy of Sciences Panel on Deterrent and Incapacitative Effects in 1978 surveyed the research on the deterrent effects of the death penalty and of criminal sanctions generally. Concerning the death penalty, that panel concluded that there was no scientific basis for believing that capital punishment was a more effective deterrent to homicide than were life sentences. Concerning sanctions generally, the panel concluded that there was no scientific basis for believing that incremental changes in penalties significantly affected their deterrent effectiveness.

It is important to stress that no one denies that penalties do have deterrent effects. The National Academy of Sciences Panel observed that it accepted the commonsense insight that, compared with no state-administered sanctions whatever, having criminal sanctions is likely to prevent crime. The policy question is always whether proposed sanctions will be more or less effective than the most likely alternative. Thus the question for proponents of increasing judges' authority to mitigate sentences is whether that change by itself, with no other changes in the severity of sentencing policies, is likely to raise crime rates. The answer is no.

Research on mandatory penalties provides little or no basis for concluding that they provide more effective deterrents than do the laws they displace. Both mandatory penalties and guidelines prohibiting mitigation for personal reasons are efforts to ensure that only the offender's crime and sometimes his criminal record influence the sentence imposed. For that reason, the U.S. Sentencing Commission often refers to its guidelines as *mandatory*. For purposes of simplicity, in the following paragraphs I use the term *mandatory penalties* to refer to both mandatory penalties and "mandatory" guidelines. If any sanctions policies should be capable of achieving discernible crime reductions, it should be mandatory penalties.

Targeted on particular offenses and promoted with promises of "Do the crime, do the time," their proponents' principal claim for them is that they will reduce crime. A second claim offered in support of mandatory penalties is that they will ensure that offenders are treated consistently. Neither claim withstands scrutiny.

With one exception that results from a statistical manipulation, the major studies of the deterrent effects of mandatory penalties conclude that no significant deterrent effects can be shown. The most famous evaluation concerned the Rockefeller Drug Law that established mandatory penalties for drug felonies. It also provided substantial funds to build new courtrooms and pay salaries for new judges and courtroom staff in order to make sure that adequate resources were available to process drug cases. The law took effect in September 1972 and was repealed as of June 30, 1976. A massive, federally funded evaluation determined that the law had not discernibly reduced drug use, drug trafficking, or drug-related health problems.

Separate evaluations of the deterrent effects of new mandatory penalty laws have also been carried out in Massachusetts, Michigan, Florida, and Pennsylvania by James Beha, Glen Pierce and William Bowers, and Colin Loftin, Milton Heumann, and David McDowall. Each study found either that no crime-preventive effect could be shown or that there was a short-term effect that quickly disappeared. The only exception is an analysis that combined data from three separate studies and then found a crime-reduction effect for only one of three offenses studied. Because it is the exception, I discuss it separately below.

The confirmatory finding was published in an article in the *Journal of Law and Criminology* by David McDowall, Colin Loftin, and Brian Wiersema. Earlier, McDowall and Loftin had collaborated on mandatory penalty studies in Florida and Michigan. In the new article, they combined the data from those studies with data from a new—to that point unpublished—mandatory penalty study in Pittsburgh and Philadelphia.

In no separate study could a deterrent effect be demonstrated. In their Detroit, Michigan, study, the authors determined that "the mandatory sentencing law did not have a preventive effect on crime." From studies in Tampa, Jacksonville, and Miami, Florida, "we concluded that the results did not support a preventive effect model." The results from the new studies in Pittsburgh and Philadelphia "do not strongly challenge the conclusion that the statutes have no preventive effect."

When the data from all six sites were combined, McDowall and his colleagues concluded that the mandatory penalty law had reduced gun homicides but not gun assaults or gun robberies. This is slightly surprising. The probability that a death will result when a gun is used in a robbery or an assault (and any homicide is, by definition, a lethal assault) should be constant in a particular place during a particular period. If, say, 3 percent of gun assaults result in deaths, a decline in deaths should mean a decline in assaults. If the number of gun homicides fell because of the mandatory penalty law, the number of gun assaults or robberies or both should also have fallen. The evaluators concluded that their inability to find falls in gun assaults or gun robberies must result from "a lack of precision in the data," rather than from an incorrect finding about homicides.

The problem with this study is that the results were obtained only by aggregating data from studies that independently found no statistically significant effect. With a much larger data set, they found an effect that was small but statistically significant. Like most social scientists, McDowall and his colleagues used a .05 significance test, which means that they were prepared to conclude that an effect could be shown only if there was less than a 5 percent chance that the finding resulted from random chance. With a small data set, an effect must be very large to be significant. A six-to-four split amount ten observations, for example, even though six is

50 percent larger than four, is not statistically significant. Among one thousand observations, a small absolute or percentage difference can be statistically significant.

Even if the six-site finding is taken at face value, it offers little support to proponents of mandatory penalties. A small deterrent effect is of little more weight than no deterrent effect when the competing values under consideration are as fundamental as the amelioration of racial disparities in our prisons and jails.

The second rationale, ensuring the consistent application of penalties to all offenders who commit a particular offense, fares little better in the face of the research evidence. The problem is that mandatories (including the federal sentencing guidelines) often dictate the imposition of penalties that the judge and everyone else involved consider too harsh. Torn between their oaths to enforce the law, and therefore to impose the harsh penalty, and their oaths to do justice, and therefore to avoid the harsh penalty, judges and juries often do the latter. Prosecutors also—despite the stereotype that they always want the harshest possible penalty—often believe that mandatory penalties are too harsh. Alone, through their charging and plea bargaining powers, or jointly with judges and defense lawyers, prosecutors often work to avoid the imposition of what they see as unduly harsh penalties.

From the refusal of judges and juries to impose mandatory death penalties in eighteenth-century England to the collaborations of judges, prosecutors, and defense lawyers in the circumvention of harsh federal sentencing guidelines today, practitioners have struggled to avoid imposing penalties they believe to be unjust. American case studies that document that phenomenon stretch over five decades, including American Bar Foundation studies in Michigan in the 1950s by Donald Newman and Robert O. Dawson, studies of the Rockefeller Drug Law in New York and of mandatory penalties for firearms offenses in Massachusetts in the 1970s, studies of mandatory penalty laws for firearms offenses in Florida and Michigan in the 1980s, and studies of compliance with the federal sentencing guidelines in the 1990s. (These studies are discussed in detail in my 1992 essay, "Mandatory Penalties," in *Crime and Justice,* Volume 16).

There is a tendency among legislators and others to ignore the foreseeable effects of mandating harsh penalties, and this has had a perverse effect. Insofar as, in theory, mandatory penalties and guidelines are supposed to make judges accountable for their decisions by setting published standards for sentences, they often have the opposite effect. That is, they drive the key decisions underground.

Because no judge can comfortably refuse to enforce an applicable law, they usually avoid mandatory penalties by means of artifice. In studies of mandatories in Michigan in the 1950s, judges refused to accept guilty pleas and instead (this is before *Gideon v. Wainwright,* 372 US 335 [1963], held that felony defendants were constitutionally entitled to legal representation) appointed counsel and instructed them to negotiate a plea bargain to avoid the mandatory penalty. Also in Michigan, in the 1970s, judges sometimes refused to accept guilty pleas to crimes subject to a mandatory penalty for gun use and instead insisted on going to trial; in their findings of fact, when they failed to mention a gun the mandatory penalty became inapplicable. Most of the modern studies of plea bargaining show that prosecutors routinely use mandatory penalty provisions as bargaining chits. A recent study in Arizona by Kay Knapp of the Institute for Rational Public Policy showed that 57 percent of felony defendants were subject to mandatory penalty provisions but that, after plea bargaining, only 15 percent of those convicted were affected by the mandatories. Studies sponsored by the U.S. Sentencing Commission found that applicable guidelines were circumvented by plea bargaining in as many as 35 percent of cases, and these were only the circumventions that were detected. A commission study of mandatory penalties found than prosecutors failed to file mandatory-bearing weapons charges in 45 percent of the drug cases to which they were applicable.

A good example of the tacit conspiracies to avoid the law that mandatory penalty provisions foster is provided by Rule 5K1 of the U.S. Commission's guidelines. Rule 5K1 provides than on motion by the prosecutor requesting a mitigated sentence because substantial assistance has been given to the prosecution, the judge is free to depart from the guidelines. No one is in a position to second-guess the prosecutor about the existence or the significance of the reported "substantial assistance." If both the judge and the prosecutor wish to sidestep a harsh applicable penalty, the 5K1 motion provides a perfect and undetectable device for doing so. The sentencing commission's speculations concerning the reasons that mandatory penalties and the commission's guidelines are so often circumvented: the practices "may reflect a greater tendency to exercise prosecutorial or judicial discretion as the severity of the penalty increases." To like effect, "the prosecutors' reasons for reducing or dismissing mandatory charges . . . may be attributable to . . . satisfaction with the sentence received."

The hypocrisies often associated with mandatory penalties are well illustrated by the findings of the American Bar Foundation's study of plea bargaining to avoid mandatory penalties for armed robbery and nighttime burglary in Michigan in the 1950s:

> Armed robbery is so often downgraded that the Michigan parole board tends to treat a conviction for unarmed robbery as prima facie evidence that the defendant had a weapon. And the frequency of altering night-time burglary to breaking and entering in the daytime led one prosecutor to remark: "You'd think all our burglaries occur at high noon."

Political Honesty

The preceding pattern of findings concerning mandatory penalties should surprise no one who is familiar with the workings of felony courts. The pattern has been known and well documented since at least the eighteenth century when English judges and juries showed they they would work hard to avoid mandatory death penalties that they believed were unjustly severe for the offenses subject to them. Because of the widespread understanding of how mandatory penalties operate, in 1970 the U.S. Congress repealed almost all mandatories then in effect for drug crimes. Why, then, in our time do politicians continue to propose them and legislators to enact them?

The answer is easy. The politician's rationale for mandatory penalties is that support for them is an indicator of toughness on crime. It is easy to stake out the low ground on crime control issues. No powerful constituency will be affronted. The general public understandably fears crime and resents criminals. At worst, opponents or prospective opponents will compete to show who is toughest. Any opponent who disagrees is likely to be disparaged as "soft on crime" and, as Michael Dukakis's experience in the 1988 presidential election shows, a calm discussion of realistic policy options is no match for allusions to Willie Horton.

In times of anticrime hysteria, the safest position on crime issues may be the preemptive strike. This is why the Bush administration's drug czar William Bennett and the Democratic Senate Judiciary Committee chairman Joseph Biden battled in the early 1990s, using obscure government reports as weapons, to establish who was tougher on drugs. It was a draw. This may also be why President Clinton in 1994 supported and aggressively promoted a crime bill that would attach the death penalty to more crimes, enact new mandatory penalties, and restrict prisoners' habeas corpus rights in federal courts—not policy proposals usually associated with liberal or moderate Democrats. This may also be why Clinton's 1994 State of the Union address to Congress endorsed the pending crime bill and proposals for mandatory life sentences for third-time violent offenders.

This is not a new problem. At times when anticrime hysteria is in the air, few elected officials are willing to resist. Late in the eighteenth century, Edmund Burke declared "that he could obtain the consent of the House of Commons to any Bill imposing the punishment of death." In July 1991, one congressman told a *New York Times* reporter, "Congressmen and senators are afraid to vote no" on punishment bills "even if they don't think it will accomplish anything." A Senate aide echoed, "It's tough to vote against tough sentences for criminals." No doubt numerous congressmen would, at least in private, have said similar things in 1993 and 1994 as the president's crime bill worked its way through the Congress.

Whether in the foreseeable future elected officials will stop pandering to people's fears and begin honestly discussing the hard choices that crime control policies pose is anyone's guess. The choices at least are clear: Continue proposing disingenuously to reduce crime through policies that we know do not work, and continue worsening the lot of disadvantaged blacks in America, or reject failed policies and cynical politics in order to reduce the racial disproportions in American prisons and jails. Honest politicians know what needs to be done. The next chapter sketches the elements of an honest sentencing policy that would stop doing disproportionate damage to black Americans.

7

"What Is to Be Done?"

The reduction of racial disparities in the criminal justice system is well within our power. There need be no trade-offs between racial justice and public safety. The program that an honest politician would follow—were visions of Willie Horton–style sloganeering not lurking—is straightforward. First, think about the foreseeable effects of crime control policy decisions on members of minority groups; when policies are likely to burden members of minority groups disproportionately, reconsider the policies. Second, to guard against racial bias in sentencing and against unjustly severe penalties in general, establish systems of presumptive sentencing guidelines for ordinary cases that set maximum penalties, scaled to the severity of offenders' crimes. Third, recognize the prudence and compassion of our predecessors, and throughout the justice system reestablish presumptions that the least punitive and least restrictive appropriate punishment should be imposed in every case. Fourth, empower judges at sentencing to mitigate sentences for all defendants, irrespective of race, ethnicity, or sex, to take account of individual circumstances. Fifth, celebrate the decent instincts of our predecessors, and reinvest in corrections programs that can help offenders rebuild their lives and enhance their own and their children's life chances. Sixth, most important of all, be honest; for as long as cynical and disingenuous appeals continue to be made by politicians to the deepest fears and basest instincts of the American people, the prospects of reducing racial disparities in the justice system will remain small.

Only the first of these proposals is directed solely at the problems of black Americans. We need not and should not have policies "for blacks only." The central problem is the link between crime and social disadvantage. Too many blacks are disadvantaged, but so are too many Hispanics, Asian Americans, Native Americans, and whites. Color-blind policies that will minimize the criminal justice system's destructive effects on poor blacks will minimize the criminal justice system's destructive effects on poor Americans of every race.

Thinking About Race

The adjuration to "think about the racial effects of contemplated policy decisions" seems so obvious as not to warrant mention. In the last decade of the twentieth century, it should go without saying that governments desire racial justice and detest racial injustice. As, however, the images conjured up by the Welfare Queen and Willie Horton attest, American politicians are not unwilling, as it is said, to "play the race card." Harvard philosopher Cornel West observed in *Race Matters* (1993) that "the Republican Party since 1968 has appealed to popular xenophobic images," playing the race card to realign the electorate along racial lines. And the foreseeable and realized burdens imposed on poor American blacks by recent social welfare and criminal justice policies make it clear that many policymakers do not much worry about the racial ramifications of their decisions.

That indifference is striking because it is so inconsistent with conventional thinking about race in other settings. In education, for example, as a policy matter, de facto segregation has long been seen as no less invidious than de jure segregation (the Supreme Court disagrees: de jure segregation is forbidden, de facto segregation is often allowed). Redistricting in a racially mixed town so that most of the white kids live in one district and go to one school, and most of the black kids live in another district and go to another school, feels wrong, even if we believe school board members when they say they were trying to follow roads or land contours or neighborhoods and deny any intent to achieve segregated schools.

Housing is another example. In many states, courts have struck down local zoning ordinances, such as minimum lot sizes and prohibitions or strict limits on multifamily housing or trailer parks, because they operate to exclude poor and minority residents. Often there is little doubt that the purposes of the zoning ordinance were free from racial bias, for example, to maintain ambience, to anticipate and avoid overcrowded public facilities, or to preserve the rural or arboreal character of a community.

In employment, likewise, federal equal opportunity laws make racial disparities in hiring, firing, and promotions a critical issue. Of course, disparities resulting from deliberate bias are forbidden. But disparities resulting from seemingly nonbiased practices are also suspect. If a preemployment screening test disproportionately eliminates from consideration members of minority groups, the employer must either eliminate the test or prove that it meaningfully measures skills or aptitudes that are demonstrably related to success on the job.

In the criminal justice system, however, the notion that racial disparities matter has not taken hold. In *Washington v. Davis,* 426 U.S. 229 (1976), a case involving disparities in Washington, D.C., police hiring practices, the Supreme Court held that the U.S. Constitution (as opposed to equal employment opportunity statutes) forbids only intentional racial disparities. Foreseeable but unintended disparities are acceptable. That decision has been construed to apply generally to policymaking in the criminal justice system.

More recently but unambiguously, the Supreme Court in *Personnel Administrator of Massachusetts v. Feeney,* 442 U.S. 256 (1979), observed: "Discriminatory purpose . . . implies that the decisionmaker . . . selected or reaffirmed a particular course of action at least in part 'because of,' not merely 'in spite of,' its adverse effects upon an identifiable group." This language was invoked by Justice Lewis Powell in the *McCleskey* case upholding the constitutionality of the death penalty against the equal protection objection that racial disparities as great as twenty-two to one, depending on the races of the offender and the victim, characterized capital sentencing in Georgia. Powell wrote that "*McCleskey* must prove that the decisionmakers in *his* case acted with discriminatory intent" (emphasis in original). This is a nearly impossible requirement. Few officials, no matter how biased, will openly acknowledge or demonstrate their racial animus. As long as officials claim to be motivated by some other legitimate purpose, the occurrence of foreseeable racial disparities creates no constitutional problem.

It need not have been so. American jurisprudence has analytical tools that could have been employed to subject disparity-causing policies to close examination. In federal equal protection law under the Fourteenth Amendment, for example, the courts have long held that explicit racial classifications by government are subject to strict scrutiny and can be upheld only on a showing of a "compelling state interest." Most other kinds of classifications are subject only to minimal scrutiny and can be justified by showing a "rational basis" for them, a standard highly deferential to government officials. A few classifications, most notably gender, are entitled to "intermediate scrutiny." In federal free speech law under the First Amendment, for another example, the courts have long held that allowable restrictions on expression must not be overbroad; that is, they must be crafted to reach the objectionable unprotected form of expression but no other. Neither compelling state interest nor overbreadth doctrines can be applied without refinement to justice system disparities, but they illustrate the kinds of tools that could have been developed to subject disparity-causing policies to close scrutiny.

Doctrines could readily be fashioned that subject disparity-causing policies to judicial review. Under current doctrine, disparities are either intentional, and thus forbidden unless they pass the "compelling state interest test," or permitted. That crude either/or approach is insufficiently sensitive to the ethical and racial dimensions of justice policy. A better approach, drawing on the criminal law's acknowledgment that knowing acts are often as morally culpable as intentional acts, would be to subject policies intended to result in racial disparities to strict scrutiny and policies known to be likely to result in disparities to intermediate scrutiny. Compelling justifications would be required for intentional disparities and very good ones for foreseeable disparities.

Objections will be raised that judicial elaboration of constitutional doctrines for review of disparity-causing or -exacerbating penal policies would be unwise and undemocratic. The failure in wisdom—given Americans' remarkable litigiousness—would be that the courts would become even more involved in policy issues than they now are and that the process of policy formulation would become even more complex and arduous than it now is. The failure in democracy would be the creation of additional impediments to the effectuation of the "public will" through the actions and policies of elected officials.

There are two answers. The first is that what distingushes constitutional governments from others is the notion that the powers of the state are limited, in part to protect minorities from abuse by majorities. Although it took nearly a century for the U.S. Supreme court in *Brown v. Board of Education,* 349 U.S. 294 (1954), to decide that the Equal Protection Clause of the Fourteenth Amendment forbade state maintenance of segregated public schools, it finally did so. Few in retrospect doubt the correctness of that decision (and many other related ones), even though at the time it was deplored as unwise and castigated as antidemocratic. When the more directly accountable branches of government fail to resolve problems of racially invidious public policies—as with public education before *Brown*—it may be necessary for the courts to do so. Prudential and political concerns no doubt would lead to judicial restraint in applying disparate-impact doctrines. The foundations of the republic, however, would be unlikely to crumble if an extreme instance of racial disparity—for example, the twenty-two-to-one racial imbalance in *McCleskey*—resulted in the decision that a policy or practice was unconstitutional on racial-disparity grounds.

Second and more important, notions of avoidance of foreseeable racial disparities need not be restricted to constitutional doctrine. A virtuous government would take account of the likely racial effects of contemplated policies. An analytic defining certain kinds of outcomes as presumptively wrong and working out the criteria that should be satisfied to overcome presumptions against racial (and other) disparities would enrich policy processes and diminish racial injustices.

If followed, the preceding suggestions would create policy processes greatly different from recent cynical efforts to use racial stereotypes to partisan advantage and recent willingness to overlook the harmful effects on different racial groups of government policies. Current patterns of racial injustice in the justice system (and the welfare system) will continue until governments reject them because they are wrong. When that day comes, a disparity-avoidance analytic will guide efforts to do better.

Even if the courts are unwilling to act, commonplace legal concepts provide tools that racially sensitive policymakers could use. Rebuttable presumptions could be observed that forbid disparity-causing policies unless it can be shown that important public policy goals could not otherwise be achieved or that their achievement would be fundamentally compromised. Here is a simple illustration, mentioned earlier, of how such a presumption would work. In the early 1970s, the U.S. Parole Commission established guidelines that would allow hearing examiners to take into account prisoners' likelihood of recidivism when recommending release dates. Research was undertaken on past parolees' recidivism to establish base expectancy rates for use in the guidelines. The seven variables that together best predicted recidivism included three—employment, education, and residence patterns—that concerned prisoners' personal characteristics. The problem was that using such variables would, in the aggregate, injure blacks. If whites on average are better educated than blacks (and they are) and if the guidelines made earlier release likely for better-educated prisoners (and they did), whites as a class would benefit and blacks as a class would suffer. When this problem was pointed out, the commission reconsidered its guidelines, eventually dropping the personal variables and discovering that another set of variables that included only criminal history information generated comparably accurate recidivism predictions. So in the end, by trying to lessen racial disparities in applying its policies, the commission did so and without compromising the pursuit of its legitimate objective to link release dates to the probability of recidivism.

The criminal justice system in America today would look vastly different if the Reagan and Bush administrations, and the state governments that followed their lead, had established and honored a rebuttable presumption against the adoption of disparity-causing policies. The War on Drugs would not have been launched, because we know that in times of moral panic, especially concerning drug use, people look for scapegoats. Because visible drug dealing and easily arrested dealers are disproportionately to be found in disorganized minority communities in the inner city, it was foreseeable that the scapegoats would disproportionately be members of minority groups. Because the best evidence available in this and other countries is that making penalties more severe has little or no effect on behavior, the harsh, penalty-enhancing policies of the

War on Drugs would have been unlikely to overcome the race-effects presumption.

That does not mean that national policies to diminish drug use and reduce their availability should not have been adopted, but that they would have looked very different. One emphasis would have been on drug treatment. At no time during the Reagan–Bush War on Drugs was treatment on demand available for all cocaine and heroin addicts who wanted it. For years, it was estimated that sixty thousand addicts in New York City alone awaited treatment at any one time. Evaluations of intensive parole and probation programs around the country by RAND Corporation researchers Joan Petersilia and Susan Turner showed that even drug-dependent offenders under supervision often could not get treatment.

Another emphasis would have been on public education and on educational programs in schools. Considerable evidence has accumulated that programs in elementary and middle schools can significantly reduce use of tobacco, alcohol, and drugs. Another RAND Corporation team headed by Phyllis Ellickson did much of the most important evaluation research. There were many such programs, but never enough. Successive administrations always insisted that 70 percent of federal funding be devoted to law enforcement, with the balance to be shared by treatment and education efforts.

Another emphasis would have been on law enforcement, but of a different sort. Rather than concentrate on arresting instantly replaceable user-dealers and confining them for many years, police would have concentrated on importers, manufacturers, and major distributors. Of course, street dealers would have been arrested; not to do so would have signaled a callous disregard of law-abiding residents of the areas in which drugs were openly sold. After arrest, however, a stiff prison sentence would not have been the preferred disposition. Spending $20,000 to $30,000 per year to confine a street-level drug dealer whose place on the corner will be filled within days after his arrest is a senseless waste of money. For drug-dependent dealers, the option of choice would have been compulsory drug treatment. A consensus now exists—among leading researchers and evidenced by surveys of knowledge by the National Institute of Medicine and the General Accounting Office—that drug treatment "works" to reduce both drug use and offending by drug-dependent offenders. The single best predictor of success is the length of time in treatment, and legal compulsion is a good way to get and keep people in treatment.

Had the emphasis of the War on Drugs been different, billions fewer dollars would have been needed for processing countless numbers of unnecessary arrests and jailing and imprisoning hundreds of thousands of unnecessary inmates. The funds freed up, along with funds diverted from source-country and extraterritorial interdiction efforts that are all but universally judged ineffective, would have gone a long way toward meeting unmet treatment needs and expanding educational programs.

Had there been a rebuttable policy presumption against disparity-causing policies, sentencing laws and policies adopted in recent years would have looked very different. The extreme example concerns the different treatments accorded to persons convicted of drug crimes involving crack cocaine and powder cocaine. Crack cocaine offenses are generally subject to much harsher penalties than is powder cocaine, even though (as a number of courts including the Minnesota Supreme Court have held) they are pharmacologically indistinguishable. The extreme difference is found in federal laws enacted in 1986 and in Section 2D1.1 of the federal sentencing guidelines, under which one gram of crack is treated as equivalent to one hundred grams of powder. In a Minnesota law that was typical of laws in many states, the possession of three grams of crack exposed a defendant to a maximum twenty-year prison sentence and, under sentencing guidelines, a presumptive sentence of forty-eight months. The same amount of powder cocaine exposed a defendant to a five-year maximum sentence and a presumptive sentence of probation, with a stayed twelve-month prison sentence to be served if probation were later revoked.

The problem with distinguishing between crack and powder cocaine in this way is that crack tends to be used and sold by blacks and powder by whites, which means that the harshest penalties are mostly experienced by blacks. In *U.S. v. Thurmond*, 54 CrL 1091 (1993), upholding the 100-to-1 rule in the federal guidelines against an equal protection challenge, the federal Court of Appeals for the Tenth Circuit cited statistics showing that 95 percent of federal crack prosecutions are brought against blacks and 40 percent of powder cocaine prosecutions are brought against whites. In *State v.*

Russell, overturning the Minnesota statute on equal protection grounds, the Minnesota Supreme Court observed that 96.6 percent of those charged under the crack statute in 1988 were black and 79.6 percent of those charged under the powder cocaine statute were white.

The sentencing distinctions between crack and powder cocaine could never have survived a rebuttable policy presumption against disparity-causing policies, but they have survived constitutional equal protection challenges in the federal courts. Through the end of 1993, every federal court of appeals that had considered the matter had rejected equal protection challenges to the 100-to-1 rule (for example, *U.S. v. Thomas,* 900 F.2d 37 [4th Cir. 1990]; *U.S. v. Frazier,* 981 F.2d 92 [3rd Cir. 1992]; *U.S. v. Lattimore,* 974 F.2d 971 [8th Cir. 1992]; and *U.S. v. Thurmond,* 54 CrL 1091 [1993]). The Minnesota Supreme Court overturned the Minnesota law under the equal protection clause of the state, not the federal, constitution, holding that there was no "rational basis" for the distinction. Early in 1994, a federal district court judge in the District of Columbia, citing "the racist origins of the Harrison Act [and] the racist implications arising from the public clamor in 1986 about crack in the inner city," declared the 100-to-1 rule unconstitutional on Eighth Amendment ("cruel and unusual punishment") grounds as applied to minor addicted participants in a crack transaction.

The distinction between crack and powder cocaine is, however, only the most extreme example of sentencing laws that could not survive a rebuttable policy presumption against disparity-causing policies. In federal and state laws, but particularly federal laws, mandatory penalties for drug crimes have proliferated since 1980. As the data on racial patterns for drug arrests presented in Chapter 3 make clear, blacks are far more likely than whites to be arrested for drug crimes and became ever more likely as the Reagan–Bush years progressed. In a 1991 report to the Congress on mandatory minimums, the U.S. Sentencing Commission observed that black defendants are more likely to be affected by them than white defendants are. In December 1993, the Bureau of Justice Statistics issued a report by Douglas C. McDonald and Kenneth E. Carlson, showing that on average federal prison sentences for blacks were 41 percent longer than for whites and that the different penalties for crack and powder cocaine were the major reason for that difference.

Even more generally, penalties for many crimes became harsher during the 1980s, and mandatory penalties were enacted for many nondrug offenses. In the federal courts, unprecedently severe sentencing guidelines were promulgated and progressively made harsher.

None of those penalty-enhancing changes would have survived the racial impact presumption. The only possible legitimate argument for them is that tougher or surer penalties will lower crime rates. As Chapter 6 explained, there is no credible evidence on which such an argument could be based, and no English-speaking national government except ours claims to believe it. The real motives for such laws, as Thomas and Mary Edsall's book on race issues in American politics shows, were to prove that candidates and officials were tough on crime and, sometimes, to use "anticrime" (or "antiwelfare") as a veiled synonym for "antiblack." None of those reasons would survive the presumption.

Individualizing Punishments

Few informed people can any longer doubt that the "just-deserts" movement and the development of rigid sentencing policies based only on the offender's crime and criminal history were mistakes. They were well-intended mistakes, aimed at reducing sentencing disparities and race and class biases in sentencing. They may have been necessary mistakes that showed us how to protect against aberrantly severe penalties and exposed the injustices that result when sentencing shifts its focus from the offender to the offense. Mistakes they were, however, and we now know how to do better.

A just sentencing policy will simultaneously ensure that offenders receive penalties no harsher than they deserve and that judges are empowered to mitigate sentences for all defendants, irrespective of race, ethnicity, or sex, to take account of individual circumstances. Such a policy would have three elements. To protect against unjustly harsh penalties, guidelines scaled to the severity of the offender's crime would set presumptive maximum sentences. To protect against unnecessarily severe sentences, judges would be directed to impose the least restrictive appropriate alternative sentence. To protect against unduly destructive sentences, judges would be empowered in every case to mitigate sentences so as to take account of defendants' special circumstances.

Upper Limits

Before just deserts entered the penal lexicon and guidelines became part of sentencing, there were few protections against the possibility that defendants would receive aberrantly severe punishments. Under the rehabilitative ideology of indeterminate sentencing, there was no necessary link between the seriousness of the offender's crimes and the duration of his sentence. In the extreme forms of indeterminate sentencing in California and Washington, felons were sentenced to prison terms ranging from one year to the statutory maximum; the parole board would decide when the prisoner could safely be released. It was possible and sometimes happened that offenders convicted of trifling crimes served lengthy prison terms.

Under the procedures of indeterminate sentencing, there was a chance but not an assurance that unduly harsh sentences would later be reduced. Until the 1980s, no American jurisdiction had a meaningful system of appellate sentence review (only two or three do now), so there was little possibility that an appellate judge would review the adequacy of the reasons for a sentence. The parole board could release a defendant at any time after he became eligible for release (usually after serving one-third of the maximum sentence), but often would not. Because unduly long sentences were often attributed to individual judges' idiosyncrasies or to racial or class animus, they were a major target of sentencing reformers.

One of the clear successes of sentencing guidelines has been a lower incidence of aberrantly harsh sentences. As the data presented in Chapter 6 demonstrated, "upward departures" from sentencing guidelines are rare in every jurisdiction for which data have been published. For a variety of reasons, including the legal presumption in favor of guidelines sentences, the one-way pressure of plea bargaining toward sentence reductions, and the availability of sentence appeals for departures, judges rarely impose sentences harsher than the applicable guidelines direct.

This is an accomplishment that adherents of every punishment theory can celebrate. Because maximum guideline sentences can be scaled to the offender's culpability or the severity of his crime, both just-deserts proponents like Andrew von Hirsch and limiting-retributivism proponents like Norval Morris should be pleased. Few offenders will receive penalties harsher than they deserve. Because the imposition of penalties harsher than public sentiment deems just will bring the law into disrepute, utilitarians like Nigel Walker and proponents of hybrid theories like H. L. A. Hart and C. L. Ten have reason to approve.

Proponents of different punishment theories disagree whether minimum penalties should also be scaled to the offender's culpability or the severity of his crime, but about maximum deserved penalties almost all agree. Thus, one uncontroversial component of a punishment system that is both generally and racially just is that it contain sentencing guidelines that set presumptive maximum sentences scaled to the differing severities of offenders' crimes.

Least Restrictive Appropriate Alternative

A second element of a punishment system that is both generally and racially just is that it direct judges to impose the least restrictive or punitive appropriate alternative sentence. Most defendants in state felony courts, whatever their race, come from disadvantaged backgrounds. Forcing judges to impose harsher penalties than they believe appropriate is to make them do more damage to disadvantaged offenders than circumstances require, in effect gratuitously to impose unnecessary suffering.

A policy that directed judges to impose the least restrictive appropriate alternative would have the rare property that every legitimate consideration would be advanced. This is the policy opposite of the zero-sum game in which one person's gain is someone else's loss. Public safety interests would be advanced. The standard would direct the least restrictive *appropriate* alternative. When an offender's demonstrated dangerousness required that he be confined for the protection of others or when an especially heinous or notorious offense outraged public opinion, no sentence short of confinement would be appropriate. Such offenders and offenses are rare, however; a policy calling for the least restrictive appropriate alternative policy would save taxpayers billions of dollars a year. Tens of thousands of offenders are confined who need not be, and hundreds of thousands are held longer than serves any legitimate public purpose. Such offenders would not escape punishment but would instead be sentenced or released from prison to an appropriate community corrections program. It costs lots of money to operate good community corrections programs, but far less than it does to run prisons. Finally, not least, such a policy would do less damage to offenders and their families.

Preference for the least restrictive alternative is an aspect of indeterminate sentencing that was mistakenly jettisoned. Both the American Bar Association's first set of Criminal Justice Standards (1967) and the American Law Institute's *Model Penal Code* (1962) favored using the least restrictive alternative. The *Model Penal Code* created presumptions in favor of probation over imprisonment and in favor of releasing prisoners on parole when they first became eligible. The code also created a presumption in favor of relatively short sentences that could be overcome only by special findings that the offender was especially dangerous or a career offender. In each case the judge could reject the presumption but had to give reasons for doing so.

There is less consensus among proponents of different punishment theories concerning the appropriateness of the least restrictive alternative approach. Utilitarians and adherents of hybrid theories would support it on grounds of "parsimony": Punishments by definition are painful; the infliction of pain, though sometimes necessary, is never a happy event; and a just punishment system would therefore never inflict more pain than is minimally required to achieve legitimate public objectives.

Some retributivists would disapprove. The most rigid retributivists would argue that for every crime there is a single appropriate punishment that in justice must be imposed. Some interpretations of Kant's writings on punishment attribute this position to him. Subtler retributivists like Andrew von Hirsch admit that in the abstract we can never agree on the single ideally appropriate punishment for any crime, but they argue that we can agree on the comparative severity of different crimes and can scale crimes to ensure that the penalties that offenders receive are proportionate to the severity of the crimes they have committed. For von Hirsch, a "principle of proportionality" means that both minimum and maximum penalties must be keyed to offense severity so that all offenders convicted of the same offense receive similar punishments and offenders convicted of different offenses receive proportionately different punishments.

That kind of analysis depends on an oversimplified view of offenders' culpability, in which the only meaningful differences among offenders concern their crimes and some consideration of their past criminal records. To the contrary, I believe that most people's intuitions about just punishment include more distinctions among offenders: between offenders who commit assaults in a moment of great emotion and those who commit assaults coolly and cruelly; between offenders without dependents and those with children who will be affected by the choice of punishment; between disadvantaged offenders who steal under pressure of want and affluent offenders who steal on a whim; between user-dealer sellers of drugs and nonuser distributors. No doubt there are countless other bases on which many people believe offenders should be distinguished.

The other argument for a rigid system of strictly proportionate sentences is that judges cannot be trusted to exercise their discretion ethically but will instead use their authority to mitigate only the sentences of affluent offenders. The principal problems with this argument are that most felons are sentenced in state felony courts and, as the data presented in Chapter 4 show, there are very few affluent offenders in state felony courts. Most of those who could conceivably benefit are disadvantaged, and many are members of minority groups.

Moreover, after twenty years of work with state and federal judges from many states, I have considerable confidence in the basic decency of most contemporary judges. This is not a Pollyannaish view. There are good and bad judges, smart and not-so-smart judges, cruel and compassionate judges. Nonetheless, with only a few exceptions who stand out because they are so rare, I have seldom encountered judges who are unaware of their immense powers over others' lives and who do not find sentencing the most difficult part of their jobs. In addition, today's judges include many more women and people from minority backgrounds. Given a choice between a system in which most offenders are treated unnecessarily harshly and one in which a few affluent offenders may be treated unduly leniently, I would opt for the latter every time.

There are two important policy implications of subscribing to a least restrictive alternative approach. First, all mandatory penalties should be repealed. For some especially serious crimes now subject to such provisions, guidelines should set presumptive minimum sentences. Most of the time, judges will impose at least the presumptive minimum sentence. In cases in which the offense or the offender's circumstances make such a penalty appear too harsh, judges would have the authority to order a lesser sentence if they give reasons for doing so. Should the prosecution wish it, the adequacy of those reasons could be examined on appeal.

Two centuries of experience with mandatory penalties demonstrate that judges and prosecutors often surreptitiously nullify mandatory penalties that they believe are too harsh. Whether that happens depends on the personalities of the officials involved and inevitably results in gross inequities among offenders. It is far better to authorize such mitigations and let them happen in the open where officials are accountable for their decisions.

Second, policies like those of the U.S. Sentencing Commission that forbid mitigation of sentences on grounds of the offenders' personal characteristics or special circumstances should also be repealed. There are only three arguments for such policies. The first, that justice requires strictly proportionate penalties based only on offenses and past criminality, was discussed a few paragraphs earlier and in Chapter 5. It lacks discernible merit and can be set aside. The second, that such policies make the application of guidelines more predictable and therefore are more effective deterrents, cannot be scientifically demonstrated and is probably wrong, as the evidence presented in Chapter 6 demonstrates. The third, that such a policy prevents preferment of middle-class offenders, is based on the fallacious belief that there are many middle-class offenders in felony courts. It too lacks merit. The result of such policies is to damage disadvantaged and minority offenders, especially those who have to some degree overcome dismal life chances. There is no ethical basis for a policy that produces such results.

Preventing Unduly Harsh Penalties

A third element of a punishment scheme that is both generally and racially just is that it would impose penalties far less severe than those now common in American courts. Offenders in American courts receive sentences expressed in years and decades that courts in other countries would mete out in weeks and years. American punishments are all but incomparably harsher than those in other countries, as the data in Table 7-1 show for punishment distributions in Sweden, the Australian State of Victoria, and American state prisons. The data are not fully comparable. Whereas the Victorian and Swedish data are for 100 percent of all incarcerative sentences, the American state data are only for state prison sentences, which means that jail sentences are not included. All the same, the difference is one of orders of magnitude. The differences in harshness result partly from the far greater politicization of crime control policy in this country than elsewhere. For two de-

Table 7-1. Distribution of Prison Sentences Imposed in Sweden, Victoria, and United States (state prisons)

Duration	Sweden (%)	Victoria(%)	American State Prisons (%) (1986)	(1991)
10+ years	0	3.6	39	43
4–10 years	1.7	19.6	25[a]	24[a]
2–4 years	3.8	36.0	25[b]	23[b]
1–2 years	5.0	23.2		
½–1 year	12.0			
$\frac{1}{6}$–½ year	28.0	13.4	10	10
under $\frac{1}{6}$ year	50.0			

[a] = 5–10 years.
[b] = 2–5 years.

Sources: Allen Beck et al., *Survey of State Prison Inmates, 1991* (Washington, D.C.: Bureau of Justice Statistics, 1993); Arie Freiberg, "Sentencing Reform in Victoria," in *The Politics of Sentencing Reform,* edited by Chris Clarkson and Rod Morgan (Oxford: Oxford University Press, 1994); Nils Jareborg, "The Swedish Sentencing Reform," in *The Politics of Sentencing Reform,* edited by Chris Clarkson and Rod Morgan (Oxford: Oxford University Press, 1994).

cades, there has been unremitting pressure for increases in penalties and no pressure at all for decreases.

An Oregon judge likened modern American crime control policy to America's Vietnam War strategy: When the addition of more troops and matériel failed to defeat the Viet Cong, the solution was always to send in more troops and matériel, and more troops and matériel, until finally we realized that that strategy would not work, and then we left. In the case of American crime control policies, we cannot leave, but we can abandon a counterproductive strategy.

At least since 1980, America has been involved in a continuous series of unsuccessful wars against drugs and crime, using strategies that cannot work and always responding to failure by attempting to pursue more aggressively our strategy of harsh penalties and wholesale incarceration. At the federal level and in most states, "crime bills" are introduced in every legislative session, calling for harsher penalties as the "solution" to the crime problem. The most recent manifestations of this syndrome are the numerous federal and state proposals for "three times and you're out" laws. Rarely are bills introduced calling for a reduction in penalties; when they are, the rationale is not the ineffectiveness or injustice of harsh penalties but that their administration has become too costly.

Partly the harsher penalties in America than elsewhere result from an aspect of national character. Americans have a remarkable ability to endure suffering by others. We lock up our citizens at rates five to fifteen times higher than those in other Western countries. Alone among Western countries, the United States retains capital punishment, and applies it with increasing frequency. The thirty-eight prisoners executed in 1993 was the largest number since 1962. Alone among major Western countries, the United States lacks a national system of medical care and a system of income maintenance that provides a minimum decent standard of living for all its citizens, especially dependent children. Since 1980, we have allowed homelessness to reach levels unparalleled in modern times. That those whose suffering we so lightly endure are disproportionately black is one of the less attractive features of our national character.

Besides the mistaken claim that harsher penalties more effectively prevent crime, a second rationale is sometimes offered for why so many of our citizens are in prison: Crime rates, it is said, are far higher in the United States than elsewhere. That turns out not to be true either, but the evidence disproving it has only recently become available.

Overall, American crime rates are comparable to those in Australia, Canada, New Zealand, and the Netherlands. Among Western countries, American rates for most crimes are among the highest, but usually are not the highest. Such comparisons have been feasible and believable only lately, with the publication of data from two international surveys of crime victimization in twenty countries. Until now, such comparisons have not been credible, as they have been based on police records that vary widely among countries in their accuracy and completeness and in how different countries' legal systems categorize different crimes. In order to avoid the limitations of official police records, the National Crime Victimization Survey began collecting data in the United States in 1973. The rationale was that information from representative national samples of Americans about crimes suffered by them or members of their families is far more likely to be complete and accurate than are police records. Building on American experience with victimization surveys and on experience in other countries, a consortium of countries was formed in the mid-1980s to conduct international victimization surveys. The surveys were carried out with funding from the participating countries, including the United States. Conspiracy theorists might wonder why the results—so inconsistent with the crime control politics of the Reagan and Bush administrations—were not widely disseminated by the federal government, which in part paid for the surveys.

The International Crime Survey is managed from the Dutch Ministry of Justice. Overall direction is given by Jan van Dijk, the Netherlands' most internationally prominent criminologist and the longtime director of the Dutch Ministry's criminology research center, and Pat Mayhew, senior principal research officer of the English Home Office's Research and Planning Unit and England's leading expert on victimization surveys (she also directs the British Crime Survey). In 1988 and again in 1991, using standardized data collection instruments for all twenty countries, thereby avoiding problems of noncomparability that would result from different legal systems' divergent definitions of crimes, researchers interviewed randomly selected samples of residents of each country. Eight countries, including the United States, participated in both years. For no crime were the American rates highest, as the comprehensive results shown in Table 7-2 reveal. In recent years, for example, auto theft rates were higher in England, Italy, Australia, New Zealand, and France. Burglary rates were higher in New Zealand and Australia. Robbery rates were higher in Spain and

Table 7-2. One-Year Victimization Rates, by Country and Offense (in %)[a]

	Thefts of Cars[b]	Thefts from Cars [b]	Burglary with Entry	Robbery and Pick- pocketing	Assaults/ Threats and Sexual Incidents
England and Wales[c]	3.3	8.7	2.5	2.1	3.5
Scotland[d]	1.2	7.7	2.0	1.4	2.1
Northern Ireland[d]	2.2	5.5	1.1	1.2	2.5
Netherlands[c]	0.5	7.6	2.2	2.7	4.5
West Germany[d]	0.5	7.6	2.2	2.7	4.4
Switzerland[d]	0.0	2.4	1.0	2.0	2.0
Belgium[c]	1.1	3.9	2.2	2.3	2.3
France[d]	2.8	7.1	2.4	2.2	2.5
Norway[d]	1.3	3.5	0.8	1.0	4.0
Finland[c]	0.7	3.6	0.6	2.4	2.5
Spain[d]	1.9	14.6	1.7	5.0	4.1
Sweden[e]	2.0	4.7	1.4	1.1	3.0
Italy[e]	3.0	7.9	2.4	2.7	1.6
Czechoslovakia[e]	1.2	7.7	4.3	3.9	4.7
Poland[e]	1.3	11.5	2.3	7.8	5.6
USA[c]	2.5	8.5	3.5	2.5	6.3
Canada[c]	1.2	8.2	3.2	1.9	6.0
Australia[c]	3.0	7.4	4.0	1.8	7.1
New Zealand[e]	2.8	7.3	4.3	1.0	6.6
Japan[c]	0.6	1.5	0.9	na	0.7

[a]Rates are the percentage of respondents aged 16 or over reporting at least one victimization.
[b]Based on car owners.
[c]Risks averaged for 1988 and 1991.
[d]Risks for 1988 only.
[e]Risks for 1991 only.

Source: Jan J. M. van Dijk and Pat Mayhew, *Criminal Victimization in the Industrialized World* (The Hague: Dutch Ministry of Justice, 1992).

comparable in Italy. Assault rates were about the same in New Zealand, Australia, Canada, and the United States.

The glaring exception, the area in which American crime rates appear to be the highest in the developed world, is violent crimes involving guns. American crime rates for homicide are far higher than elsewhere, as are rates for robberies and assaults involving guns. Because gun crimes are comparatively rare in most countries, they were not investigated in the International Crime Survey. Countless researchers, preeminently including economist Philip J. Cook of Duke University and law professor Franklin E. Zimring of the University of California at Berkeley, have demonstrated that violent crimes in which firearms are used are far more likely to be fatal or seriously injurious than are violent crimes involving other weapons or no weapons at all. The old saw, "Guns don't kill people, people kill people," is nonsense. Much violent crime is impulsive, and few people outside the National Rifle Association doubt that a violent impulse in the presence of a loaded firearm is far more likely to cause death or injury than is a violent impulse elsewhere.

Guns are so prevalent in America not because the American public supports unrestrained gun ownership but because elected officials have long feared the National Rifle Association. This is shown by a long series of public opinion surveys. The "Brady Bill," requiring a seven-day waiting period before completing a handgun purchase, squeaked through Congress late in 1993 after many years of rejection. Yet a 1993 Gallup poll showed that by 88 percent to 11 percent, Americans supported a seven-day waiting period before a buyer takes possession of a gun. Fourteen different National Opinion Research Center surveys from 1973 to 1991 showed that from 69 to 81 percent of Americans favored conditioning gun ownership on prior possession of a police gun permit. The "opposes" ranged from 18 to 29 percent. The highest high (81 percent for) and the lowest low (18 percent against) were in 1991. A March 1993 Gallup poll showed that 70 percent of Americans believed that laws governing the sale of firearms should be made "more strict." A March 1991 Gallup poll showed that Americans opposed the complete prohibition of handguns by only a 10 percent margin (53 percent to 43). The same poll showed that more than 80 percent of Americans supported the registration of all handguns. So even though America has the highest rates of gun crime of any developed country, the problem lies not in underlying rates of crime but in underlying rates of gun ownership. The long-term solution lies not in sentencing policy but in gun control policy.

Revivifying Treatment

A fourth element of a punishment scheme that is both racially and socially just is that it would invest in human capital. It would provide services to offenders, for their sake and ours, sometimes—as in the case of drug and sex-offender treatment—whether or not they wanted the services. The knowledge exists to provide effective services to offenders, although the will and the money to do so have long been lacking. A series of issues warrant mention. First is the mythology that "nothing works." Second is whether helping services can fairly be provided to offenders that are not available to nonoffenders. Third is paying for the services to offenders.

Nothing Works

The "nothing works" mythology has done enormous damage because it has given politicians a rationale for investing less in educational, vocational, and other services to offenders. Robert Martinson's provocatively titled 1974 *Public Interest* article, "What Works—Questions and Answers About Prison Reform," did not conclude that nothing works. Nor did the 1975 book *The Effectiveness of Correctional Treatment—A Survey of Correctional Treatment Studies,* by Douglas Lipton, Robert Martinson, and Judith Wilks, from which it derived. Before his death, Martinson tried to set the record straight in an article in the *Hofstra Law Review,* to explain what he really meant, but it was too late.

What Martinson and his colleagues determined, and what two National Academy of Science Panels chaired by Lee Sechrest confirmed, was that existing correctional treatment evaluations did not convincingly demonstrate that correctional treatment programs reduced recidivism. Martinson and his successors found hints here and there that particular programs had positive effects for particular kinds of offenders. Overall, however, they decided that the available research rarely provided a basis for rejecting the evaluators' "null hypothesis" that interventions have no effect.

In its time, the original Lipton, Martinson, and Wilks analysis was important and responsible. Their work started in the 1960s when indeterminate sentencing systems were ubiquitous in America. The broad discretions accorded to judges, corrections officials, and parole boards were based on the premise that rehabilitation was the main rationale for sentencing and corrections and that offenders' rehabilitative prospects and progress should be determinative considerations in decision making.

Efforts therefore to establish the effectiveness of correctional treatment programs were important, as was the conclusion that earlier assumptions about rehabilitative effectiveness were unfounded. It became clear that indeterminate sentencing gave officials too much unregulated power over other human beings. Partly as a result, indeterminate sentencing has gone into eclipse, and grandiose rehabilitative claims are seldom made.

In retrospect, it was naive and simplistic to ask or answer global questions about correctional treatment effectiveness. We would not consider such questions useful in relation to medical or psychiatric or environmental measures. We do not ask, "Does medical treatment work?" but, instead, whether a particular treatment delivered in a particular way helps a particular ailment according to particular criteria.

Better questions generate better answers. We now know, on the basis of sound experimental studies using control or comparison groups, that some kinds of sex-offender treatment reduce later offending by some kinds of sex offenders, that all kinds of drug treatment reduce later drug abuse and drug-related offending by some kinds of drug abusers, and that a variety of programs for young offenders reduce their later offending.

For drug-abusing offenders, particularly, the case for increased investment in drug treatment is powerful. From the Justice Department's Drug Use Forecasting (DUF) data from urinalyses of arrested felons, we know that one-half to three-fourths in many cities test positive for recent drug use. From both ethnographic and statistical studies of drug-using offenders, we know that high levels of drug use and high levels of offending are strongly associated. When drug use declines, offending declines. From treatment evaluation studies, we know that participation in well-run methadone maintenance programs and therapeutic communities can demonstrably reduce both later drug use and later criminality of drug-dependent offenders. Finally, also from drug treatment evaluations, we know that the best predictor of successful treatment is time in treatment, even when coerced by legal compulsion.

Together, our knowledge of drug treatment effectiveness argues powerfully for providing treatment on demand for all drug-dependent offenders who want it, and compulsory treatment for many drug-dependent offenders who do not.

The case for greatly increased public investment in services for offenders, however, is far broader than that. Given the argument for the informal mitigation of punishment for disadvantaged offenders that was advanced in Chapter 6, and well-established links among disadvantaged childhoods, race, and crime, a rational crime policy would give high priority to helping disadvantaged adults develop the skills needed to rebuild their lives and enhance the life chances of their children. The case is strong for remedial education, for life skills training, for parenting training, and for vocational training. Such programs are far less expensive to operate than prisons and jails are and far more likely to advance the causes of public safety and racial justice.

Less Eligibility

Proposals for services for offenders sometimes meet with the objection that is it unjust to offer benefits to offenders that are not provided to the least well-off law-abiding citizens. This is sometimes referred to as the principle of less eligibility, from its most famous formulation by the English social reformers Beatrice and Sidney Webb: "The condition of the pauper should be less eligible than that of the lowest grade of independent labourer." Although the notion has surface plausibility, it need not be an impediment to expanded services for disadvantaged offenders.

The principle of less eligibility, first articulated in the 1834 report of a British Royal Commission on the English poor laws and in the contemporaneous writings of Jeremy Bentham, has been applied to both paupers and prisoners. Concerning paupers, the claim is that "poverty relief" or welfare benefits should not allow a standard of living superior to that of the poorest nonrecipient. Concerning offenders, the comparison is with the least well-off nonoffender.

The principle comes in descriptive and prescriptive versions. The descriptive version expresses the political prediction that public opinion will not long countenance policies that favor the unworthy over the worthy. The prescriptive version takes two forms. To utilitarians like Jeremy Bentham, violation of the principle would create perverse incentives. Why should a poor man work barely to survive if the poor laws will feed him adequately without work? This is the crux of the modern conservative's objection to supplying more than the most primitive and uncomfortable housing to the homeless and of Charles Murray's objections to social welfare programs in general. To others, less eligibility is a principle of justice. Satisfactions should be distributed according to merit, and so a disadvantaged person who works or lives a law-abiding life deserves more from life than does a disadvantaged person who does not work or commits crimes.

These are powerful but simple claims that have little relevance in the complex world in which we live. The descriptive version of the less-eligibility principle must be wrong because it is routinely violated. For example, governments spend far more housing a young adult offender in a prison, $25,000 to $35,000 per year, than the out-of-pocket cost of supporting him for a year and educating him in a community college. Government pays little or nothing for his law-abiding brother's support or education. Governments spend staggering amounts—$32,000 per year per family in hotels and $38,000 per year per family in apartment-style shelters in New York City in 1993—to run shelters for the homeless and pay nothing to help others nearly as badly off find housing. For many offenders, prisons provide a safer environment, better meals, superior medical care, and better educational opportunities than would be available on the streets.

There is a psychologically powerful reason why the descriptive "lesser-eligibility" doctrine does not prevent providing services to offenders. Few people choose to give up their liberty and to subject themselves to the pervasive controls and limited privacy of imprisonment or intensive community corrections programs. Offsetting the "benefits" of decent medical care, reliable meals, and the knowledge that a prisoner's stay is costing taxpayers $25,000 a year is the awareness that convicted felons bear a damaging stigma and that imprisonment is for nearly everyone a miserable experience.

The prescriptive versions of the less-eligibility doctrine fare little better. Given the numbers of black males, especially in the inner city, whose lives are invaded by the criminal justice system, it is difficult to contend that utilitarian incentives to conformity are working. Similarly, given the social pathologies afflicting urban areas of concentrated poverty, it is difficult to assert with a straight face that those who commit crimes do so principally because of defects in their characters. The conditions of life affecting the urban black underclass, the temptations that crime and drug abuse represent to impoverished people, and the extraordinary racial disproportions characterizing the criminal justice system are fundamental problems confronting modern America. The argument that we should not act to ameliorate them because mistaken inferences might be drawn about individual persons' comparative worthiness misses the point.

Finding Money

Paying for major increases in human capital investment would be easy if governments stopped throwing money at crime control policies that are fruitless, wasteful, and cruel. Senator Everett Dirksen's "A billion here, a billion there, after a while you are talking about real money" was said some time ago, but it still has merit. If American incarceration rates fell to twice that of the next highest Western nation, that is, to around 225 per 100,000 population, our prison and jail population would fall from 1.5 million to under 600,000. This is not unimaginable. In 1980, when crime rates were about the same as in 1993, state and federal prisons and jails housed slightly fewer than 500,000 inmates. At the modest estimate of $25,000 operating costs per year per prisoner, lowering the number of inmates by 900,000 would save county, state, and federal governments $22.5 billion a year.

Reducing demonstrably ineffective source-country and extraterritorial interdiction components of current antidrug efforts to half their current levels might save a more modest $2 billion per year. Substantial reductions in the number of arrests and prosecutions of user-dealers would permit substantial savings in police and prosecutorial costs, or substantial redirection of effort toward violent crimes generally and family violence particularly, and to enforcement of other currently underenforced laws like those prohibiting consumer fraud and criminal violations of environmental laws.

These changes in policy direction are feasible and achievable without significant threats to public safety. Fewer than half of state prisoners in 1991, for example, had been convicted of violent crimes. Of violent offenders in prison, many had been there for long periods and had passed the periods in their lives when they were likely to be violent again. Countless evaluations of nonincarcerative correctional programs show that sending people to prison does not reduce the chances that they will reoffend after they are released. Offenders held in prison have recidivism rates equal to or higher than those of comparable offenders who are placed on ordinary probation or in intermediate sanctions like intensive supervision, day reporting centers, and house arrest with or without electronic monitoring. Thus, incarceration does not reduce prisoners' later criminality and may even increase it. This leaves the incapacitation of dangerous offenders as the only plausible basis for confining large numbers of people. Responses to some notorious offenders will also require some prison space, but not much. Half a million prison beds—or 600,000 if we want to adjust for population growth—should easily accommodate legitimate American needs for penal confinement.

Incapacitation is the one penal purpose that imprisonment can unarguably serve. The objective should be to devise ways to ensure that prisons are used for incapacitative purposes. This involves two steps: first, deciding what kinds of crimes we most want to prevent and, second, figuring out how to prevent them.

A sensible penal policy would focus on violence and sex crimes, as these are the crimes that Americans most fear. Yet in 1990, only a quarter of those sent to prison had committed violent (including sexual) crimes, and nearly a third each were property and drug offenders.

Current policies of indiscriminate imprisonment have the counterproductive effect of limiting the prisons' capacity to incapacitate violent and sexual offenders. Twenty consecutive years of increases in prison populations have meant that facilities are always crowded. In order to maintain populations at controllable levels and sometimes to comply with federal court orders establishing population caps, current prisoners must often be released to make room for new arrivals.

In a variety of ways, less pressure on prison beds might well result in a safer America. States like North Carolina, Texas, and Florida could abandon their current practices of releasing violent offenders early in order to make room for newly arriving property and drug offenders. Abandoning current policies of mass arrests of user-dealers might make the inner city a less dangerous place, thereby reducing the felt need of participants in the drug markets to use violence to protect themselves. Lessening the destructive effects of imprisonment on the life chances of disadvantaged property and drug offenders would allow more of them to move earlier into law-abiding lives in which the chances of their using violence would be fewer.

Such abrupt changes of policy direction are possible, as other countries have shown. In Margaret Thatcher's England, drug control policies in the late 1980s were moving in the direction of American-style moralistic prohibition. When the relations between intravenous drug use and AIDS became clear, English policy changed course toward a harm-reduction approach that gave greater priority to AIDS prevention. Practices unthinkable a few years earlier, like heroin maintenance and needle exchange programs, became acceptable. West Germans in the 1960s decided that too many people were in prison and, in particular, that sentences under six months served little purpose. Legislation was enacted to replace most short sentences with fines. In 1968, roughly a quarter of convicted offenders were sentenced to imprisonment. Two years later the percentage of convicted offenders sentenced directly to prison had fallen to 7 percent. The number of prison admissions had fallen from 136,000 to 42,000. In 1989, the figures were 6 percent and 33,000.

Doing Justice

Nothing in the criminal justice system's power can bring racial and social justice in America into harmony. The problems are too great, and the justice system's capacities are too limited.

The solutions to those problems lie elsewhere—in universal health care; a universal Social Security–like system of income support; adequate public education; assurance of decent, affordable housing; reinvestment in the cities; and a full-employment economy with government as the employer of last resort. The goal should be to make sure that every child, whoever his or her parents and whatever their race or class, has a reasonable chance to live a satisfying, productive, and law-abiding life. That is a full agenda. Its recitation should make clear the implausibility of any hope that the justice system can be the engine driving those changes.

What the justice system can do is cause less harm. The entanglement of extraordinary numbers of black American males in the justice system's tentacles damages them, their children, and their communities. The actions we take in the name of public safety are self-deluding, because we will not lower crime rates by means of punishment when the conditions that cause crime continue to fester. As long as our crime control policies treat symptoms and not ailments, they are doomed to fail.

The Reagan and Bush administrations' crime control policies might have been tolerable if all they did was waste money. They did, after all, create and continue to support hundreds of thousands of new jobs in police departments, courts, prosecutors' and public defenders' offices, and corrections. We have a long and venerable tradition of supporting otherwise dubious programs—in public works spending, location of military installations, award of defense contracts—principally to create and protect jobs. Unfortunately, recent crime control policies do more than waste money. They waste lives.

Contemporary crime control policies fundamentally impede the movement of disadvantaged black Americans into the social and economic mainstream of modern America. Although reasonable people can differ in the extent to which they attribute the conditions of the black urban underclass to contemporary racism and to changing economic and social structural pressures in modern America, reasonable people cannot disagree that the disadvantages suffered by black Americans in 1970 were preponderantly the product of centuries of American racism. That a majority of black Americans have overcome a legacy of racism and the recurrent recessions of the past two decades is to be celebrated. That a minority have not and are far worse off in 1994 than in 1970 is to be lamented. That our crime control policies have made the lives and life chances of that minority even worse than they otherwise would have been is shameful.

Some readers will recognize that the phrase "malign neglect" used in this book to characterize policymakers' indifference to the racial effects of their policies, is a play on Daniel Patrick Moynihan's suggestion in the early 1970s that black Americans would benefit from a period of "benign neglect" by government. All people in the end want the same things for themselves and their children, he argued, and the best course might be for government to stop meddling and let black Americans get on with the job of achieving those things.

We have recently lived through twelve years of national crime control and welfare policies of malign neglect of the well-being of black Americans. Conservative politicians have cynically played on white Americans' fears and on racial stereotypes, exemplified by the Welfare Queen and Willie Horton. Policies have been promoted that have failed to achieve their ostensible objectives, because they could not, and that have foreseeably and cruelly impeded the efforts of too many disadvantaged blacks to live satisfying lives.

In his 1986 book, *Family and Nation,* Moynihan described a meeting on drug policy with the austere director-general of the French Sûreté and others, which he attended as a representative of the Nixon administration. Moynihan had described heroin problems in black ghettos in New York City to the Frenchmen and explained that something had to be done. The French participants' "bewilderment was scarcely concealed. The Americans were just *now* coming to tell us about a plague ravaging their cities, their youth" (emphasis in original). The director-general said little during the meeting or a subsequent elaborate meal. As the luncheon guests departed, Moynihan reports, the director-general "looked straight at me, and asked in a tone of incredulity tinged with disdain, 'What kind of people are you?' " Historians will someday look back at the tangled problems of race, poverty, crime, and punishment in America in the Reagan–Bush years and wonder what kind of people we were.

References

Findings of specific studies are identified in the text by mention of the authors' names. Full bibliographical information is provided here. Data from statistical series and sources routinely compiled and reported by the federal government are generally not attributed to a specific source (except in figures and tables). Data on victimization and reported crime rates are drawn respectively from Bureau of Justice Statistics reports from the National Crime Victimization Survey (e.g., *Criminal Victimization in the United States—1992*) and from the Federal Bureau of Investigation's Uniform Crime Reports based on police data (e.g., *Crime in the United States—1992*). Data on jail and prison populations are drawn from Bureau of Justice Statistics reports on these subjects that are listed among the references. Data on population trends, social welfare spending and caseloads, and the demographic composition of social welfare caseloads are drawn from *The Green Book,* an overview of federal entitlement programs published annually by the U.S. House of Representatives Committee on Ways and Means and from the *Statistical Abstract of the United States,* published annually by the U.S. Department of Commerce.

Abadinsky, Harold. 1989. *Drug Abuse: An Introduction.* Chicago: Nelson-Hall.

Allen-Hagen, Barbara. 1991. *Public Juvenile Facilities, Children in Custody 1989.* Washington, D.C.: U.S. Department of Justice, Office of Juvenile Justice and Delinquency Prevention.

Alterman, Eric. 1989. "G.O.P. Chairman Atwater: Playing Hardball." *New York Times Magazine,* April 30, p. 30.

American Bar Association. 1968. *Standards Relating to Sentencing Alternatives and Procedures.* Chicago: American Bar Association.

American Friends Service Committee. 1971. *Struggle for Justice.* New York: Hill & Wang.

American Law Institute. 1962. *Model Penal Code (Proposed Official Draft)*. Philadelphia: American Law Institute.

Andenaes, Johannes. 1974. *Punishment and Deterrence*. Ann Arbor: University of Michigan Press.

Anderson, Elijah. 1990. *Streetwise: Race, Class, and Change in an Urban Community*. Chicago: University of Chicago Press.

Anglin, M. Douglas, and Yih-Ing Hser. 1990. "Treatment of Drug Abuse." In *Drugs and Crime,* edited by Michael Tonry and James Q. Wilson. Volume 13 of *Crime and Justice: A Review of Research,* edited by Michael Tonry and Norval Morris. Chicago: University of Chicago Press.

Ashford, Kathryn, and Craig Mosbaek. 1991. *First Year Report on Implementation of Sentencing Guidelines*. Portland: Oregon Criminal Justice Council.

Associated Press. 1991. "Gravely Ill, Atwater Offers Apology." *New York Times,* January 13, sec. 1, pt. 1, p. 16.

Austin, James, and Aaron David McVey. 1989. *The Impact of the War on Drugs*. San Francisco: National Council on Crime and Delinquency.

Australia Law Reform Commission. 1980. *Sentencing of Federal Offenders*. Canberra: Australian Government Publishing Service.

Ayres, Drummond. 1991. "Drug Raids Tarnish a University That Prizes Its Ties To Jefferson." *New York Times,* March 24, p. A20.

Barr, William P. 1992. "The Case for More Incarceration." Washington, D.C.: U.S. Department of Justice, Office of Policy Development.

Bazelon, David. 1976a. "The Morality of the Criminal Law." *Southern California Law Review* 49:385–405.

———. 1976b. "The Morality of the Criminal Law: A Rejoinder to Professor Morse." *Southern California Law Review* 49:1,269–74.

———. 1988. *Questioning Authority*. New York: Knopf.

Beck, Allen, et al. 1993. *Survey of State Prison Inmates, 1991.* Washington, D.C.: Bureau of Justice Statistics.

Beha, James A. II. 1977. " 'And Nobody Can Get You Out': The Impact of a Mandatory Prison Sentence for the Illegal Carrying of a Firearm on the Use of Firearms and on the Administration of Criminal Justice in Boston." *Boston University Law Review* 57:96–146 (pt. 1), 289–333 (pt. 2).

Bell, Derrick. 1992. *Faces at the Bottom of the Well—The Permanence of Racism*. New York: Basic Books.

Bentham, Jeremy. 1843. *The Works of Jeremy Bentham,* vol. 4, edited by John Bowring. London: Simpkin, Marshall.

Berlin, Isaiah. 1969. *Four Essays on Liberty*. Oxford: Oxford University Press.

Blumstein, Alfred. 1982. "On the Racial Disproportionality of United States' Prison Populations." *Journal of Criminal Law and Criminology* 73: 1259–81.

———. 1988. "Prison Populations: A System out of Control?" In *Crime and Justice,* vol. 10, edited by Michael Tonry and Norval Morris. Chicago: University of Chicago Press.

———. 1993a. "Making Rationality Relevant: The American Society of Criminology 1992 Presidential Address." *Criminology,* January 1993.

———. 1993b. "Racial Disproportionality of U.S. Prison Populations Revisited." *University of Colorado Law Review* 64:743–60.

Blumstein, Alfred, Jacqueline Cohen, Susan E. Martin, and Michael Tonry, eds. 1983. *Research on Sentencing: The Search For Reform.* 2 vols. Report of the National Academy of Sciences Panel on Sentencing Research. Washington, D.C.: National Academy Press.

Blumstein, Alfred, Jacqueline Cohen, and Daniel Nagin. 1978. *Deterrence and Incapacitation.* Report of the National Academy of Sciences Panel on Research on Deterrent and Incapacitative Effects. Washington, D.C.: National Academy Press.

Blundy, David. 1988. "Prisoner Who Held the White House Key." *Sunday Telegraph,* November 13, p. 11.

Bonnie, Richard J., and Charles Whitebread. 1974. *The Marihuana Conviction: A History of Marihuana Prohibition in the United States.* Charlottesville: University Press of Virginia.

Botvin, Gilbert J. 1990. "Substance Abuse Prevention: Theory, Practice, and Effectiveness." In *Drugs and Crime,* edited by Michael Tonry and James Q. Wilson. Volume 13 of *Crime and Justice: A Review of Research,* edited by Michael Tonry and Norval Morris. Chicago: University of Chicago Press.

Bourgois, Philippe. 1989. "In Search of Horatio Alger: Culture and Ideology in the Crack Economy." *Contemporary Drug Problems* 1989: 619–49.

Boxill, Bernard. 1989. "Is Further Civil Rights Legislation Irrelevant to Black Progress?" In *Race: Twentieth Century Dilemmas, Twenty-first Century Prognoses,* edited by Wilson A. Van Horne and Thomas V. Tonnesen. Milwaukee: Institute on Race and Ethnicity.

Broder, David S. 1981. "Still Learning to Be the Opposition." *Washington Post,* February 15, p. C7.

Brownstein, Paul, et al. 1989. *Patterns of Substance Use and Delinquency Among Inner City Adolescents.* Washington, D.C.: Urban Institute.

Bureau of Justice Statistics. 1984. *The 1983 Jail Census.* Washington, D.C.: U.S. Department of Justice, Bureau of Justice Statistics.

————. 1985. *Jail Inmates, 1983*. Washington, D.C.: U.S. Department of Justice, Bureau of Justice Statistics.

————. 1987. *Correctional Populations in the United States, 1985*. Washington, D.C.: U.S. Department of Justice, Bureau of Justice Statistics.

————. 1989a. *Correctional Populations in the United States, 1986*. Washington, D.C.: U.S. Department of Justice, Bureau of Justice Statistics.

————. 1989b. *Correctional Populations in the United States, 1987*. Washington, D.C.: U.S. Department of Justice, Bureau of Justice Statistics.

————. 1991a. *Census of Local Jails, 1988*. Washington, D.C.: U.S. Department of Justice, Bureau of Justice Statistics.

————. 1991b. *Correctional Populations in the United States, 1988*. Washington, D.C.: U.S. Department of Justice, Bureau of Justice Statistics.

————. 1991c. *Correctional Populations in the United States, 1989*. Washington, D.C.: U.S. Department of Justice, Bureau of Justice Statistics.

————. 1992a. *Jail Inmates, 1991*. Washington, D.C.: U.S. Department of Justice, Bureau of Justice Statistics.

————. 1992b. *Drugs, Crime, and the Justice System*. Washington, D.C.: U.S. Department of Justice, Bureau of Justice Statistics.

————. 1993. *Correctional Populations in the United States, 1991*. Washington, D.C.: U.S. Department of Justice, Bureau of Justice Statistics.

————. Various years. *Prisoners in [1993 and various years]*. Washington, D.C.: U.S. Department of Justice, Bureau of Justice Statistics.

————. Various years. *Sourcebook of Criminal Justice Statistics—[1992 and various years]*. Washington, D.C.: U.S. Government Printing Office.

Cahalan, Margaret Werner. 1986. *Historical Corrections Statistics in the United States, 1850–1984*. Washington, D.C.: U.S. Department of Justice, Bureau of Justice Statistics.

Canadian Sentencing Commission. 1987. *Sentencing Reform: A Canadian Approach*. Ottawa: Canadian Government Publishing Centre.

Center on Juvenile and Criminal Justice. 1990. *Young African American Men and the Criminal Justice System in California*. San Francisco: Center on Juvenile and Criminal Justice.

Chaiken, Marcia, ed. 1988. *Street Level Enforcement: Examining the Issues*. Washington, D.C.: U.S. Government Printing Office.

Chaiken, Jan M., and Marcia R. Chaiken. 1982. *Varieties of Criminal Behavior*. Santa Monica, Calif.: RAND Corporation.

————. 1990 "Drugs and Predatory Crime." In *Drugs and Crime,* edited by Michael Tonry and James Q. Wilson. Volume 13 of *Crime and Justice: A Review of Research,* edited by Michael Tonry and Norval Morris. Chicago: University of Chicago Press.

Clark, Stover. 1992. "Pennsylvania Corrections in Context." *Overcrowded Times* 3(4): 4–5.

Clarke, Stevens H. 1992. "North Carolina Prisons Growing." *Overcrowded Times* 3(4):1, 11–13.

Cohen, Mark. 1988. "Pain, Suffering and Jury Awards: A Study of the Cost of Crime to Victims." *Law and Society Review* 22:537–55.

Cohen, Richard. 1993. "Common Ground on Crime." *Washington Post,* December 21, p. A23.

Committee on Justice and the Solicitor General. 1993. *Crime Prevention in Canada: Toward A National Strategy.* Ottawa: Canada Communication Group.

Committee on Ways and Means, U.S. House of Representatives. 1993. *Overview of Entitlement Programs: 1993 Green Book.* Washington, D.C.: U.S. Government Printing Office.

Correctional Association of New York. 1990. *Imprisoned Generation: Young Men Under Criminal Justice Custody in New York State.* New York: Correctional Association of New York.

Cose, Ellis. 1993. *The Rage of a Privileged Class.* New York: HarperCollins.

Courtwright, David T. 1982. *Dark Paradise: Opiate Addiction in America Before 1940.* Cambridge: Harvard University Press.

Currie, Elliot. 1993. *Reckoning—Drugs, the Cities, and the American Future.* New York: Hill & Wang.

Curtis, Lynn. 1975. *Violence, Race, and Culture.* Lexington, Mass.: Heath.

Dailey, Debra L. 1993. "Prison and Race in Minnesota." *Colorado Law Review* 64: 761–80.

Dawson, Robert O. 1969. *Sentencing.* Boston: Little, Brown.

Delgado, Richard. 1985. "Rotten Social Background: Should the Criminal Law Recognize a Defense of Severe Environmental Deprivation?" *Journal of Law and Inequality* 3:9–90.

DeParle, Jason. 1990. "Talk of Government Being out to Get Blacks Falls on More Attentive Ears." *New York Times,* October 29, p. B7.

DiIulio, John J. 1990. "Crime and Punishment in Wisconsin." *Wisconsin Policy Research Institute Report* 3(7):1–56.

———. 1991. *No Escape: The Future of American Corrections.* New York: Basic Books.

———. 1994. "Let 'Em Rot." *Wall Street Journal,* January 26, ed. page.

DiIulio, John J., and Anne M. Diehl. 1991. "Does Prison Pay?" Unpublished manuscript. Center of Domestic and Comparative Policy Studies, Princeton University.

Doble, John, Stephen Immerwahr, and Amy Richardson. 1991. *Punishing Criminals: The People of Delaware Consider the Options.* New York: Edna McConnell Clark Foundation.

Doble, John, and Josh Klein. 1989. *Punishing Criminals: The Public's View. An Alabama Survey.* New York: Edna McConnell Clark Foundation.

Dressler, Joshua. 1988. "Reflections on Excusing Wrongdoers: Moral Theory, New Excuses, and the MPC." *Rutgers Law Review* 19:671–716.

Du Bois, W. E. B. 1899. "The Negro Criminal." In Samuel L. Myers and Margaret C. Simms. 1988. *The Economics of Race and Crime.* New Brunswick, N.J.: Transaction Books.

Duff, Antony. 1986. *Trials and Punishments.* Cambridge: Cambridge University Press.

Dugger, Celia. 1993. "Homeless Shelters Drain Money from Housing, Experts Say." *New York Times,* July 26, p. B1.

Edin, Kathryn, and Christopher Jencks. 1992. "Reforming Welfare." Chap. 5 in *Rethinking Social Policy* by Christopher Jencks. Cambridge, Mass.: Harvard University Press.

Edsall, Thomas, and Mary Edsall. 1991. *Chain Reaction: The Impact of Race, Rights, and Taxes on American Politics.* New York: Norton.

Ellickson, Phyllis L., and Robert M. Bell. 1990. *Prospects for Preventing Drug Use Among Young Adolescents.* Santa Monica, Calif.: RAND Corporation.

Elliott, Delbert S. 1993. "Longitudinal Research in Criminology: Promise and Practice." In *Cross-National Longitudinal Research on Human Development and Criminal Behavior,* edited by E. G. Weitekamp and H.-J. Kerner. London: Kluwer.

Ellwood, David T. 1988. *Poor Support: Poverty in the American Family.* New York: Basic Books.

Fagan, Jeffrey. 1993. "The Political Economy of Drug Dealing Among Urban Gangs." In *Drugs and the Community,* edited by Robert C. Davis, Arthur J. Lurigio, and Dennis P. Rosenbaum. Springfield, Ill.: Thomas.

Federal Bureau of Investigation. Various Years. *Uniform Crime Reports for the United States—[1993 and various years].* Washington, D.C.: U.S. Government Printing Office.

Ferraro, Thomas. 1990. "Bush Releases Upbeat Report, Says Drug War 'Paying Off'," United Press International, December 19.

Fishkin, James S. 1983. *Justice, Equal Opportunity, and the Family.* New Haven, Conn.: Yale University Press.

Flanagan, Timothy J., and Kathleen Maguire, eds. 1990. *Sourcebook of Criminal Justice Statistics—1989.* Washington, D.C.: U.S. Government Printing Office.

———, eds. 1992. *Sourcebook of Criminal Justice Statistics, 1991.* Washington, D.C.: U.S. Government Printing Office.

Flowers, Ronald. 1990. *Minorities and Criminality.* Westport, Conn.: Greenwood Press.

Fogel, David. 1975. *We Are the Living Proof.* Cincinnati: Anderson.

Frankel, Marvin. 1973. *Criminal Sentences—Law Without Order.* New York: Hill & Wang.

Freiberg, Arie. 1994. "Sentencing Reform in Victoria: A Case Study." In *The Politics of Sentencing Reform,* edited by Chris Clarkson and Rod Morgan. Oxford: Oxford University Press.

Garland, David. 1991. "Sociological Perspectives on Punishment." In *Crime and Justice: A Review of Research,* vol. 14, edited by Michael Tonry. Chicago: University of Chicago Press.

Georges-Abeyie, D., ed. 1985. *The Criminal Justice System and Blacks.* New York: Clark Boardman.

Gerstein, Dean R., and Henrik J. Jarwood, eds. 1990. *Treating Drug Problems.* Report of the Committee for Substance Abuse Coverage Study, Division of Health Care Services, National Institute of Medicine. Washington, D.C.: National Academy Press.

Gilder, George. 1981. *Wealth and Poverty.* New York: Basic Books.

Gilliard, Darrell K. 1992. *National Corrections Reporting Program, 1987.* Washington, D.C.: U.S. Department of Justice, Bureau of Justice Statistics.

Gladwell, Malcolm. 1993. "N.Y. Crack Epidemic Appears to Wane: Seeing Drug's Destructiveness, Younger People Are Turning Away," *Washington Post,* May 31, p. A1.

Glueck, Sheldon. 1962. *Law and Psychiatry: Cold War or Entente Cordiale?* Baltimore: Johns Hopkins Press.

Greenwood, Peter W., ed. 1986. *Intervention Strategies for Chronic Juvenile Offenders: Some New Perspectives.* Westport, Conn.: Greenwood Press.

Greenwood, Peter W. 1987. *The Vision Quest Program: An Evaluation.* Santa Monica, Calif.: RAND Corporation.

———. 1988. *Correctional Programs for Chronic Juvenile Offenders: Characteristics of Three Exemplary Programs.* Santa Monica, Calif.: RAND Corporation.

Greenwood, Peter W., with Allan Abrahamse. 1982. *Selective Incapacitation.* Santa Monica, Calif.: RAND Corporation.

Greenwood, Peter W., Elizabeth Piper Deschenes, and John Adams. 1993. *Chronic Juvenile Offenders.* Santa Monica, Calif.: RAND Corporation.

Grossman, James R. 1989. *Land of Hope: Chicago, Black Southerners, and the Great Migration.* Chicago: University of Chicago Press.

Haaga, John G., Richard Scott, and Jennifer Hawes-Dawson. 1992. *Drug Use in the Detroit Metropolitan Area.* Santa Monica, Calif.: RAND Corporation.

Hacker, Andrew. 1992. *Two Nations: Black and White, Separate, Hostile, Unequal.* New York: Scribner.

Hagan, John. 1974. "Extra-Legal Attributes and Criminal Sentencing." *Law and Society Review* 8: 357—83.

Hagan, John, and Kristin Bumiller. 1983. "Making Sense of Sentencing: A Review and Critique of Sentencing Research." In *Research on Sentencing: The Search for Reform,* vol. 2, edited by Alfred Blumstein, Jacqueline Cohen, Susan Martin, and Michael Tonry. Washington, D.C.: National Academy Press.

Hart, H. L. A. 1968. *Punishment and Responsibility.* Oxford: Oxford University Press.

Hawkins, Darnell F. 1985. "Trends in Black–White Imprisonment: Changing Conceptions of Race or Changing Conceptions of Social Control?" *Crime and Social Justice* 24:187–209.

———. 1986. "Race, Crime Type, and Imprisonment." *Justice Quarterly* 3:251–69.

Heumann, Milton, and Colin Loftin. 1979. "Mandatory Sentencing and the Abolition of Plea Bargaining: The Michigan Felony Firearms Statute." *Law and Society Review* 13:393–430.

Hill, John L. 1988. "Freedom, Determinism, and the Externalization of Responsibility in the Law: A Philosophical Analysis." *Georgetown Law Journal* 76:2045–73.

Hindelang, Michael. 1976. *Criminal Victimization in Eight American Cities: A Descriptive Analysis of Common Theft and Assault.* Washington, D.C.: Law Enforcement Assistance Administration.

———. 1978. "Race and Involvement in Common Law Personal Crimes." *American Sociological Review* 43:93–109.

Holmes, Steven A. 1994. "Prominent Blacks Meet to Search for an Answer to Mounting Crime." *New York Times,* January 8, p. A1.

Home Office. 1990. *Crime, Justice, and Protecting the Public.* London: H. M. Stationery Office.

Honderich, Ted. 1989. *Punishment: The Supposed Justifications.* Cambridge: Polity Press.

Ifill, Gwen. 1991. "Senate's Rule for Its Anti-Crime Bill: The Tougher the Provision, the Better." *New York Times,* July 8, p. A6.

Inciardi, James A., ed. 1993. *Drug Treatment and Criminal Justice.* Newbury Park, Calif.: Sage.

Jankowski, Louis W. 1992. *Correctional Populations in the United States, 1990.* Washington, D.C.: U.S. Department of Justice, Bureau of Justice Statistics.

Jareborg, Nils. 1994. "The Swedish Sentencing Reform." In *The Politics of Sentencing Reform,* edited by Chris Clarkson and Rod Morgan. Oxford: Oxford University Press.

Jaynes, David Gerald, and Robin M. Williams, Jr., eds. 1989. *A Common Destiny: Blacks and American Society.* Committee on the Status of Black Americans, National Research Council. Washington, D.C.: National Academy Press.

Jencks, Christopher. 1992. *Rethinking Social Policy.* Cambridge, Mass.: Harvard University Press.

Johns, Christina Jacqueline. 1992. *Power, Ideology, and the War on Drugs.* New York: Praeger.

Johnson, Bruce D., Terry Williams, Kojo A. Dei, and Harry Sanabria. 1990. "Drug Abuse in the Inner City: Impact on Hard-Drug Users and the Community." In *Drugs and Crime,* edited by Michael Tonry and James Q. Wilson. Volume 13 of *Crime and Justice: A Review of Research,* edited by Michael Tonry and Norval Morris. Chicago: University of Chicago Press.

Johnson, Guy B. 1941. "The Negro and Crime." *Annals of the American Academy of Political and Social Science.* 271:93–104.

Johnston, Lloyd D., Patrick M. O'Malley, and Jerald G. Bachman. 1992. *Smoking, Drinking, and Illicit Drug Use Among American Secondary School Students, College Students, and Young Adults, 1975–1991.* Volume 1: *Secondary Students.* Volume 2: *College Students and Young Adults.* Washington, D.C.: U.S. Government Printing Office.

Joint Committee on New York Drug Law Evaluation. 1978. *The Nation's Toughest Drug Law: Evaluating the New York Experience.* A Project of the Association of the Bar of the City of New York and the Drug Abuse Council. Washington, D.C.: U.S. Government Printing Office.

Kandel, Denise B. 1991. "The Social Demography of Drug Use." *Milbank Quarterly* 69:365–414.

Kant, Immanuel. 1964. *Groundwork of the Metaphysics of Morals,* translated by H. J. Paton. New York: Harper Torchbooks. (originally published 1797)

Klaus, Patsy. 1994. *The Costs of Crime to Victims.* Washington, D.C.: Bureau of Justice Statistics.

Kleck, Gary. 1981. "Racial Discrimination in Criminal Sentencing: A Critical Evaluation of the Evidence with Additional Evidence on the Death Penalty." *American Sociological Review* 46:783–805.

Kleiman, Mark A. R. 1992. *Against Excess.* New York: Basic Books.

Kleiman, Mark A. R., and David Cavanagh. 1990. "A Cost–Benefit Analysis of Prison Cell Construction and Alternative Sanctions." Working Paper 90-06-03, prepared for the National Institute of Justice. Guggenheim Program in Criminal Justice Policy and Management. Cambridge, Mass.: Harvard University, Kennedy School of Government.

Kleiman, Mark A. R., and Kerry D. Smith. 1990. "State and Local Drug Enforcement: In Search of a Strategy." In *Drugs and Crime,* edited by Michael Tonry and James Q. Wilson. Volume 13 of *Crime and Justice: A Review of Research,* edited by Michael Tonry and Norval Morris. Chicago: University of Chicago Press.

Klein, Stephen, Joan Petersilia, and Susan Turner. 1990. "Race and Imprisonment Decisions in California." *Science* 247:812–16.

Knapp, Kay A. 1984. *The Impact of the Minnesota Sentencing Guidelines— Three Year Evaluation.* St. Paul: Minnesota Sentencing Guidelines Commission.

———. 1991. "Arizona: Unprincipled Sentencing, Mandatory Minimums, and Prison Crowding." *Overcrowded Times* 2(5):10–12.

Krisberg, Barry, and Robert DeComo. 1992. *National Juvenile Custody Trends 1978–89.* Washington, D.C.: U.S. Department of Justice, Office of Juvenile Justice and Delinquency Prevention.

Langan, Patrick A. 1985. "Racism on Trial: New Evidence to Explain the Racial Composition of Prisons in the United States." *Journal of Criminal Law and Criminology* 76:666–83.

———. 1991. *Race of Persons Admitted to State and Federal Institutions, 1926–86.* Washington, D.C.: U.S. Department of Justice, Bureau of Justice Statistics.

Laws, Richard D., ed. 1989. *Relapse Prevention with Sex Offenders.* New York: Guilford Press.

Lemann, Nicholas. 1991. *The Promised Land—The Great Black Migration and How It Changed America.* New York: Knopf.

Leuw, Ed. 1991. "Drugs and Drug Policy in the Netherlands." In *Crime and Justice: A Review of Research,* Vol. 14, edited by Michael Tonry. Chicago: University of Chicago Press.

Lieberson, Stanley. 1980. *A Piece of the Pie—Blacks and White Immigrants Since 1880.* Berkeley and Los Angeles: University of California Press.

Lipton, Douglas, Robert Martinson, and Judith Wilks. 1975. *The Effectiveness of Correctional Treatment—A Survey of Correctional Treatment Studies.* New York: Praeger.

Loftin, Colin, and David McDowall. 1981. " 'One with a Gun Gets You Two': Mandatory Sentencing and Firearms Violence in Detroit." *Annals of the American Academy of Political and Social Science* 455:150.

———. 1984. "The Deterrent Effects of the Florida Felony Firearm Law." *Journal of Criminal Law and Criminology* 75:250–59.

Loftin, Colin, Milton Heumann, and David McDowall. 1983. "Mandatory Sentencing and Firearms Violence: Evaluating an Alternative to Gun Control." *Law and Society Review* 17:287–318.

Lusane, Clarence, with Dennis Desmond. 1991. *Pipe Dream Blues: Racism and the War on Drugs.* Boston: South End Press.

Lynch, Michael J., and E. Brett Patterson. 1991. *Race and Criminal Justice.* New York: Harrow & Heston.

MacCoun, Robert, and Peter Reuter. 1992. "Are the Wages of Sin $30 an Hour? Economic Aspects of Street-Level Drug Dealing." *Crime and Delinquency* 38(4):477–91.

McDonald, Douglas C., and Kenneth E. Carlson. 1993. *Sentencing in the Federal Courts: Does Race Matter?* Washington, D.C.: U.S. Department of Justice, Bureau of Justice Statistics.

McDowall, David, Colin Loftin, and Brian Wiersema. 1992. "A Comparative Study of the Preventive Effects of Mandatory Sentencing Laws for Gun Crimes." *Journal of Criminal Law & Criminology* 83:378–94.

Maclean, B., and D. Milanovic, eds. 1990. *Racism, Empiricism, and Criminal Justice.* Vancouver, B.C.: Collective.

McNeely, R. L., and Carl E. Pope. 1981. *Race, Crime, and Criminal Justice.* Beverly Hills, Calif.: Sage.

McNulty, Timothy J. 1990. "U.S. Report Finds Teen Drug Use Still Falling." *Chicago Tribune,* February 14, 1990, p. A8.

Maguire, Kathleen, Ann L. Pastore, and Timothy Flanagan. 1993. *Sourcebook of Criminal Justice Statistics—1992.* Washington, D.C.: U.S. Government Printing Office.

Majority Staffs of the Senate Judiciary Committee and the International Narcotics Control Commerce. 1990. *Fighting Drug Abuse: A National Strategy.*

Mann, Coramae Richey. 1993. *Unequal Justice—A Question of Color.* Bloomington: Indiana University Press.

Margolick, David. 1994. "Falsely Accused: In a Humiliating Arrest, a Black Judge Finds Lessons of Law and Race Relations." *New York Times,* January 7, p. A23.

Marshall, W. L. 1993. "The Treatment of Sex Offenders—What Does the Outcome Data Tell Us?" *Journal of Interpersonal Violence* 8(4):524–30.

Martin, Susan E., Lee B. Sechrest, and Robin Redner, eds. 1981. *New Directions in the Rehabilitation of Criminal Offenders.* Washington, D.C.: National Academy Press.

Martinson, Robert. 1974. "What Works—Questions and Answers About Prison Reform." *Public Interest* 35(2):22–54.

———. 1979. "New Findings, New Views: A Note of Caution Regarding Sentencing Reform." *Hofstra Law Review* 7:243–58.

Massing, Michael. 1993. "What Ever Happened to the 'War on Drugs.' " *New York Review of Books,* June 11, p. 46.

Mauer, Marc. 1990. *Young Black Men and the Criminal Justice System: A Growing National Problem*. Washington, D.C.: The Sentencing Project.

Mead, Lawrence. 1986. *Beyond Entitlement: The Social Obligations of Citizenship*. New York: Free Press.

———. 1992. *Dependency Politics: Non-Working Poverty in the U.S..* New York: Basic Books.

Miller, Dan. 1977. "The Chutzpa Queen; Favorite Reagan Target as Welfare Cheat Remains Unflappable at Trial in Chicago." *Washington Post*, March 13, p. A3.

Miller, Jerome G. 1992a. "42% of Black D.C. Males, 18 to 35, Under Criminal Justice System Control." *Overcrowded Times* 3(3):1, 11.

———. 1992b. "56 Percent of Young Black Males in Baltimore Under Justice System Control." *Overcrowded Times* 3(6):1, 10, 16.

———. 1992c. *Hobbling a Generation: Young African American Males in the Criminal Justice System of America's Cities: Baltimore, Maryland*. Alexandria, Va.: National Center on Institutions and Alternatives.

———. 1992d. *Hobbling a Generation: Young African American Males in Washington, D.C.'s Criminal Justice System*. Alexandria, Va.: National Center on Institutions and Alternatives.

Miller, Warren E., and Santa A. Traugott. 1989. *American National Election Studies Data Sourcebook, 1952–1986*. Cambridge: Harvard University Press.

Minnesota Sentencing Guidelines Commission. 1980. *Report to The Legislature*. St. Paul: Minnesota Sentencing Guidelines Commission.

———. 1991. *Summary of 1989 Sentencing Practices for Convicted Felons*. St. Paul: Minnesota Sentencing Guidelines Commission.

Moore, Mark H. 1990. "Supply Reduction and Drug Law Enforcement." In *Drugs and Crime*, edited by Michael Tonry and James Q. Wilson. Volume 13 of *Crime and Justice: A Review of Research*, edited by Michael Tonry and Norval Morris. Chicago: University of Chicago Press.

Moore, Michael. 1984. *Law and Psychiatry: Rethinking the Relationship*. Cambridge: Cambridge University Press.

———. 1985. "Causation and the Excuses." *California Law Review* 73:1091–1149.

———. 1994. "Retributivism and Proportionate Punishment: The Special Case of Double Jeopardy." In *Penal Theory and Penal Practice*, edited by R. A. Duff and Sandra Marshall. Manchester: Manchester University Press.

Morris, Norval. 1968. "Psychiatry and the Dangerous Criminal." *Southern California Law Review* 41:514–47.

————. 1974. *The Future of Imprisonment*. Chicago: University of Chicago Press.

Morris, Norval, and Michael Tonry. 1990. *Between Prison and Probation: Intermediate Punishments in a Rational Sentencing System*. New York: Oxford University Press.

Morse, Stephen. 1976. "The Twilight of Welfare Criminology: A Reply to Judge Bazelon." *Southern California Law Review* 49:1247–69.

Moynihan, Daniel Patrick. 1965. *The Negro Family: The Case for National Action*. Washington, D.C.: Office of Policy Planning and Research, U.S. Department of Labor.

————. 1986. *Family and Nation*. New York: Harcourt Brace Jovanovich.

————. 1993. "Iatrogenic Government—Social Policy and Drug Research." *American Scholar* 62(3):351–62.

Murphy, Jeffrey. 1973. "Marxism and Retribution." *Philosophy and Public Affairs* 2:217–43.

Murray, Charles. 1984. *Losing Ground—American Social Policy, 1950–1980*. New York: Basic Books.

Musto, David. 1987a. "Remarks." In *Drugs and Crime: Workshop Proceedings,* edited by Jeffrey Roth, Michael Tonry, and Norval Morris. A Report of the 1986 National Academy of Sciences Conference on Drugs and Crime Research. Washington, D.C.: National Academy of Sciences.

————. 1987b. *The American Disease: Origins of Narcotic Control*. Expanded edition (orig. 1973). New York: Oxford University Press.

————. 1989. "How America Lost Its First Drug War." *Insight,* November 20, pp. 8–17.

Myers, S., and M. Simms, eds. 1988. *The Economics of Race and Crime*. New Brunswick, N.J.: Transaction Books.

Myrdal, Gunnar. 1944. *An American Dilemma—The Negro Problem and Modern Democracy*. New York: Harper & Row.

Nagel, Ilene H., and Stephen Schulhofer. 1992. "A Tale of Three Cities: An Empirical Study of Charging and Bargaining Practices Under the Federal Sentencing Guidelines." *Southern California Law Review* 66:501–66.

Nagin, Daniel. 1978. "General Deterrence: A Review of the Empirical Evidence." In *Deterrence and Incapacitation,* edited by Alfred Blumstein, Jacqueline Cohen, and Daniel Nagin. Washington, D.C.: National Academy Press.

National Academy of Sciences Panel on Research on Deterrent and Incapacitative Effects. See Blumstein, Cohen, and Nagin 1978.

National Academy of Sciences Panel on Research on Rehabilitative Techniques. See Sechrest, White, and Brown 1979 and Martin, Sechrest and Redner 1981.

National Academy of Sciences Panel on Sentencing Research. See Blumstein, Cohen, Martin, and Tonry 1983.

National Academy of Sciences Panel on The Understanding and Control of Violence. See Reiss and Roth 1993.

National Institute on Drug Abuse. 1991. *National Household Survey on Drug Abuse: Population Estimates 1990.* Washington, D.C.: U.S. Government Printing Office.

National Institute of Justice. 1992. *Drug Use Forecasting—1991 Annual Report.* Washington, D.C.: National Institute of Justice.

————. 1993. *Drug Use Forecasting—1992 Annual Report.* Washington, D.C.: National Institute of Justice.

Newman, Donald. 1966. *Conviction.* Boston: Little, Brown.

Office of National Drug Control Policy. 1989. *National Drug Control Strategy—September 1989.* Washington, D.C.: Office of National Drug Control Policy.

————. 1990. *National Drug Control Strategy—January 1990.* Washington, D.C.: Office of National Drug Control Policy.

Owens, Charles E., and Jimmy Bell. 1977. *Blacks and Criminal Justice.* Lexington, Mass.: Heath.

Packer, Herbert. 1968. *The Limits of the Criminal Sanction.* Palo Alto: Stanford University Press.

Padilla, Felix. 1992. *The Gang as an American Enterprise.* New Brunswick, N.J.: Rutgers University Press.

Pearson, Geoffrey. 1991. "Drug-Control Policies in Britain." In *Crime and Justice: A Review of Research,* vol. 14, edited by Michael Tonry. Chicago: University of Chicago Press.

Peeples, Faith, and Rolf Loeber. 1994. "Do Individual Factors and Neighborhood Context Explain Ethnic Differences in Juvenile Delinquency?" Unpublished manuscript, Western Psychiatric Institute and Clinic, School of Medicine, University of Pittsburgh.

Pennsylvania Commission on Sentencing. 1993. *Sentencing in Pennsylvania—1991.* Harrisburg: Pennsylvania Commission on Sentencing.

Perkins, Craig. 1992. *National Corrections Reporting Program, 1989.* Washington, D.C.: U.S. Department of Justice, Bureau of Justice Statistics.

————. 1993. *National Corrections Reporting Program, 1990.* Washington, D.C.: U.S. Department of Justice, Bureau of Justice Statistics.

Perkins, Craig, and Darrell K. Gilliard. 1992. *National Corrections Reporting Program, 1988.* Washington, D.C.: U.S. Department of Justice, Bureau of Justice Statistics.

Petersilia, Joan, and Susan Turner. 1985. *Guideline-Based Justice: The Implications for Racial Minorities.* Santa Monica, Calif.: RAND Corporation.

Pierce, Glen L., and William J. Bowers. 1981. "The Bartley–Fox Gun Law's Short-Term Impact on Crime in Boston." *Annals of the American Academy of Political and Social Science* 455:120–32.

Pillsbury, Samuel H. 1992. "The Meaning of Deserved Punishment: An Essay on Choice, Character, and Responsibility." *Indiana Law Journal* 67:719–52.

President's Commission on Law Enforcement and Administration of Justice. 1967. *The Challenge of Crime in a Free Society.* Washington, D.C.: U.S. Government Printing Office.

President's Commission on Model State Drug Laws. 1993. *Final Report.* Washington, D.C.: U.S. Government Printing Office.

Quinsey, V. L., G. T. Harris, M. E. Rice, and M. L. Lalumiere. 1993. "Assessing Treatment Efficacy in Outcome Studies of Sex Offenders." *Journal of Interpersonal Violence* 8(4):512–23.

Raines, Howell. 1991. "Grady's Gift." *New York Times Magazine,* December 1, p. 50.

Reiss, Albert J., Jr., and Jeffrey Roth. 1993. *Understanding and Controlling Violence.* Report of the National Academy of Sciences Panel on the Understanding and Control of Violence. Washington, D.C.: National Academy Press.

Reuter, Peter. 1988. "Can the Borders Be Sealed?" *Public Interest* 92:51–65.

Reuter, Peter, Gordon Crawford, and Jonathan Cave. 1988. *Sealing the Borders: The Effects of Increased Military Participation in Drug Interdiction.* Report R-3594-USDP. Santa Monica, Calif.: RAND Corporation.

Reuter, Peter, Robert MacCoun, and Patrick Murphy. 1990. *Money from Crime: A Study of Drug Dealing in Washington, D.C.* Santa Monica, Calif.: RAND Corporation.

Roberts, Julian V. 1992. "Public Opinion, Crime, and Criminal Justice." In *Crime and Justice: A Review of Research,* vol. 16, edited by Michael Tonry. Chicago: University of Chicago Press.

Rossman, David, Paul Froyd, Glen L. Pierce, John McDevitt, and William J. Bowers. 1979. *The Impact of the Mandatory Gun Law in Massachusetts.* Report to the National Institute of Law Enforcement and Criminal Justice, Law Enforcement Assistance Administration, U.S. Department of Justice, Washington, D.C.

Sampson, Robert, and William Julius Wilson. 1994. "Race, Crime, and Urban Inequality." In *Crime and Inequality,* edited by John Hagan. Chicago: University of Chicago Press.

Schulhofer, Stephen J., and Ilene Nagel. 1989. "Negotiated Pleas Under the Federal Sentencing Guidelines: The First Fifteen Months." *American Criminal Law Review* 27:231–88.

Sechrest, Lee B., Susan O. White, and Elizabeth D. Brown, eds. 1979. *The Rehabilitation of Criminal Offenders.* Washington, D.C.: National Academy of Sciences.

Sellin, Thorsten. 1928. "The Negro Criminal: A Statistical Note." *Annals of the American Academy of Political and Social Science* 140:52–64.

———. 1935. "Race Prejudice in the Administration of Justice." *American Journal of Sociology* 41:212–17.

Sherman, Lawrence. 1990. "Police Crackdowns: Initial and Residual Deterrence." In *Crime and Justice: A Review of Research,* vol. 12, edited by Michael Tonry and Norval Morris. Chicago: University of Chicago Press.

Smith, Douglas A., Nanette Graham, and Bonney Adams. 1991. "Minorities and the Police." In *Race and Criminal Justice,* edited by Michael Lynch and E. Britt Patterson. New York: Harrow & Heston.

Snell, Tracy L. 1993. *Correctional Populations in the United States, 1991.* Washington, D.C.: Bureau of Justice Statistics.

Snyder, Howard N. 1990. *Growth in Minority Detentions Attributed to Drug Law Violators.* OJJDP Update on Statistics. Washington, D.C.: U.S. Department of Justice, Office of Juvenile Justice and Delinquency Prevention.

Staples, Brent. 1994. *Parallel Time: Growing up in Black and White.* New York: Pantheon Books.

Stephen, James Fitzjames. 1964. *A History of the Criminal Law of England, Vol. 2.* New York: Franklin. (originally published 1883)

Stith, Kate, and Steve Y. Koh. 1993. "The Politics of Sentencing Reform: The Legislative History of the Federal Sentencing Guidelines." *Wake Forest Law Review* 28:223–90.

Sullivan, Mercer. 1989. *Getting Paid: Youth Crime and Work in the Inner City.* Ithaca, N.Y.: Cornell University Press.

Ten, C. L. 1987. *Crime, Guilt, and Punishment.* Oxford: Clarendon Press.

Tonry, Michael. 1988. "Structuring Sentencing." In *Crime and Justice: A Review of Research,* vol. 10, edited by Michael Tonry and Norval Morris. Chicago: University of Chicago Press.

———. 1992. "Mandatory Penalties." In *Crime and Justice: A Review of Research,* vol. 16, edited by Michael Tonry. Chicago: University of Chicago Press.

———. 1993. "Sentencing Commissions and Their Guidelines." In *Crime and Justice: A Review of Research,* vol. 17, edited by Michael Tonry. Chicago: University of Chicago Press.

———. 1994. "Racial Disproportion in U.S. Prisons." *British Journal of Criminology* 34:97–115.

Trebach, Arnold, and James Inciardi. 1993. *Legalize It?: Debating American Drug Policy*. Washington, D.C.: American University Press.

Twentieth Century Fund Task Force on Criminal Sentencing. 1976. *Fair and Certain Punishment*. New York: McGraw-Hill.

Uhlman, Thomas. 1979. *Racial Justice*. Lexington, Mass.: Heath.

U.S. Congress. House. Committee on Ways and Means. 1993. *Overview of Entitlement Programs—1993 Green Book*. Washington, D.C.: U.S. Government Printing Office.

U.S. Department of Commerce. Various years. *Statistical Abstract of the United States [1993 and various years]*. Washington, D.C.: U.S. Government Printing Office.

U.S. Department of Justice. 1991. "Attorney General's Summit on Law Enforcement Responses to Violent Crime: Public Safety in the Nineties." Conference Summary. Washington, D.C.: Bureau of Justice Statistics.

———. 1992. "Operation Weed and Seed." Washington, D.C.: U.S. Department of Justice.

U.S. General Accounting Office. 1990. *Drug Abuse: Research on Treatment May Not Address Current Needs*. Washington, D.C.: U.S. General Accounting Office.

U.S. Sentencing Commission. 1991a. *The Federal Sentencing Guidelines: A Report on the Operation of the Guidelines System and Short-Term Impacts on Disparity in Sentencing, Use of Incarceration, and Prosecutorial Discretion and Plea Bargaining*. Washington, D.C.: U.S. Sentencing Commission.

———. 1991b. *Special Report to the Congress: Mandatory Minimum Penalties in the Federal Criminal Justice System*. Washington, D.C.: U.S. Sentencing Commission.

———. 1992. *Annual Report—1991*. Washington, D.C.: U.S. Sentencing Commission.

van den Haag, Ernst. 1975. *Punishing Criminals: Concerning a Very Old and Painful Question*. New York: Basic Books.

van Dijk, Jan J. M., and Pat Mayhew. 1992. *Criminal Victimisation in the Industrialized World*. The Hague: Dutch Ministry of Justice.

von Hirsch, Andrew. 1976. *Doing Justice*. New York: Hill & Wang.

———. 1986. *Past and Future Crimes*. Brunswick, N.J.: Rutgers University Press.

Walker, Nigel. 1991. *Why Punish?* Oxford: Oxford University Press.

Walker, Nigel, and Mike Hough. 1988. *Public Attitudes to Sentencing: Surveys from Five Countries*. Aldershot: Gower.

Washington State Sentencing Guidelines Commission. 1992. *A Statistical Summary of Adult Felony Sentencing*. Olympia: Washington State Sentencing Guidelines Commission.

Webb, Sidney, and Beatrice Webb. 1910. *English Poor Law Policy*. London: Longmans, Green.

Weigend, Thomas. 1992. "Germany Reduces Use of Prison Sentences." *Overcrowded Times* 3(2):1, 11–13.

———. 1993. "In Germany, Fines Often Imposed In Lieu of Prosecution." *Overcrowded Times* 4(1):1, 15–16.

West, Cornel. 1993. *Race Matters*. Boston: Beacon Press.

Wilbanks, William. 1987. *The Myth of a Racist Criminal Justice System*. Monterey, Calif.: Brooks/Cole.

Williams, Terry. 1989. *The Cocaine Kids: The Inside Story of a Teenage Drug Ring*. Reading, Mass.: Addison-Wesley.

Wilson, James Q. 1975. *Thinking About Crime*. New York: Basic Books.

———. 1990. "Drugs and Crime." In *Drugs and Crime,* edited by Michael Tonry and James Q. Wilson. Volume 13 of *Crime and Justice: A Review of Research,* edited by Michael Tonry and Norval Morris. Chicago: University of Chicago Press.

Wilson, William Julius. 1978. *The Declining Significance of Race*. Chicago: University of Chicago Press.

———. 1987. *The Truly Disadvantaged: The Inner City, the Underclass, and Public Policy*. Chicago: University of Chicago Press.

Wolfe, Tom. 1987. *Bonfire of the Vanities*. New York: Farrar, Straus and Giroux.

Wolfgang, Marvin, and B. Cohen. 1970. *Crime and Race*. New York: Institute of Human Relations Press.

Wolfgang, Marvin, Robert Figlio, and Thorsten Sellin. 1972. *Delinquency in a Birth Cohort*. Chicago: University of Chicago Press.

Wood, Floris W. 1990. *An American Profile: Opinions and Behavior, 1972–1989*. New York: Gale Research.

Wootton, Barbara. 1963. *Crime and the Criminal Law*. London: Sweet & Maxwell.

Zedlewski, Edwin. 1987. "Making Confinement Decisions." Research in Brief Series. Washington, D.C.: National Institute of Justice.

Zimring, Franklin E. 1976. "Making the Punishment Fit the Crime: A Consumer's Guide to Sentencing Reform." *Hastings Center Report* 6(6): 13–21.

Zimring, Franklin E., and Gordon Hawkins. 1991. *The Scale of Imprisonment*. Chicago: University of Chicago Press.

———. 1992. *The Search for Rational Drug Control*. Cambridge: Cambridge University Press.

Index

229